THE COMPLETE **IDIOT'S** GUIDE® TO

Best Practices for Small Business

by Gina Abudi and Brandon Toropov

ALPHA

A member of Penguin Group (USA) Inc.

This book is dedicated to small business owners everywhere.

ALPHA BOOKS

Published by the Penguin Group

Penguin Group (USA) Inc., 375 Hudson Street, New York, New York 10014, USA

Penguin Group (Canada), 90 Eglinton Avenue East, Suite 700, Toronto, Ontario M4P 2Y3, Canada (a division of Pearson Penguin Canada Inc.)

Penguin Books Ltd., 80 Strand, London WC2R 0RL, England

Penguin Ireland, 25 St. Stephen's Green, Dublin 2, Ireland (a division of Penguin Books Ltd.)

Penguin Group (Australia), 250 Camberwell Road, Camberwell, Victoria 3124, Australia (a division of Pearson Australia Group Pty. Ltd.)

Penguin Books India Pvt. Ltd., 11 Community Centre, Panchsheel Park, New Delhi—110 017, India

Penguin Group (NZ), 67 Apollo Drive, Rosedale, North Shore, Auckland 1311, New Zealand (a division of Pearson New Zealand Ltd.)

Penguin Books (South Africa) (Pty.) Ltd., 24 Sturdee Avenue, Rosebank, Johannesburg 2196, South Africa

Penguin Books Ltd., Registered Offices: 80 Strand, London WC2R 0RL, England

Copyright © 2011 by Gina Abudi and Brandon Toropov

International Standard Book Number: 978-1-59257-993-8

Library of Congress Catalog Card Number: 2011904910

13 12 11   8 7 6 5 4 3 2 1

Interpretation of the printing code: The rightmost number of the first series of numbers is the year of the book's printing; the rightmost number of the second series of numbers is the number of the book's printing. For example, a printing code of 11-1 shows that the first printing occurred in 2011.

Printed in the United States of America

Note: This publication contains the opinions and ideas of its authors. It is intended to provide helpful and informative material on the subject matter covered. It is sold with the understanding that the authors and publisher are not engaged in rendering professional services in the book. If the reader requires personal assistance or advice, a competent professional should be consulted.

The authors and publisher specifically disclaim any responsibility for any liability, loss, or risk, personal or otherwise, which is incurred as a consequence, directly or indirectly, of the use and application of any of the contents of this book.

Most Alpha books are available at special quantity discounts for bulk purchases for sales promotions, premiums, fund-raising, or educational use. Special books, or book excerpts, can also be created to fit specific needs.

For details, write: Special Markets, Alpha Books, 375 Hudson Street, New York, NY 10014.

Publisher: *Marie Butler-Knight*

Associate Publisher: *Mike Sanders*

Executive Managing Editor: *Billy Fields*

Acquisitions Editor: *Paul Dinas*

Development Editor: *Jennifer Moore*

Senior Production Editor: *Kayla Dugger*

Copy Editor: *Jaime Julian Wagner*

Cover Designer: *Rebecca Batchelor*

Book Designers: *William Thomas, Rebecca Batchelor*

Indexer: *Celia McCoy*

Layout: *Ayanna Lacey*

Senior Proofreader: *Laura Caddell*

Contents

Appendixes

Introduction

Starting and running a small business presents a never-ending series of big challenges. But you can make overcoming those challenges a whole lot easier once you know what other small business owners have done to address them. That's where this book comes in.

Most small businesses fail within their first couple of years. The business owners who run these businesses often look back on their experiences and feel as though their enterprise failed because they themselves failed. They tell themselves that, on their own, they should have been able to answer every question, anticipate every problem, plan for every new situation, stay ahead of the competition, turn a profit, and (of course) keep customers happy, all at the same time. What these entrepreneurs may not realize, however, is that they were asking too much of themselves, and that this expectation, in and of itself, is a major contributing factor to the high failure rates of small businesses.

You don't have to know everything, do everything, and predict everything all by yourself. You and your business can benefit from the insights, experiences, and labor-saving innovations of others who have walked this path before you. We call these tested insights, experiences, and innovations "best practices," and we have collected, in this one volume, as many that seemed relevant to us, as small business owners, as we could find.

This book leverages our experience, and the experience of dozens of other entrepreneurs we learned from and interviewed over the years, to identify the best practices most essential to small business owners. It provides you with an accessible, in-depth understanding of the critical best practice you need to consider before starting your business during those first few crucial years and also later on as you consider growth. It offers proven best practices for small businesses in every area—best practices that relate to technology, human resources, sales, marketing, and even social media.

Between these covers you will find resources meant to help you move your small business forward, regardless of what stage of growth it currently occupies. Whether you're in the initial planning stages, considering expansion of a successful business model, or anywhere in between, you will find help here.

We have designed this book first and foremost as a tool to help you to plan more effectively. Both of us actually run small businesses, and we are well aware of the need for effective tools that support planning, both upfront planning and the kind of planning that must take place when you encounter major change—whether that change takes the form of competitive pressures, developing a new product or service, expanding your business by hiring additional staff, or any other change that affects your daily operations. The book addresses five specific planning areas.

In **Part 1, The Basics About Best Practices,** we discuss what you need to know about best practices and how to implement them as you make plans to support your growing business. This part provides you with what you need to know to implement best practices effectively in your own business.

Part 2, Best Practices for the Perfect Start-Up, helps you get your business started. It isn't easy, when you are first kicking off a new business, to be prepared for every eventuality. Inevitably, there will be things you won't think of. That is why it is so essential to get others involved—they may see something you have missed. These chapters will guide you in thinking ahead about your business's needs and offer insights about when and where to seek professional advice in setting up your initial business plan.

In **Part 3, Best Practices for the First Two Years,** we move to those very crucial first two years of your business. These first couple of years can make or break your business. After you have launched your business, you will quickly learn that the planning part never goes away. Short- and long-term planning are essential to your business's success. And you can't just stick those plans in a file cabinet and never look at them again. You will want to use them on an ongoing basis as tools for running your business and meeting your strategic objectives. In this part, you'll also learn about the most important personnel, marketing, and sales priorities during those critical early years.

Part 4, Best Practices for Running Your Business, will guide you in the task of continuing to grow a successful business. It will help you plan and set up the infrastructure of your business—your systems for accounting, managing employees, meeting insurance needs, protecting yourself and your business against lawsuits, protecting your intellectual property, and planning for your technology needs now and in the future. Throughout this part we provide suggestions for whom to call on when you need some expertise to ensure you are making the right decisions.

In **Part 5, Best Practices for Bringing in Revenue,** we focus on a perennial concern of small businesses: making money. Here, we help you set up and execute plans for getting the right sales staff in place, giving them the right incentives, and selling your products and services. We also share best practices for creating a marketing and service plan that is built around the voice of your customer. This part provides suggestions and recommendations for developing true partnerships with your customers—partnerships that will help your business gain a strong foothold in your industry and effectively compete with—and win against—the competition.

We wrap up the book with **Part 6, Best Practices for Growing Your Business,** which focuses on growing and expanding your business over time and keeping it moving in the right direction. Here you'll find best practices for expanding intelligently and for building a sustainable culture of innovation within your company.

Look to the appendixes for a complete glossary and resources for additional information that will guide you in both your business planning efforts and in growing your business over time.

Extras

Throughout the book, we offer tips for implementing the various best practices by means of a series of helpful sidebars.

BEST PRACTICE

Here, you'll find specific information about a particularly important best practice.

DEFINITION

This sidebar offers information about important business and management terms.

BUSINESS BUSTER

This sidebar offers warnings and cautions about common small business mistakes.

PRACTICE MAKES PERFECT

Here, you will find pragmatic advice on applying a best practice in your business.

Acknowledgments

I would like to thank the two most important people in my life who have supported me through the writing of this book and in my endeavors as an independent consultant: my husband, Yusuf Abudi, and my mother, Fay Schmidt. Their undying support and encouragement has pushed me through many challenges. Throughout my entire life I have relied on the council of my mother and continue to do so today—she is one smart woman. My husband is always by my side supporting my efforts and regularly acting as a sounding board as I bounce ideas and sometimes wild dreams off of him—he helps keep me grounded. I'd also like to thank the following people who contributed to this book by spending time with me working through ideas: Henry Gregor of Strategic Visions who provided me information on the many challenges start-ups face that he has experienced in working with his own clients, and Kathleen Allen of Melanson Health who helped me formulate my thoughts and the content on corporate structures and tax issues for small businesses. A big thank-you goes out to all my friends, colleagues, and social media network connections who frequently asked me how the book was coming along and told me how excited they were for me. And finally, I want to express my thanks to my agent, Gene Brissie; to Paul Dinas, our acquiring editor; and to all the editors on this book.

—Gina

My thanks go out first to my wife Haneen, whose patience and support on this and all my projects has been, as usual, indispensable. I also want to thank my agent Gene Brissie, without whose help this book would never have come into existence; Jennifer Moore, our development editor; Kayla Dugger, our production editor; and Paul Dinas, our acquiring editor, whose belief in this project, and in us, made everything possible.

—Brandon

Trademarks

All terms mentioned in this book that are known to be or are suspected of being trademarks or service marks have been appropriately capitalized. Alpha Books and Penguin Group (USA) Inc. cannot attest to the accuracy of this information. Use of a term in this book should not be regarded as affecting the validity of any trademark or service mark.

The Basics About Best Practices

What are best practices? Why should small business owners bother learning about them and implementing them? Where can they be found? What kinds of ideas will you learn about in this book?

In this part, you find out how to select, troubleshoot, and make the most of a good idea that may be relevant to the unique set of circumstances faced by your small business. You'll also discover how to determine whether or not the idea is actually delivering the results you seek.

Best Practice Basics

In This Chapter

- Understanding what best practices are all about
- Putting best practices to use for your business
- Reaping the benefits of best practices
- Researching the best practices of others

CustomerSoft is a start-up company that sells customer relationship management (CRM) software. Thanks to a great product, this start-up has established a position in the marketplace, but the CEO, Ethan, is perpetually in search of good salespeople.

The company's annual retention rate is less than 15 percent—a terrible figure—and only half of its established salespeople are hitting their quotas. One night, the CEO shares his problems with a good friend, Cecelia, who is CEO of another company. Cecelia's company does not compete with CustomerSoft, but it does have similar long sales cycles and complex buying patterns.

Ethan tells Cecelia what's working and what's not in his sales department and asks her for some advice. Because they are good friends, Cecelia gives Ethan three great pieces of advice that he might otherwise have had to pay a consultant tens of thousands of dollars to get.

The first of those three pieces of advice Cecelia offers sounds brutal:

"Get rid of salespeople who have had six months or more to get up and running with your company but have nothing to show for it," she tells the CustomerSoft CEO. "They are not capable of managing a long, coalition-driven sales process, which is what people who sell for you have to do. Cut your losses and fire these people today.

The rest of the sales department is demoralized because you are subsidizing poor performers." Even though it's tough advice, the minute he hears it, Ethan knows it is right.

Cecelia's second suggestion is just as direct:

"Start an aggressive new hiring campaign, but hire people who are real strategists and diplomats. Those are the sellers who can handle a complex sales cycle like yours. Your big problem is that you've been making 'gut decisions' about hiring in the sales department, and your gut has been pointing you toward the wrong people. In addition to looking for relevant experience on the resumé, which you haven't really been doing up to this point, you should confirm that any new applicant you consider hiring has the right temperament and personality for this job. Not every salesperson can handle a sales cycle of 24 months, so I think you should do some personality testing to confirm that you've got the right person."

Cecelia's third piece of advice seems just as relevant and useful as the first two suggestions:

"Put any new salesperson you hire on a 90-day probation, and enforce that probation. Make a list of the key performance indicators you'd like to see the person make progress on over the first three months, share that list with the new hire, and assign a mentor to help the new person get up to speed. Check in every week. If the metrics aren't there, cut your losses and refuse to give the person a full-time position with your company."

These three suggestions—fire nonperformers, do a personality assessment as part of a new hiring blitz, and set up a meaningful probationary period for new hires—are not ideas that Cecelia came up with out of thin air. She has actually used them in her own company, and she shared them with Ethan because they're directly relevant to his business. These are good ideas, yes, but they're more than that. They are *best practices*.

What Is a Best Practice?

Better hires. More consistency in manufactured products. Better customer service. Reduced time to market. Improved efficiency. These are the outcomes we want to deliver in our business. Best practices show us what we can do to make those outcomes happen.

DEFINITION

A **best practice** is a specific method that improves the performance of a team or an organization and can be replicated or adapted elsewhere. Best practices often take the form of guidelines, principles, or ideas that are endorsed by a person or governing body that attests to the viability of the best practice.

Best practices are a specific way of working—through processes, procedures, and standards—to achieve a business's goals and objectives. A best practice is considered the most effective way for either a group or an individual to achieve a particular outcome.

For instance, a manufacturing company will likely use APICS, the best practices espoused by The Association for Operations Management. APICS stands for "Advancing Productivity, Innovation, and Competitive Success" and provides manufacturing companies with best practices and standards relating to production, inventory, supply chain, materials management, purchasing, and logistics. Similarly, consulting firms that provide project management services rely on the Project Management Institute's *Project Management Body of Knowledge* (PMBOK) for best practices and standards for managing projects.

PRACTICE MAKES PERFECT

Best practices go back many years. The Association for Operations Management was established in 1957, the Retail Leaders Industry Association (RLIA) was established in 1969, the Project Management Institute was founded in 1969, and the American Bar Association was founded in 1878. All of these industry associations were established to support the efforts of businesses in these industries, regardless of their size.

Best practices are not static; they change as ways of doing business change and as rules and regulations change on the local, national, and international level. Best practices also change as individuals and businesses learn of better ways to accomplish their goals.

As new industries—or variations on industries—develop, best practices will arise to support that industry. For instance, the "green" businesses working to reduce carbon emissions and minimize other environmental impacts are continually developing best practices for going green, particularly as new regulations require industries to reduce emissions. One such best practice is the Leadership in Energy and Environment Design (LEED) framework, used by the construction industry as a guideline for designing and building "green" buildings.

The Benefits for Small Businesses

Best practices are available for nearly every aspect of your business, including how you manage people, how you handle your finances, the technology you put in place to run your business, how you manufacture new products, and how you manage sales and marketing efforts.

By using the best practices of larger businesses, a small business can run more efficiently, increase profits, be innovative, and improve customer satisfaction. Too often, however, owners of smaller businesses don't believe that their industry's best practices will work for them. Smaller businesses can often benefit from the best practices of their industry and those of larger businesses, but they will likely need to "tweak" those best practices to get them to work optimally. This book provides you with many insights on the ongoing task of adapting the right practices for your business's unique needs.

Don't Reinvent the Wheel

Competitors, even very large competitors, can teach you a lot. Don't overlook what others are already doing in your industry. Don't waste precious time and resources trying to create solutions that others have already found. Using the best practices of others in your industry with minor adjustments to fit your way of doing business can save you a significant amount of time and money in the long run.

BUSINESS BUSTER

Trying to take a unique approach to solving business problems can result in costly errors and tarnish your business's reputation. Look into the best practices that are specific to your industry. Undoubtedly, someone before you has encountered some version of the same problem and has resolved it successfully.

Start slowly at first. Take a particular process in your business—how you manage customer service calls on your product, for example—and learn how other businesses effectively manage their customer service calls.

Suppose that your company manufactures and sells car seats for infants and young children. Your customer service department is responsible for handling phone calls from customers who have bought car seats and have questions about installing them. You would like to see a reduction in the amount of time it takes your reps to answer incoming calls; currently, the phone rings four to five times before your customer service department answers. You would like to improve that to a maximum of two rings prior to a customer call being answered.

To improve that business practice, you should take the following steps:

1. Research the best practices of other companies, as well as your competitors' current practices, for answering incoming customer service calls.

2. Analyze the data collected to determine what practices apply to your business.

3. Develop a new process to respond to customer calls using industry best practices, adjusting for your business.

4. Pilot test the new process with some of the customer service representatives.

5. Roll out the new process to all customer service representatives and measure the impact on customer service via surveys.

By drawing on data from industry groups and competitors, you can shorten the amount of time it takes to implement best practices in your own business. Rather than starting from scratch, look and see what is already in place out there. Undoubtedly any aspect of your business you are trying to improve has already been addressed by another business.

Best Practices from Industry Groups

Here's one best practice we feel strongly about: join a local chapter of your industry's business organization. Such industry groups provide member organizations with access to a variety of resources, including conferences, newsletters, and industry experts. Additionally, many industry associations provide education for their members through webinars and instructor-led courses, including the possibility of certification. For example, the Project Management Institute (www.pmi.org) provides certification of project management expertise, such as the Project Management Professional (PMP) designation.

Your first stop for research into best practices should be the association group for your particular industry, almost all of which gather data on what member businesses are doing. Many industry associations hold annual conferences where business leaders discuss best practices their companies have adopted and how they have impacted sales and customer service. Use these conferences to gather information about what has worked elsewhere and how you might use this information for your own business.

Tailoring Best Practices to Your Needs

There is a right way and a wrong way to apply best practices from within your industry. Although you might be in the same industry as another business, there are always some key differences, whether it's the type of products you're developing, how you interact with customers, or how you measure employee performance. Don't assume that what works for other businesses within your industry will work for your business without some adjustment to suit your unique needs.

For example, suppose you hear that one of your competitors is successfully using newsletters to generate interest in their products and increase sales. You are having a hard time increasing profits in a down economy and are eager to try out this approach. If your competitor is doing it, it should work for you, too, right? Not necessarily. So what do you do? First, do a bit of research.

PRACTICE MAKES PERFECT

Before applying a best practice in your business, run a pilot test. Ask a handful of employees who will use that new process or procedure (the best practice) to try it out. This enables you to work out any issues before rolling it out to all employees in your business.

Sign up for the newsletter from your competitor. Take a good look at what is included and how often the newsletter is published. Research other companies in your industry that use newsletters. Try to find out why they started sending newsletters and how they have benefitted from using them. Many companies are willing to share what works for them and what doesn't as long as you are not a direct competitor.

If, after researching the newsletter, it still looks like a good idea, do a bit of planning next. As a best practice, consider the following questions:

- What should be included in a newsletter to customers?

- How often will the newsletter be sent?

- Will it be a paper-based newsletter or sent via e-mail?

- What is the objective of the newsletter?

By thinking through these questions and answering them specifically for your business—and not just based on what companies in your industry are doing—you will be in a better position to determine if newsletters will increase sales and profits for your company.

When you decide to survey your current customers, use the survey to help you gather data to answer the preceding questions; in addition, ask customers about current newsletters they receive and what features of those newsletters are most appealing. You might ask the following questions:

- Are the newsletters you like paper-based or sent via e-mail?

- What about the newsletter appeals to you?

- If you could change one thing about the newsletter you receive, what would you change and why?

- If you could add one thing to the newsletter you receive, what would you add and why?

Let's assume that after gathering this data you have learned the following:

- Your customers prefer newsletters to be sent via e-mail.

- They are interested in coupons or other discounts included in the newsletter.

- They enjoy reading customer testimonials.

- They want to be the first to learn about new products and services.

By including this information in your newsletter, you have met the customer's needs and established a best practice for your business on the use of newsletters.

Benchmarking

Benchmark your current processes and practices against similar companies' processes and practices to understand how your business is currently performing. What is being done well and what needs work?

DEFINITION

A **benchmark** is a measure of your business's processes, procedures, and practices against the processes, procedures, and practices of companies considered the best at what they do in those particular areas you are measuring.

One particularly good way to benchmark your performance is by surveying your current and prospective customers. Additionally, surveying members of an industry association to which you belong is a good way to understand how they do business.

Let's look at another example. Assume your business provides financial services to other businesses. You have heard from a few potential customers that they have decided to go with another company rather than yours for financial services. You've asked those businesses to tell you what company they've chosen and why they made that selection. Additionally, you have decided to send a survey, through a third party, to ask the following questions of companies that purchase financial services:

• What companies do you purchase financial services from?

• Why do you purchase financial services from those companies?

• What is of key importance in selecting a financial services firm?

• What is of key importance to you in remaining with that company?

As you gather and analyze data, you will learn why companies buy from other companies—maybe they offer discounts or additional services or do a better job of responding to inquiries—and why they remain with that company for extended periods of time—maybe that company provides high-quality customer service or reduces fees for long-standing customers. Analyzing this kind of information can help you identify new ways you can improve upon what you currently do in your own business.

Best Practices from Outside Your Industry

Don't discount best practices from outside of your industry. Businesses in other industries also have customer service departments, hire employees, and use technology for efficiencies, yet you'd be surprised how often small businesses focus solely on their own industry to gather best practices.

Looking outside your industry doesn't have to be an onerous process. To find out about best practices outside your industry, look to research conducted by companies such as McKinsey & Company, Inc., Forrester Research, and IDG Research Services. Research from these companies is frequently free to members, or can be purchased by nonmembers:

• McKinsey & Company, Inc. (www.mckinseyquarterly.com) publishes a quarterly magazine that provides research on best practices in a variety of industries.

- Companies might choose to hire IDG Research Services (www.idgresearch. com) to help determine whether or not a new product will be of value to the marketplace.

- Forrester Research (www.forrester.com) sells research through their website.

These are just a few examples of websites you can visit to purchase extensive research to help your business make decisions on new products and services and to better reach out to your customer base.

PRACTICE MAKES PERFECT

By expanding your research of best practices to industries outside of your own, you are likely to find new ways of doing business that your competition isn't aware of, thereby giving your business a competitive advantage.

Let's consider another example. Suppose your business sells invitations for parties, weddings, and holiday events. You want to find out what the best practices are for presenting your product at events such as wedding expos and craft fairs. You currently find that attending such events doesn't help your business attract any new customers, and you'd like to use these events to increase your customer base.

In addition to looking at how others in your industry promote their products at expos, you are also looking outside your industry. You research how other businesses, such as software companies and training providers, display their products and focus on their services at events. You talk with vendors to get their perspective on best practices for displaying products. Additionally, you talk to other small businesses you have met through the Chamber of Commerce about creative ways to present products to potential customers at conferences and exhibits.

You learn that many businesses offer free samples of their products in a variety of designs, hang posters with customer testimonials, and offer a 20 percent expo discount. You adopt these best practices for your next expo and gain four new customers whose orders total more than $5,000.

The Benefits of Best Practices

Implementing best practices enables you to improve how your business functions overall. Even for the smallest business, best practices can bring efficiencies that enable the business to grow in the most effective way possible.

Improving Performance

By improving internal performance in areas such as design, production, sales, operations, accounting, and customer service, small businesses can begin to see quick increases in productivity, a reduction in time to market for new products and services, and short-term improvement in the quality of the products that reach the market. Improving the way work is done within the business also makes it easier to attain long-term strategic goals.

In addition, getting into the habit of capturing *lessons learned* from specific projects, and then sharing those lessons with others within your company, tends to improve business efficiencies.

DEFINITION

Lessons learned is a best practice that entails capturing and sharing information from past projects, such as problems that occurred and challenges that were faced. By sharing lessons learned, small businesses can improve how the work is done and increase efficiencies within the business.

Creating Customer Value

Creating customer value enables you to retain your current customers, increase your rate of referrals from current customers, and attract new customers to your business. Obviously, this is an important competitive advantage.

Use surveys and conversations to find out what value you bring to your customers and what else you can do to increase that value. Creating value for your customers earns you their loyalty and increased business.

Reducing Costs

No company can afford to throw money out the window, but keeping costs down is particularly important for small businesses. Not surprisingly, best practices that help small businesses cut costs tend to be among the most popular. You will find a number of such best practices in this book.

The Least You Need to Know

- Best practices are methods recognized by various industries to help businesses achieve specific goals or objectives.

- Don't reinvent the wheel. There is a great deal of information already out there on improving business performance. Find it and use what is applicable for your business.

- Look both inside and outside your industry for best practices.

- Use best practices to improve efficiencies, reduce costs, increase profitability, develop new products and services, and engage your customers.

- Modify the best practices of others to suit your particular business needs.

The Art of Implementation

In This Chapter

* Implementing best practices in your business
* Communicating with your employees about best practices
* Managing change initiatives
* Evaluating and revising your best practices

Let's assume you come across a best practice—either in this book or from another source—that you want to put into practice. How do you go about doing so? What are the most common implementation mistakes, and how can you avoid them?

Let's look at an example. Your business sells magazine subscriptions to other businesses. You have read that one of the ways a large magazine subscription service retains new customers is by adding a free six-month subscription to a magazine with the purchase of a full-year subscription at a discounted rate—effectively giving six additional months to new customers at no cost. You have read that the large company has been very successful at this initiative and, in fact, has increased its annual retention rate by 20 percent after adopting this practice. This is certainly a best practice for them, but will it work for your smaller business?

You really do not know what *your* potential customers want—you haven't asked them yet! Additionally, the margins associated with implementing such an initiative might not work for your smaller business. Can you really afford to offer this service?

A bit of research on your part—in this case a survey out to potential customers of your product—will give you a better idea of what will (and won't) work for your business.

This chapter shows you how to implement a best practice successfully within your business, and also shows you how to avoid some of the most common pitfalls.

Driving Best Practices Through Your Business

Driving best practices throughout any business is a difficult task that requires significant planning. But rather than thinking of planning as extra work, frame it as managing an important project on which your business's success depends. In fact, that is just what you are doing. Best practices have the potential to take your business to the next level … or hold it back. Which outcome you experience depends on your ability to communicate the ideas effectively, win buy-in from your staff, consider the risks, and help employees adjust to the inevitable changes they will face in doing their jobs.

DEFINITION

Driving best practices refers to the practice of deciding upon and implementing best practices throughout the organization in a structured manner. Best practices may be driven from the top down (manager down to individual contributor) or driven from the bottom up.

During the initial planning stages of implementing any best practice, you must think about these questions:

- What are you trying to accomplish?
- Is this the right time for you to get started? How do you know?
- What can be done now and will have the most impact?
- What should be phased in later?
- Who needs to be involved in the effort?
- How will these changes affect other aspects of your business?

There are likely many areas where you can improve your business. You can't do everything at once, though, so you must prioritize by focusing on those areas that will have the most positive impact on your business in the short term—in other words, where you will get the biggest bang for your buck.

Once you have addressed these questions, develop a project plan that includes these key components:

- **Problem statement:** What are you trying to solve by implementing new best practices into your business?

- **Schedule and budget:** What is the timeline for implementing the best practices, and what are the initial budget requirements?

- **Resource needs and responsibilities:** Who on the staff should be involved, and what are their roles and responsibilities for this initiative?

- **Risk plan:** What could go wrong, and how will you address it if it does go wrong? What will be the impact on the business?

- **Communication plan:** How will you communicate these changes, and the reasons for them, throughout your business? How will you communicate to customers and vendors?

- **Change management plan:** What are your plans for dealing with a potentially significant change in the business? How will you help employees adjust and accept the change? How much time will people need to adjust?

- **Evaluation:** How will you evaluate whether the best practice that was implemented was a success and improved your business performance? How much time needs to pass before you can evaluate it?

Understanding Your Responsibilities

As the business owner, you need to ensure not only that you have set up the right plan, but also that you have chosen the right people to help you implement that plan. In some cases, you might find that the best people to implement a change are those who are actually doing the work on a daily basis. More often, you will provide the strategy and oversee the employees who implement the best practice plan you initiate.

BUSINESS BUSTER

Failing to involve your employees in the process of implementing best practices will ensure failure!

Think of yourself as the cheerleader for this effort, not the quarterback! You need to draw the broad outlines of the plan, delegate appropriate authority to the right people, hold them accountable, inspire them, and check in regularly to assess the team's progress. Your own list of responsibilities is already quite long. It includes ...

- Determining what you are (and aren't) going to measure to determine whether or not the initiative is a success.
- Analyzing the data gathered and modifying it to fit your business.
- Leading the effort to implement the new best practice.
- Evaluating the success of the new best practice and sharing your findings with the team.

While you will be relying on others to do some of the work, it is important that you, as the business owner, assume the ultimate responsibility for the success or failure of this effort. Let's look at an example of a business owner's responsibility in such an initiative.

Suppose you own a small business that creates custom gift baskets. Last holiday season you had a difficult time keeping up with orders and, out of 100 baskets shipped, 25 of them did not arrive on time, which meant that you had to issue full refunds to those customers. This has occurred two years in a row, and you don't want to have the same problem this year. Let's walk through your responsibilities as a business owner in improving the process of shipping your product during busy seasons.

First, you have determined that the process in need of improvement is the delivery of your products to your customers. Currently, 25 percent of your shipments during the holiday season are late. That is the baseline you are measuring against.

You appoint a team leader to head up a small group of employees to research shipping practices of other small local businesses, such as bookstores, gift shops, and flower shops. Additionally, you ask them to research how larger organizations such as Amazon. com, PC Connection, and other larger companies manage their shipping of product to customers. They do this research by reviewing websites where information on shipping is included and making telephone calls to local businesses to talk with the business owners.

Using the information they found, you and the team then start brainstorming ways to adapt it to your situation, market position, and available resources. Here are the initiatives you and the team come up with:

- Setting up accounts with a variety of companies, including UPS, FedEx, and the U.S. Postal Service

- Hiring temporary employees during the busy season

- Offering discounts to customers who order early

- Setting a "drop dead" date: all orders placed before that date are guaranteed to arrive on time; orders placed after that date can only be delivered on time for an extra charge

Notice that you do this brainstorming with the input of the employees who will actually be doing the work.

You and the team have also learned that many of the smaller businesses that ship products have staff who are specifically responsible for shipping rather than relying on all employees to help do the job. To help ensure success on the best practice being implemented for shipping during the busy season, you set up a department devoted to the task.

Your next step is to measure the success of your new practice for shipping with the goal of improving upon your late shipment rate of 25 percent.

As you can see in the example, by focusing on improving shipping, a vital component to this particular business's growth has been identified. By improving shipment of product, this business will increase profits (no refunding customers for late shipments) and increase customer satisfaction overall.

Getting Employees Involved

Of key importance in any best practice initiative is ensuring that the relevant employees are involved in the process from the start. Whether you are adapting a best practice from this book, from a competitor in your industry, or from someone operating outside your industry, you must bear in mind that whatever changes are eventually made will affect how someone in your organization performs his or her job and interacts with your customers. Happy employees really do lead you to happy customers, so be sure you involve and engage all the members of the team that your new initiative will affect.

Involving employees is not optional. You *must* get your employees on board with the process of reviewing practices and making changes. You need to engage them—or at the very least, consult them—about everything connected to the best practice that will affect them.

> **BEST PRACTICE**
>
> According to author and speaker Tom Peters, if you are going to have a "Wow!" organization, you need to remember that the most important part of your business is the employees. They are the ones who are actually doing the work to ensure your business's success. Get them involved!

One way to bring employees on board is to ask for their input on how the business is performing today and to identify opportunities for improvement. Ask your employees what resources they need to better perform in their roles and provide improved service to customers. What are some ways they have thought of to improve how they work? No doubt they have some ideas and may already be implementing some of those ideas individually.

Employees need to feel that they are part of the business and invested in its success. By encouraging them to find ways to improve how work is done, and carefully listening to their ideas, you will find that they are more committed to the plans you propose and that they have a greater stake in the business and its success.

Using Consultants and Other Experts

Depending on the size of the effort you are undertaking, you may want to get consultants involved in the process. There are many such experts whose specialty is implementing best practices within a given field.

Many (perhaps most) small businesses do not have the budget necessary to bring in outside consultants. In fact, it's likely that you bought this book because it represented a cost-effective alternative to developing a customized best practices plan with the help of a consultant.

If you do decide to use a consultant or other external best practice expert, we recommend you follow these best practices:

- Choose consultants who have demonstrated experience in your particular industry.

- Check the references! Don't limit yourself to the names they provide as references; dig a bit deeper and do your own research.

- Learn about their methodology for researching, modifying, and implementing best practices in similar businesses.

- Be clear about your expectations and be realistic about what you can expect from the consultant.

- Ensure they develop and follow a project plan and provide regular status reports to you.

Most of all, remember that *you* are the expert on your business, not the consultant. The consultant will bring expertise in researching and implementing best practices, but you will need to partner with the consultant to bring the expertise about your particular business and its goals.

PRACTICE MAKES PERFECT

If you have identified a number of processes in your business to improve upon, you might want to call in a consultant for the first project. Work side-by-side with the consultant to learn the ropes so you can lead the other best practice initiatives yourself.

Be willing to think outside the box when it comes to getting outside help. Do you have any friends or family members who also run small businesses? Have they recently implemented best practices within their business? What are their lessons learned?

Don't stop there. If you have friends and family members working for large corporations or nonprofit organizations, see how much of their expertise is relevant to your business. What are some of their best practices in areas you are looking to improve, such as manufacturing your product, shipping, customer service, selecting vendors, and so on? What can you learn from how larger organizations get the work done?

Communication Is Key!

In every best practice implementation initiative, internal communication is a critical factor in your success. You cannot over-communicate with your employees.

Failure to communicate early and often as you implement best practices increases your chances of wasting your company's valuable resources.

There are a variety of ways to ensure you are getting your message across and that your employees are willing to participate in the discussion and offer their opinions and suggestions. Certainly consider any or all of the following communication methods:

- E-mail
- Department or functional area group meetings
- All-staff meetings
- Water cooler conversations
- Internal company website
- Surveys to your employees
- Casual conversations
- And the classic medium for great employee ideas: the suggestion box

Don't pick just one way to communicate; use a variety of methods. You'll find you get increasingly more information as individuals become more willing to share information. You'll also learn which employees are not quite on board or are worried about changes, which will give you an opportunity to follow up with them individually in a casual conversation.

Preparing Your Workforce for Change

Change management is a key issue in best practice implementation. Most of us are uncomfortable with sudden change, especially when we feel it is thrust upon us. Unanticipated change often makes us afraid of what the future holds—and makes us wonder whether or not we can be a part of that future.

DEFINITION

Change management is a structured way to get employees to move toward a new way of performing their jobs. It's the management skill of introducing people to change and gaining their acceptance as it takes place.

When employees are fully prepared for an impending change, they are more relaxed and accepting of that change. When anxiety levels are lower, you are more likely to experience a successful transition from "the way we were" to the way things need to be.

When planning a best practice implementation and considering the change management implications, think about these questions:

- What is the employees' comfort level with moving to the new best practice?

- Have employees been through any similar changes in the business before, or has it been status quo until now?

- Who among the staff appears the most comfortable with change? These are the individuals who are always looking for new ways to do their job or willing to take on other responsibilities.

By answering these questions, you have a better understanding of who on your staff can help to lead the charge of implementing best practices and who needs more hand-holding to be comfortable with the changes ahead.

BEST PRACTICE

As a best practice in managing change, set the timeline for implementation based not on those who are most comfortable with change but rather on those who need the most guidance and support in adjusting their roles and expectations.

Once you have some employees who support your initiative, use those individuals to help you get the others on board with the changes that are underway. Employees may feel more comfortable with change when they know other employees support it.

Take the time necessary to ensure that all employees are comfortable with the changes and confident in their abilities to do the job as it will now need to be done. This includes providing the training for any new software or technology that might now be required for their job and ensuring they have support as they begin using new best practices and processes. Ideally, you should provide your people with the time to learn all the new components of their job before you hold them accountable for attaining major new goals.

Staging Best Practice Implementation

Staged implementation enables you to roll out the new best practices and processes slowly throughout the business. Using such an approach enables you to work out kinks that may arise and make adjustments and modifications before everyone in the business is affected. Staged implementation also enables you to keep the rest of the business running smoothly when you are planning a particularly large best practice implementation process.

Let's look at an example. Your business is a local winery. You want to change your wine production process to expand your operation. By changing your process, you'll be able to bottle more wine to meet increasing customer demand. You currently have two production lines.

Rather than convert both production lines for the new process, you decide to take a staged approach and convert one line to work with the new process and keep one line running under the old process. This enables you to keep production running to meet customer demand for your product while trying out the new process for production on the second manufacturing line. This gives you an opportunity to work out any potential issues and ensure a successful implementation when you roll out the new process for production throughout your business.

When contemplating a staged implementation approach, consider these best practices:

- Ask employees who support the upcoming change to help by being part of the pilot team, but also include a few employees who are uncomfortable with the process so you can help increase their comfort level.

- Choose a less-busy time period for the pilot team to implement the new best practices so stress levels will be lower.

- Provide enough time to ensure that any issues that arise can be addressed and corrected before the full rollout.

- Have the individuals who are part of the pilot team available to assist the other employees after rollout.

Use these best practices to ensure a smooth transition to the new way of getting things done in your business.

Measure, Revise, and Refine

Best practices change as business needs and objectives change. Changes in competition for a product or service, changing demands of the customer, or a combination of the two, are likely to create the need for you to change the way your business operates and the best practices that make your business a success.

For example, if you find that competitors are coming out with new products regularly and significantly ahead of your introduction of new products, you should look at your development practices and processes and revise them to decrease the time it takes your business to introduce new products.

Of critical importance in any best practice implementation is consistently evaluating how well the best practice is working for your business and making revisions as necessary to keep working toward perfection.

PRACTICE MAKES PERFECT

Don't expect the first rollout of a new best practice to be perfect. Once employees start using the process, they will begin to encounter problems. Work with your employees to make modifications and adjustments until the process runs smoothly.

Don't hesitate to adopt the recommendations and suggestions of those doing the job. The employees who are using the new best practice day in and day out will have the best insight on how to improve upon what is being done.

Is What You're Doing Working?

Evaluate your best practices on a regular basis. Depending on your business that may be monthly, quarterly, twice a year, or annually. The more changes you make in your business, the more frequently you will want to evaluate your practices for getting work done.

Of course, you need to ensure that any best practices are aligned to your specific objectives. Set metrics to measure your progress. For example, if you want to increase your potential sales leads by 20 percent quarterly and have put new practices in place to meet that objective, you'll want to evaluate monthly how you are progressing toward the objective. If, after the second month, you only see a 1 or 2 percent increase in leads, you'll want to look at how you might adjust your new practices to get closer to meeting your goal.

When evaluating your new best practices, don't forget to take into consideration the comments of those who are using those new practices on a daily basis to perform their roles. Ask for their input on how things are going, what's working, and what's not. What additional changes might be made to continue to improve their job performance?

Consider conducting business impact and return-on-investment (ROI) studies of best practices within key areas of your business. This will help you to understand the effectiveness of the best practice by showing the monetary value of what was implemented and rolled out.

Time to Update Your Best Practices

Your best practices need to be updated as your business grows, the economy changes, new industry regulations are adopted, and new competitors enter the marketplace. When you experience any of these changes, you need to review your practices to determine whether you need to update them to remain competitive.

> **BEST PRACTICE**
>
> Keep abreast of what is going on in your industry and external to your industry that may impact how customers purchase your products and services. This may be an indicator of the need to update your practices to continue to be a viable business.

When you are ready to update your best practices, look again at what others are doing around you. What changes have they made to remain successful? Select a team of your best employees from a variety of areas throughout the business to help in updating your best practices.

The Least You Need to Know

- Choose to implement best practices that will have the most impact on your business.
- Get your employees involved in implementing best practices; they will be the most impacted by the changes.
- Communicate with your staff throughout the entire process using a variety of channels.
- If you decide to use external resources and consultants, remember that they are there to provide guidance but that you are the expert in your business.
- Evaluate your best practices regularly and make any necessary adjustments and changes to remain competitive and viable.

Best Practices for the Perfect Start-Up

What are the most common mistakes entrepreneurs make when launching a new business? How do you avoid them? What are the most important opportunities? What tools, processes, and documents will help you to get your business started on the right foot?

Every big, successful business was once a small, start-up business. The challenge lies in getting that business off the launching pad and onto the right trajectory. In this part of the book, you learn how to avoid the most common pitfalls, create the right plans, and set a strategy that makes sense for your new business.

Starting Your Business

In This Chapter

- Differentiating your business from competitors
- Doing your research to ensure a successful launch
- Structuring your business legally
- Considering your business's core requirements

Too often small businesses fail simply because the owner didn't do upfront planning and carefully map out details about the business or the environment in which it will be operating. Questions you'll need to consider include: Why do you think your idea is a good one? Who else is in your vicinity doing the same thing you want to do? What do you bring to the business that someone else does not?

People want to go into business for themselves for a variety of reasons. Some people simply want to be their own boss. Others want to earn more money. And some people want to have the freedom to come and go as they please. These are all valid reasons for starting a business, but don't jump in assuming it is going to be easy; it most assuredly will not be!

This chapter covers the diverse best practices essential for starting a business. It helps you ensure you have considered all the planning essentials prior to jumping in and launching your own business.

Refining Your Business Idea

What is the purpose of your business? Will you manufacture products, sell consulting services, open a local diner, or embrace any of a million other ideas? Regardless of what your business will be, you need to spend significant time refining your initial business idea to ensure the business you launch meets a need in the marketplace.

BUSINESS BUSTER

According to the U.S. Small Business Administration (SBA), 50 percent of small businesses fail in the first five years. There are a variety of reasons for this high failure rate; we believe it is due largely to poor business planning. Don't be a statistic! Take the time to plan for your company to succeed.

As a best practice, start by asking yourself the following questions:

Do you have money set aside for emergencies? What will you do if your business doesn't make money immediately? It is unlikely you'll be profitable in the first year, and maybe not even for a couple of years—how will you pay your bills during that time?

What excites you? Think about what you like to do. If you could do anything and not worry about money, what would you do? Maybe there is an idea in there. Do you love to travel? Maybe you could open a small travel agency. Do you love dogs? Maybe you could open a doggie day care or a pet shop.

Are you self-motivated? You need to be a self-starter. No one will be telling you what to do and when to do it; you'll need the discipline to do the work that needs to be done in the time it needs to be done.

Do you have the time needed to invest in starting a business? We aren't talking about a 40-hour work week; you'll be spending a significant amount of time working on your business. Where are you now with your family and other commitments? Given where you are right now in your life, does it make sense to branch out on your own and start a business?

Starting a business is not easy. It requires a significant amount of planning and commitment on your end. While starting a small business means you are your own boss and make your own decisions, it also means you bear the risk for whatever might go wrong in the business, including poor decisions. You'll need a lot of knowledge in many areas, including human resources, basic legal issues, contracts, negotiating, and technology. Of course you can (and will) call on experts to help you; but the broader your knowledge base, the less risk you'll face—you won't have to rely as much on others to do things that will have an impact on your business and its future.

Once you have settled upon an idea for starting a business, you'll need to take some time up front to refine that idea to increase the likelihood of your business's success. Let's look at an example.

Assume you are considering opening a small deli. You'll need to think through whether your idea is a good one based on factors such as:

- What will make your deli special

- Local competition

- Potential customers

- Available locations

- Financing options

- Available resources, such as employees

The following sections consider each of these issues in turn.

What's So Special About Your Company?

What's so special about your idea to open a deli? Why would someone come to you for their breakfast or lunch? What can you bring to the deli business that would make your deli stand out from others and draw in customers?

BEST PRACTICE

Before starting your business, visit similar businesses and understand what their challenges are. You might go outside your local area so that these other businesses do not see you as a competitor and will be willing to talk with you.

Maybe your deli will offer a make-your-own-sandwich station where customers are provided a setup similar to a salad bar. Perhaps your deli will offer a variety of ethnic sandwiches or sandwiches named after local celebrities. Or maybe you will cater to a growing Muslim population in your area by offering halal meat for your sandwiches.

The point is that your idea must have something special about it. Your business has to stand out!

Who Else Is Out There?

It is very unlikely you will come up with a business idea that doesn't already exist somewhere. The key is to ensure that no one located nearby is doing exactly the same thing you want to do. Consider who your competition might be and how you would compete effectively against them.

Let's assume that your competition for the local deli is a pizza shop that also sells sub sandwiches. You'll need to differentiate yourself from the pizza shop. You might decide to do so by offering a variety of sandwiches they don't offer along with soups and salads for lunch and pastries for breakfast. Additionally, while they are strictly a take-out joint, you might offer seating for customers along with wireless Internet access and small meeting areas. Now there's a reason to visit your shop rather than grab a piece of pizza.

Don't assume you already know everything there is to know about the competition. When analyzing other businesses that do some or all of what you want to do, take the following issues into account:

- **Location:** What similar businesses exist within a specific radius? The radius you focus on will depend greatly on the type of business. In addition, the ability of many businesses to sell products and services online makes geography increasingly less relevant in determining who the competition is.

- **Customer base:** Who are the potential customers and how many of them are within the area (or a reasonable driving distance)? If you are very unique—for example, the only shop within a 50-mile radius that sells model trains—you have an even larger potential for customers. However, if you are a small deli, it is unlikely people will come from farther than 5 miles or so.

- **Longevity:** How long has your competition been in business? Are they new in the area or have they been in business for several years (and therefore have a solid base of customers that have been with them a while)? How loyal are those customers?

- **Look outside the box:** You may have competition that is not obvious at first glance. For example, when considering competition for your deli, a local ice cream shop that also sells sandwiches may be competition for you. Don't forget fast-food establishments like Wendy's or McDonald's. Even a local Target or Costco may sell food that may compete with your deli.

Study the businesses that compete with you. Purchase their products. How is the quality? How do they interact with customers? Do they seem to know customers personally? If you bought something from them, would you want to buy again?

Do Your Homework!

Your work is not done just because you know who the competition is and how you are different from them. One powerful best practice for small business planning is to answer these questions on paper:

- What will be your product(s) or services(s)?

- Who will you market and sell your product to?

- What will be your differentiators? What is the benefit for customers to purchase from you? What added value will you bring to your product or service?

- Where will you get necessary capital to start?

At this stage, of course, you are only creating initial draft answers, but it's important that you get them down in black and white. Your answers may well change as you build your business plan (which we discuss in Chapter 4), but you should begin writing these ideas down now.

Market Research

You'll need to do additional research about your particular industry and understand its potential. Is it a growing industry? (If it is shrinking instead of growing, you will face higher levels of competition.) What changes are likely to occur in the short and long term? Does it make sense to have another company—yours—offer products or services in that particular industry? If so, why?

Let's look at another example. Assume that you want to open a business that helps companies develop and optimize their websites. As part of the IT industry, you would want to consider the size of this industry. Certainly an increasing number of companies are developing websites and doing business over the web. Given that, is there room for additional entrants? How will you compete effectively in a business where it doesn't matter if you are local? Companies will hire others to do this work regardless of location. You may well be competing with companies in Manhattan, Mumbai, or somewhere in between. Where will you fit in? Many small companies and individuals already provide this service locally; what makes you exceptional? What value will you bring to the industry and the customers?

> **BUSINESS BUSTER**
>
> Many small businesses fail because of insufficient research. When you think you have done enough and are ready to move forward, that's when you should stop, invest some more time, and make sure you have considered all possible competitors and challenges within your industry.

Small Business Economics 101

In order to start your business and run it effectively, you'll need to know some basic business economics. In-depth information on economics is beyond the scope of this book, but we cover some basics for you to consider when starting your own business.

Supply and Demand

One factor that will have a huge effect on your business is, of course, the behavior of your customer. Customers control supply and demand in the marketplace.

Let's look at an example. You own a small fruit and vegetable store that sells only organic products from local farmers. Recently there have been reports in the news that show that eating organic produce is healthier. Since those reports have come out, demand for organic fruits and vegetables has increased. This is great for your business, but it also means an increase in competition—chain supermarkets are now offering more organic produce than ever before. In addition, because of increased demand for your products, you can't keep enough organic produce on your shelves for your customers, so you must adjust your inventory to meet customer needs.

You can increase your pricing because there is a stronger demand for the product and less supply. However, as new entrants begin to sell the same product and therefore increase supply in the marketplace, you will have to drop your prices.

Supply and demand is an economic model that explains pricing equilibrium in the marketplace. To get a sense of how this pricing equilibrium works, let's assume that this year Florida was hit with severe frost in the winter months that damaged half of the state's orange crop. While the demand for orange juice has not changed, the supply has been drastically affected by the frost and damaged crops. Due to the limited supply of orange juice, the price will increase. The same number of people are competing for a dramatically smaller number of oranges. If we reverse this example and assume this year was the best year ever for orange production and there were very few damaged oranges, the demand remains static, but the supply of oranges increases. In this scenario, there is likely to be a glut in the market of oranges, effectively lowering the price of orange juice in the marketplace.

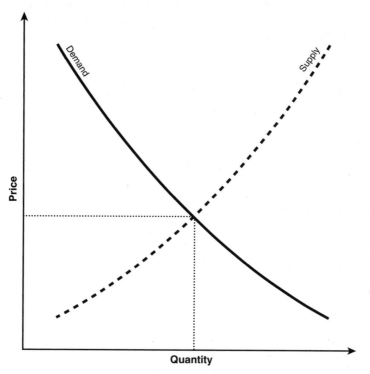

A sample supply and demand curve.

As the preceding graph shows, as supply increases, demand will decrease; when price increases, demand will decrease. The intersection of supply and demand shows the balance, or pricing equilibrium, in the marketplace.

Going back to our example of the organic local food store, as customers realize there is more supply of organic produce, they will begin to demand lower prices. In other words, if customers can now find organic produce at several markets, they will begin to shop based on price. If, as a smaller business, you are able to order produce specifically to meet your customer's needs and to ensure you have the highest quality product, you may be able to retain your higher price structure *and* effectively compete against the chain supermarkets. Alternatively, you might find another differentiator that a larger supermarket cannot provide: maybe you'll offer cooking classes for your customers, provide organic ready-made meals, or offer other product lines (such as organic cosmetics and local handmade food gifts such as jams and jellies).

BUSINESS BUSTER

Many small businesses find it difficult to hold on when mega-stores step into the marketplace. Those small businesses that do survive are innovative and constantly on the move.

Barriers to Entry

Some businesses are more affected by supply and demand than others because of their particular product or service. For instance, let's say you want to run a small company that delivers training for Microsoft certification using Microsoft Official Curriculum. There are a number of potential challenges to consider, including:

- Competition—a flooded marketplace

- Government regulations and licensing

- Price sensitivity—customers are indifferent as to who they purchase from and shop solely on price

- Location—customers want local trainers as they will not pay for travel

Your problems stem from the fact that the customer is indifferent about where they purchase this training since the goal of the training is simply to obtain certification. Because everyone is using Microsoft's Official Curriculum, there is no difference in material. Trainers must be certified, and while some trainers are more competent than others, it is difficult to sell the customer on the value of having a better trainer. Additionally, there are many e-learning offerings that help people get certified. So where does this leave you? Competing with countless other trainers with few, if any, ways to differentiate yourself!

BEST PRACTICE

The process of comparing your business to your competition doesn't end once you get your business off the ground. You must constantly innovate to ensure a successful long-term business. Set up regular sessions with key employees to analyze what your competition is doing and how you compare.

In some situations, government policies and licensing requirements affects your ability to offer a product or service as a small business. For example, to start a radio station, the Federal Communications Commission requires a license, and it would be difficult, given the large barrier to entry into the marketplace from current radio stations, for a smaller business to obtain such a license. Many larger stations may work together to keep you out of the marketplace and, in some industries (such as this one), they may have the power to do so.

Another potential barrier to entering an industry as a new player in the market is the competition. More established firms have a brand name and have built up their reputation in the marketplace. It may be difficult for new companies to enter that market and gain some of that market share. It doesn't mean you shouldn't try—we are not trying to discourage you! But these are all things to consider as you think about starting your own business. If you are entering an industry with heavy competition from big players, make sure you have a niche for your business—something that will make you stand out from the others and intrigue and draw customers.

Cost Structure

An additional component of success for any business is understanding your cost structure—specifically *fixed costs* and *variable costs*. We have seen too many businesses led by individuals who don't have a grasp of the costs involved in running their business.

DEFINITION

Fixed costs, also called *sunk costs,* include overhead and things like lease payments and salaries of employees. **Variable costs** vary depending on your output; they can include materials required to manufacture products or seasonal employees.

Without a complete understanding of your cost structure, you will find it difficult to obtain financing and investment in your business, control costs, and effectively manage your business.

Let's look at an example. Your business produces engines for lawn mowers and other such equipment. Your variable costs have increased by 20 percent over the last year, mainly due to the increase in demand and shortage of supply of a particular component for the engines you produce. You need to reduce costs overall. You cannot lower your fixed costs as business is increasing, and you need the employees you have as well as the manufacturing facilities. You'll need to review your variable costs. Your options include:

- Purchasing materials on a just-in-time basis (continuous forecasting). By continuously forecasting your needs, you only purchase materials exactly when needed, in (ideally) the exact quantity needed; you therefore do not store materials, which increases costs.

- Negotiating better contracts with suppliers (i.e., multi-source suppliers rather than single-source suppliers).

These are the kinds of issues you'll need to be familiar with, and be ready to address, long before you launch your business. (See Chapter 12 for more ways to cut costs in your business.)

Legal Ownership Options

According to the U.S. Census Bureau report in 2007, there were more than 27 million businesses registered in the United States. Of these, only 5.75 million have paid employees. The balance—the vast majority—are *sole proprietorships* with no paid employees.

DEFINITION

A **sole proprietorship** is a business that is run by one individual. In a sole proprietorship, there is no legal difference between the individual owner and the business; they are one and the same. All assets and debts related to the business are owned by the individual.

Small businesses operating within the United States can form a variety of different types of partnerships and corporations. Your decision on how to legally organize your business will be based on many factors, including …

- The size of your business.

- Your expectations for growth and expansion.

- Your future plans for the business. (Do you eventually want to sell it?)

- Risk associated with your business—you may need the protections of a corporation.

- Your need for investment from outside sources.

Sole Proprietorships

Sole proprietorships are not an official form of legal ownership, as they do not require any special forms or filings to be completed with either state or federal government. However, you might still have to obtain business licenses or permits, depending on your particular business (such as if you are running a daycare business). Depending on state and local zoning board requirements, you might also be required to register your business as a sole proprietorship if you are running a business out of your home.

When people pay for the products or services of a sole proprietor, they write a check out to the individual directly rather than to a company name, and the business owner can deposit this check in a personal checking account.

A sole proprietorship is certainly the simplest way to run your small business. When filing tax returns, all income can be reported as personal income, along with any deductions for your small business, on Schedule C. Therefore, taxes are certainly much simpler in a sole proprietorship.

A disadvantage to a sole proprietorship is that your assets—even your personal assets such as your home—are unprotected if you are unable to pay your debts. There is no difference between you personally and your sole proprietorship. If your business runs into debt that you cannot get out from under, you are personally responsible for that debt as the individual owner. In such situations, if you file bankruptcy, you would need to file personal bankruptcy as the sole proprietor of the business, a step that would, of course, affect your personal assets.

While a sole proprietorship may be a good option initially in starting off your business, as you grow and hire employees, look to expand your business with investment money, or want to take advantage of deductions permitted other businesses, you may want to consider other legal ownership options.

Partnerships

Two or more individuals are able to form partnerships; however, one individual can form a limited liability company (LLC). Depending on the type of partnership entity you select, you have total liability to limited liability.

In a general partnership, all parties are liable based on the percentage of the business they own. For example, if you own 40 percent of a business and your partner owns 60 percent, you are responsible for 40 percent of the debt and your partner is responsible for 60 percent.

An LLC provides more protections under the law than a general partnership but is more flexible than a corporation (less record-keeping and administrative requirements). Therefore, registering as an LLC is frequently a good choice for smaller businesses.

Professional limited liability partnership (PLLP), limited liability partnership (LLP), or professional limited liability company (PLLC) are usually reserved for licensed professionals such as a doctors, lawyers, accountants, architects, or engineers. A small law firm may have five partners who have formed a PLLP, LLP, or PLLC.

Corporations

Corporations are much more formal entities that offer more protections for its members (stockholders) under the law. Corporations are a separate legal entity from its stockholders and can enter into agreements and contracts without the members personally entering into those agreements. The members (or stockholders) of the corporation have very limited liability—only to the extent of their initial monetary contribution into the corporation. For example, a stockholder who has paid $30 per share for 1,000 shares of stock is only liable for $30,000, the initial amount paid per share.

Corporations pay higher taxes than any other business entity. In many cases, corporations have an easier time obtaining investment money because there is a sense of security in dealing with a formal entity on the part of investors.

Understanding Your Business's Core Needs

Your business will have certain unique requirements for getting started. If you are going to be selling homemade products such as soaps, candles, or jams and jellies, you will want to do some or all of the following as part of the launch of your business:

- Secure a table or booth at local craft fairs (especially around the holidays).

- Secure a storefront location to sell your product.

- Develop an e-commerce website so people can purchase from you online.

You need to understand the core needs of your particular business in order to have a successful launch. If you are selling photographs, a website presence alone may be sufficient to get started, with a long-term goal of opening a storefront location when you have more profits to invest back into the business. If you are opening a dry-cleaning business, you'll need a storefront location but might not need a website initially.

Now let's look in more depth at some of the specifics you will want to consider prior to launching your business.

What Are the Cash Requirements?

Every business will have some cash requirements. Consider the cash requirements for your particular business and how to obtain that cash if you don't already have it on hand. You'll need cash on hand to …

- Pay yourself until your business makes a profit.

- Sign a lease for space for a storefront location.

- Purchase supplies or products.

- Obtain permits and licenses.

- Implement technology such as computers, servers, and e-commerce software.

- Secure health insurance and business insurance.

- Market your business (website design, e-mail blasts, direct mail).

Think carefully about your cash requirements. Consider every possibility and then add a bit extra on top of it, just in case. Ideally, you will want enough cash to keep your business running for 12 to 18 weeks while you work to make your business profitable. This provides you the security you need to keep moving forward and get through the rough patches.

Let's look at an example. You want to open a dry-cleaning business. Here are the costs you'll need to cover to get the business off the ground:

- Leases for equipment and building
- Business insurance and maintenance
- Permits/licenses
- Costs associated with incorporating the business
- Employees' salary and health insurance costs
- Utility costs
- Advertising and other marketing
- Supplies

In addition, you'll need money to live on for at least a year. You estimate you'll need $350,000 set aside for the business for the first year.

BUSINESS BUSTER

Too often small business owners jump into starting their own business without having a complete understanding of the costs involved. This is a frequent cause of business failure. Spend time talking with other small business owners in your industry and doing your homework carefully so that you fully understand what you are getting into.

As a best practice when starting a new business, check with a number of sources for information on costs associated with starting that particular business. Your local Chamber of Commerce, business and industry associations, and the U.S. Small Business Administration (SBA) are all sources of information on business start-up costs. Additionally, speak with a proprietor of the type of business you are starting to get his perspective on what it takes to start a business. By being well-prepared for what is involved, you increase your chances of success, and you'll be much more relaxed when the inevitable hiccups occur.

Should You Invest Your Own Money?

Now that you have an idea of how much money you'll need to invest in your business, and how much you'll need to hold on to in order to stay afloat while your business is getting off the ground, you'll need to determine where you're going to get that money. Chapter 4 includes information on funding your start-up; in this section we help you decide whether to invest your own money and how to decide how much to invest.

Let's start by assuming you will need to invest some of your own money to start your business. This will show investors that you are serious and committed to making the business a success. However, before you jump in and invest your own finances, think about how much you need to live on while your business gets going. If you have a spouse who is bringing in a regular paycheck, or you plan to work full time and start your business on the side, you'll likely need less (or nothing) set aside to pay yourself. However, if you won't have any income outside of your new business, you need to be sure you can cover your expenses.

Here's an example. You are opening a store that sells handmade crafts, and you need $200,000 to get started. You have $150,000 in savings. You will have no other income once you start your new business except for what the new business generates. Given that, you decide to invest $50,000, apply for financing for the balance of $150,000 and hold $100,000 to live on during the first year.

Your decision to invest your own money will be based on a variety of factors, including …

- Availability of financing.
- Your ability to sustain yourself financially during the start-up phase.
- Other household income.

Many entrepreneurs choose not to relinquish control of their business by selling stock or seeking venture capital (VC). For some companies, such as the analytics software giant SAS, the price of such financing is simply too high. If retaining control over all timelines and decision-making processes is important to you, you may want to go it alone, financing the business out of your own savings or out of the company's cash flow. This is not necessarily an easy path, but it has proved to be the best one for some businesses.

Lease, Buy, or Go Virtual?

Another major decision you'll need to make for your business is whether to lease space, buy property and a building, or have a virtual business where everything is done online. Your choice will be based on the type of business you are opening and the amount of money you have for investment. Some businesses are more conducive than others to being completely virtual.

> **BEST PRACTICE**
>
> If you are unsure about the best location for your business, you should lease rather than purchase. Ideally, choose a location that is already set up for your particular business. If you are opening a restaurant, look for a space that has already housed a restaurant. This requires less retrofitting on your part and saves you money.

Let's look at a few examples.

Own: You are interested in opening a small gift shop in an area with high tourist traffic. You notice that there is a small gift shop for sale in your town. The owner of the gift shop owns the building in which the shop is located and is selling both the business and the building. You decide to pursue the option of purchasing the business since it has been operating for over five years and seems to do quite well. Additionally, you have significant money of your own to invest in the business and are willing to take more risks.

Lease: You are interested in opening a hardware business. The previous one closed about a year and a half ago, and the building it was in has remained empty for that time period. The owner of the building is willing to either sell or lease you the building. The shop requires little retrofitting since it was previously a hardware store. You decide to pursue the option of leasing the business as it will be easier for you to manage financially and you are concerned about taking on too much risk.

Virtual: You are interested in starting a business doing event photography. You have no need for a storefront location and will instead run the business out of your home for at least the first year. You decide to launch your business with a website. You have money to invest in building a website and marketing your business, which will cost no more than $20,000.

In your initial planning for your business, consider your options for leasing, buying, or running your business solely online. What are your competitors doing? Does one path work better for you initially? Can you expand as you start to make a profit?

The Least You Need to Know

- Do your homework up front so you know exactly what you are getting into.
- Consider getting professional advice on how to best organize your business.
- Identify what distinguishes your business from the competition by answering the question, "Why are you special?"
- When you think you have done enough market research, do more! Be prepared to invest significant amounts of time in the planning stage of starting a business.
- Anticipate keeping at least 12 to 18 months' worth of cash on hand while you work to make your business profitable.
- If you are unsure about the best location for your business, lease rather than purchase.

Getting Down to Business

In This Chapter

- Developing and utilizing your business plan
- Understanding your options for funding
- Creating a realistic budget
- Getting the expertise you need

While a good business plan does not ensure your business will be successful, it does show that you have thought everything through carefully.

This chapter focuses on best practices for developing a business plan that helps you make the right decisions about your business and improves your chances of getting the investment support you need. You'll also find out about best practices that relate to funding for your business, developing your initial budget for the business, and finding the expert advice you need.

Creating Your Business Plan

A business plan is a formal document that includes information on the goals and objectives of your business and explains why you believe you can reach those goals. It also includes your detailed plan for meeting those goals by means of specific research, production, marketing, and sales initiatives.

Your business plan's biggest value lies in the fact that it forces you to think strategically about your business ideas and their viability. This is why we believe that even if you are not looking for investment in your business, you should develop a business plan anyway!

Your business plan should include research that shows why you have chosen the right industry to be in. It should also show how you will create value for customers and deal with competitive challenges.

> **PRACTICE MAKES PERFECT**
>
> Share your business plan with a trusted advisor and ask for feedback. Does the reviewer see the value in your business idea? Are there any serious gaps in the plan or flaws that you overlooked? A second set of eyes can make all the difference, especially if you are using the plan to secure investment monies or a bank loan.

Entrepreneurs also frequently use business plans when they are ready to take their companies to the next level. For example, let's assume that you own a deli and have been in business for a few years. You are considering expanding your deli into a full restaurant that's open for lunch and dinner with increased seating capacity. A business plan will help you to effectively develop the road map for achieving your goals. Think of the plan as a decision-making tool.

Companies also use business plans when they are interested in expanding their product lines or increasing their service offerings. In addition, you can use your business plan to track your progress against the goals and objectives you set when you started the business.

Use the plan to think about the good and the bad aspects of doing business. Don't just focus on all the great things you think will happen!

You should plan on spending at least a few weeks developing and refining your business plan.

The Goal and the Audience

There are many possible audiences for your business plan, depending on your objectives. If you are looking to expand your business and want to get investment from outside resources, you should target your business plan toward banks, investment capital firms, and others who might invest in your business growth.

You might also share portions of your business plan with employees so they understand your vision for the business. You could use the plan to set goals and objectives for specific departments to achieve in a set time period or in meetings with potential purchasers of your business or additional business partners.

What to Include in Your Plan

Your business plan will include the following basic information:

- A general description of your business

- Your products or services and target customers

- How you will market and sell your products or services

- A competitive analysis

- Your operational plan

- Key vendors and suppliers

- Management staff/partners

- Financial plan and budget

- Growth plans

- Investment needs

You should also include information on the vision you have for your business, your mission statement, the industry you will be part of, the strengths you personally bring to the business (your background and experience), how you will legally structure your business, and any licenses or permits required for your business.

You will also want to ensure that your business plan addresses needs related to technology, location, e-commerce, website development, insurance, and resources.

BEST PRACTICE

Include an executive summary section in your business plan—no more than two to three pages—that explains the key points of the business plan, with the details in the business plan itself. Go to www.score.org/index.html for a wide variety of resources and business plan templates for small business owners.

Your budget and financial plans need to clearly capture the costs of running your business, keeping in mind that costs go far beyond money. Think about time and internal resources, too. For example, what will be required to secure a single customer for your product or service? Suppose you will be selling consulting services to help businesses market their products. You know you will need a business development resource—someone to seek out customers for your business. You estimate it will cost you between $3,000 and $5,000 to secure a customer and will require at least a three- to six-month time frame to close the deal. Once you have the customer, you will need an account manager to maintain the customer relationship. These are all part of your cost of doing business, along with salaries and benefits, marketing, leases, equipment purchases, and so on.

The operational section in your business plan should discuss how your products are produced, your customer service initiatives, how you will manage inventory, and costs associated with production of the product.

How to Stand Out from the Crowd

The competition for business financing is tough. Your plan might be sitting on an investor's desk along with hundreds of other plans. What are you going to do to stand out from the crowd? What will make your business plan more attractive to a potential investor?

Certainly, ensuring that your business plan is professionally developed, well written, and free of spelling and grammar errors will help. And ensuring your plan is complete and includes details about your business—risks/rewards, short- and long-term goals—is a must. What else can you do to stand out from the crowd? Here are some suggestions that have worked for other businesses seeking financing:

Include a video. A 5- to 10-minute video of you presenting your plan enables the viewer to make a connection with you. You become more than just a piece of paper with data—you're a real person explaining your goals and why you would like investment in your business. You can even upload your video to YouTube! However, you should ensure that it reaches only a small group or an individual (such as a bank officer) and is accessible only via a special link; you don't want it to show up on public searches. This can be a very powerful technique for communicating with lenders and investors.

Have stellar references and/or recommendations. If you have already offered your services to others informally, ask for letters of recommendation to include in the business plan.

Include a product sample. If you have a prototype of the product you want to manufacture, allow the investors an opportunity to view it. This will show that you have made some personal investment in developing the product.

BEST PRACTICE

If you have already lined up potential customers, include that information in your business plan. This demonstrates a starting point for your business and will be attractive to potential investors.

To stand out from the crowd, you must ensure that your plan shows that you have done your homework—that you know what is involved in branching out on your own to offer your products and services and that you are prepared for the risks and challenges ahead of you. Your plan shouldn't be overly optimistic; make sure it is realistic.

You'll also want to show that you know how to execute your business idea. It is all well and good to have a great idea, but if you are unable to execute it—and have no proof that you are able to do so—what's the use of showing anyone your plan? If you have a product idea, test the idea out with potential customers to determine their level of interest. If you have an idea for a new service, interview prospective buyers and find out exactly how willing they are to purchase and use it. Include concise summaries of the results of your tests and interviews in your business plan. There's no reason for anyone to believe your business can succeed unless you have tested the market-worthiness of your idea!

Remember that your plan is not static; it will change. New competitors in the marketplace, economic changes, new products or services, and significant growth are all situations that will require you to revisit your business plan and update it so it continues to be relevant.

As a best practice, review your business plan at least annually to ensure it is still viable and accurately describes your business and its objectives. However, if the industry you are in is rapidly changing, you may want to review your plan quarterly.

Finding Start-Up Funding

Finding money to start a business is not an easy task. You must be able to prove that you have looked closely at all the financial contingencies and created plans for dealing with them. You should also be prepared for your personal credit to be scrutinized closely. Be sure you have accurate, updated, and verifiable information for the following items:

- Profit and loss statement for your business

- Cash flow analysis (including the point at which it becomes positive)

- Balance sheet
- Costs associated with your business—fixed and variable
- Break-even analysis

We discuss each of these documents in detail later in Chapter 12.

You will certainly need to go beyond a year in your figures—you should plan for a three- to five-year range. If you are launching a start-up, much of this information will be guesswork, but those projections should be realistic. Any assumptions you make should be documented so that potential investors can understand your thinking. As a start-up, use your past experience and knowledge since you don't have real numbers to show. Being realistic about your business finances demonstrates that you are prepared for the many challenges that lie ahead.

For any investment request you make, be sure that you are able to clearly describe what you want the money for, who else is involved in the initiative (your partners and their backgrounds), your current finances, how much money you are seeking, and how you will manage that investment.

BEST PRACTICE

Prior to applying for a business loan, make sure all your ducks are in a row. Review your credit reports and ensure that your accounts payable and receivable are current. The lender will need to be confident in your abilities to run the business, make good use of the loan monies, and pay them back in a timely manner.

If you plan to invest some of your own money in your start-up business, make this clear in your business plan. Investors like to see where all of the money is coming from for the business, and investing some of your own cash makes it a more attractive investment for them.

When going for funding, expect to have to provide proof that you are able to pay your debts (if you have a poor credit history, you'll find it difficult to secure funding). You may also have to put up collateral, in the form of your intellectual property (IP), your personal home, or other significant assets, for your business loan. For instance, if your company develops programs for critical skills training such as negotiating, communicating, and managing others, that training content is your IP. You can use that IP to help you secure a loan for your business.

There are numerous options for financing your business, including self-financing, personal loans from banks and credit unions, investments from venture capital firms, small business loans, microloans, and loans from friends and family. The following sections look at each of these more closely.

Self-Financing

What is your ability to finance some or all of your business opportunity? For some businesses, you may need very little financing to get started—just some supplies and the ability to pay yourself. For instance, let's say you want to open a consulting business specializing in helping companies and individuals manage their computers, including technical support, purchasing of computers, and setup and maintenance of systems. You do not need office space; you'll be at client sites or working from your home. You'll be working by yourself, at least initially. You already have a few customers lined up, so you have a head start. You'll need financing to purchase equipment, to pay your bills, and to do a bit of advertising of your services. You'll need about $100,000 to get started. You have $50,000 in savings and decide to finance the rest through a home equity loan.

Other options for self-financing include borrowing against your 401(k) (if you are currently employed and will keep your job as you start off in your own business), an IRA, or life insurance policies with a cash value. There are risks with all of these options, and you'll want to be clear about those risks.

PRACTICE MAKES PERFECT

Ask advisors, such as your accountant or attorney, to help you by reviewing the information you are pulling together to get financing for your business. Find someone to practice your pitch on, so when you go for that loan or investment monies, you are polished, professional, and relaxed.

Bank and Credit Union Loans

The recent economic meltdown has made borrowing money from banks much more difficult than ever before, putting lots of pressure on small businesses trying to start off or stay afloat. You may have better luck with credit unions, especially if you are a longtime customer.

Banks and credit unions both will want to know what you need the loan for and will certainly be interested in your ability to pay back that loan. You'll need to present a business plan when applying for either a bank or credit union loan.

Many banks offer loans backed by the U.S. Small Business Administration (SBA) loan programs. SBA-backed loans provide a guarantee to the bank loaning the money, meaning that the SBA will pay a percentage of the loan to the bank if you default on the loan. We discuss the SBA program and other small business loans later in this chapter.

Before applying for a bank loan, make sure all your finances are in order. You'll need impeccable record-keeping! This is also true of credit union loans. The more prepared you are, the more likely you will be successful in securing the loan. Remember, appearing unprepared is a sign of risk for most banks.

Venture Capital

Your choice of venture capital (VC) firm to approach to fund your start-up (or the expansion of your business) will depend on your business and what stage of development you are in. VC firms provide financial funding to start-up firms with high potential for future success. The partners of the VC firm make their investment back (with interest) through owning equity in the business in which they are investing those monies. Many VC firms also provide oversight of business operations to ensure the appropriate use of the investment monies.

VC firms fund at various stages of a business. They provide seed money to businesses at the very early stages of start-up. Seed money is frequently provided to enable development of a prototype of a product or to introduce and test out a new service. Investors who provide seed money are sometimes called angel investors. Angel investors may agree to invest in a new business where a regular VC firm may not.

Some VC firms provide financing to help new businesses market their products or services, develop products, and hire the right resources for the early stages of the business. This is frequently called start-up funding.

The next two rounds of funding by a VC firm are called first-round and second-round funding. First-round funding is for a business that is ready to begin to sell their product or service and continue development on their product. Second-round funding helps start-up businesses to market and sell their products by hiring the right resources to do so. At the second-round funding, many start-ups are still not making any profit and the VC funds are paying the bills for the business while they are trying to become profitable.

All of this funding takes place in the early stages of a new business before they are making any profits. Once a start-up business is making a profit, they may partner with a VC firm to get funding to expand their business with new products and services.

BEST PRACTICE

Do your homework carefully before approaching a VC firm about funding your business. Do they work in your industry? Do they fund your type of business? How much control will they want over your business? Doing your research up front will save you considerable time and effort in what is not an easy process. The National Venture Capital Association (www.NVCA.org) provides a directory for entrepreneurs on member VC firms.

As a best practice, consider the following questions prior to approaching a VC firm to get funding for your business:

- Have you done your homework to prove the viability of your idea?
- Do you have the right team (you and your partners) in place to manage the business?
- What are you bringing to the table? Are you investing any money yourself?
- Why should they invest in you and your idea?

When you apply for VC funding, expect to be grilled on the thinking behind your business plan, your ideas, and the viability of both. The VC investors want to know what is in it for them—they want a return on their money in a reasonable period of time. Expect to hear some "no's," but don't give up—you have many options!

You may also want to consider the website Prosper (www.prosper.com). This site connects individuals who need to borrow money with those willing to invest. Similarly, Lending Club (www.lendingclub.com) is a peer lending service that partners individuals looking for investment money with those interested in investing in them. For small businesses in an economy where business loans are not easy to get, Prosper and Lending Club are two great options to help you finance the expansion of your business!

Small Business Loans

The U.S. SBA provides a variety of loans, often through banks and other lending institutions, for small businesses. Frequently the SBA is willing to loan smaller amounts than a bank or VC firm.

One option for an SBA-backed loan is the 7(a) Loan Program. This is the SBA's primary loan program and provides banks and other lending institutions a guarantee that the SBA will cover a portion of the loan should the borrower default. This is also a flexible loan program, as it enables borrowing for a variety of purposes for small businesses. SBA loans are applied for through a bank or lending institution directly, not through the SBA. These types of loans have the following requirements:

- Your business is a for-profit company.

- You do business in the United States.

- You are an eligible business.

- The loan is being used to either establish a new business or expand an existing business.

- You are unable to get funds from other sources.

- You have a good personal credit history.

There are a few different types of 7(a) loans, including loans for international trade or special purposes. The SBA website provides all the information you need on 7(a) loans, including requirements, how to apply, terms, and minimum and maximum loan amounts.

The SBA also provides a CDC/504 Loan Program. This is a longer-term financing option for small businesses to provide monies for brick-and-mortar operations. It may be used to purchase land to build facilities or for improvements to existing facilities. It may also be used to purchase machinery and other equipment for manufacturing. The CDC/504 loans are frequently used to expand and grow existing small businesses.

SBA Microloans

Microloans are short-term loans to small businesses that don't need a large investment—no more than $35,000—but do need some support to get started in their endeavor. These loans can be used for working capital or to purchase supplies, inventory, and equipment for a business.

Let's look at an example. You want to open a business making pottery to sell to other businesses. You need help in purchasing the materials and equipment—such as an oven and the clay—to make the pottery. You only need $20,000, and you have collateral to cover the loan. A microloan may be perfect for you.

The SBA is the largest source for small business financing and should not be overlooked as you think about funding opportunities. SBA loans come through banks; the SBA does not loan directly to business owners. However, the loans are backed by the SBA. This section provides only a very brief overview of your SBA loan options. Visit SBA's website for a variety of resources to help small businesses.

Friends and Family

Don't discount friends and family for small loans. You may be able to borrow money from them at a very low interest rate (or, if you are lucky, no interest!). Be just as buttoned-up here as if you were applying for a bank loan. Walk through your business plan with them!

According to Henry Gregor, author of *Business Genesis: A Strategic Approach to Starting a Business* (www.strategicvisions.org), many smaller companies turn to bootstrapping to get themselves started. Bootstrap financing is a way of acquiring funds without raising equity or getting a loan from a bank. It may include borrowing from friends or family, using credit cards, selling personal assets, or using the business owner's personal savings.

BUSINESS BUSTER

If you borrow money from banks and use the funds differently than you stated you would, the bank might be able to call the total amount of the loan, requiring you to pay it back in full immediately.

Developing Your Initial Budget

The initial budget for your business needs to be focused on what you plan to spend to get your business started and any revenue you expect to receive. Your expenses will probably exceed any revenue, especially in the first year. In fact, you may find for the first year that you have no revenue at all! Given that many start-ups are unprofitable for an extended period, this is to be expected. Your goal in budgeting for your business is to keep your expenses as lean as possible to get through those tricky first years.

> **BEST PRACTICE**
>
> If you have never created a detailed budget before, seek the help of an accountant to develop the budget for your business. This is an important document that will help guide your business decisions and accurately forecast your finances.

A budget helps you to understand the expenses involved in running your business and how those expenses compare to the revenue you are bringing in. You can't fully understand your profitability without understanding the expenses associated with the revenue.

For example, let's assume that you are considering selling a product for $20. When you look at the costs of creating, marketing, and selling that product, you realize that it costs you $19. That leaves you a profit of only $1! And what happens if you want to, or have to, provide a discount? You have no wiggle room at all. You need to consider how to either reduce the cost of developing and marketing the product or to increase the price of the product to increase your profit. A budget will help you to look at all your costs to see where you can make some changes to increase profitability.

What You Should Include

Your initial budget should cover at least the first two years of your business operations and should include information about the following start-up expenses:

- Real estate purchases (such as buying a business storefront)

- Capital equipment purchases or leases (computers, furniture, etc.)

- Lease costs for facilities, which might include utilities, security deposits, and tenant improvements to the rented facility

- Administrative costs such as professional services fees, salaries and benefits, fees for legal structuring of your business, licenses and permits, and business insurance

- Inventory and other supplies

- Sales and marketing costs

- Any other start-up expenses associated with your particular business

Break down all of your expenses into fixed expenses (such as rent, utilities, and lease payments) and variable expenses (such as production costs, income taxes, bank fees, and materials).

As a best practice, if you are developing a product, ensure your variable costs are shown per unit. That enables better analysis of your cost per development of a single unit.

Your budget should include the estimated monthly sales of your product or service. For a start-up business, this can be a bit tricky—you don't yet know what your sales will be. Of course, you have done your homework and likely have an idea of your sales. Include in your initial budget:

- Best-case scenario (high estimates of sales for the year)

- Worst-case scenario (low estimates of sales for the year)

- Probable-case scenario (estimates of sales between the worst- and best-case predictions)

Let's look at an example of best-, worst-, and probable-case scenarios. Your business will be selling coffee from around the world. Based on your market research (and a promise from friends and family to purchase your product!) you predict the following sales for the first year you are in business:

Sales of Coffee Product—One Year

Best Case	Worst Case	Probable Case
$150,000	$25,000	$75,000

In the preceding table, you see three estimates for sales of coffee product for the first year: predicted sales in the best-case, worst-case, and probable-case scenarios.

You should then break your estimated sales down further throughout the 12 months of the year based on factors that might affect your business, such as seasonality or time to market your product.

Looking at the probable-case scenario, your 12-month sales would look like this:

12-Month Breakdown of Sales: Probable-Case Scenario
Sales of Coffee Product ($)

Jan.	Feb.	Mar.	Apr.	May	June
2,150	2,530	2,990	3,500	4,200	4,900

July	Aug.	Sept.	Oct.	Nov.	Dec.
5,300	6,800	8,080	9,600	11,200	13,730

Of course, making sales doesn't mean you are making a profit. You would then take your sales, subtract your costs, and determine your profit for the month and for the year.

You must also address the painful fact that you will probably not collect all of your money. Sad but true: not every customer will pay his or her bill. Certainly some businesses have fewer worries about collections than others. For instance, you may request only cash or credit or debit card payment for coffee purchases. This may mean that you collect 100 percent of sales (or perhaps 99 percent if you aren't diligent about checking credit cards!). However, you may also accept checks, which may bounce and reduce your collections.

If you assume you will collect 90 percent of all sales, and you predict that you will make $5,000 in sales for the month, you can assume you will only collect $4,500.

Balancing Needs: Now and Later

As you'll begin to see when you develop your initial budget, you may not be able to sustain all the expenses during the critical first year or so of your business. The question is: what can you do without?

Suppose you have built your initial budget and found that your expenses are way over what you can afford, by about $20,000 a month. You have some great ideas but want to find a way to reduce expenses so that you feel more comfortable managing your finances while you try to secure a loan. You want to also ensure that any cuts you make in your budget do not affect the professionalism of your business. You decide that you can take the following steps to reduce your expenses:

- **Do it yourself.** Instead of paying someone else to create brochures for your consulting services, you decide to create the brochures yourself and print them as you need them. Additionally, rather than having a printer typeset and print your business cards, you find that, with the right supplies, you can print professional-quality cards yourself.

- **Postpone hiring personnel.** You decide to hold off on hiring a salesperson and make the sales yourself at first. Once business picks up and revenue starts coming in, you'll consider hiring a sales rep.

- **Reduce marketing costs.** Rather than promote your services in print publications and newspapers, you decide to focus on social media and press releases.

- **Postpone expenses for renting office space.** Since you are a consultant and will be traveling to company sites, you really do not need an office space. You can easily work out of your home with a few simple adjustments like adding a business line and fax line.

Making these changes enables you to adjust your initial budget so that you feel more comfortable with the expenses you'll have to cover while you are getting customers and bringing in sales.

PRACTICE MAKES PERFECT

Refer to your budget regularly to plan for your business, control your costs, and evaluate how you are performing against your estimates. Make adjustments as necessary. Think of your budget—like your business plan—as a living document!

Developing your initial budget before you actually start your business gives you a detailed account of what you will need to cover each month in expenses and how much you'll be able to pull for a salary for yourself. The lower your expenses, the fewer worries you will have about meeting your commitments, and the better you can manage your business as it grows. What's more, your business will look better when you apply for that business loan! However, remember that your budget is a living document and is not set in stone. If some fantastic opportunity comes up and it makes sense for you to take advantage of it, you should consider reworking your budget.

What Can You Do Yourself?

You may want to seek a professional review of your business plan to ensure it is complete and would be well received by any potential investors or bankers. However, there are some areas you should be able to handle yourself given all the resources available on the Internet and in print. These include:

- Creating the initial business plan

- Developing your initial budget

- Researching options for loans and investment

Remember that you are the expert in your business. If something you hear from someone else just doesn't make sense given your business idea and plans, get a second opinion.

Filling in the Resource Blanks

Your resources include accountants, attorneys, other small business owners in your industry and external to your industry, advisors from SCORE (you'll learn more about SCORE later on in this book), your local Chamber of Commerce, and your local banker or credit union representative. Many consultants provide advice to individuals starting businesses. If you seek out the advice of such a consultant, ensure that they have worked in your particular industry before; that way, they will better be able to support your efforts and be a sounding board as you run your ideas by them.

Seek advice from other business owners on what challenges they faced in starting their business and how they managed to secure business loans or investment monies. What documentation and information did they find was most useful in stating their case to secure monies for their business?

The more you know at the outset, the more likely you are of running a successful business with growth potential.

When to Hire the Experts

Some areas of your business are better left to the experts. For example, if you are unsure about what taxes you need to pay (and most of us are), you will want to hire an accountant to be sure your books are set up properly and you make the required tax payments.

If your business is strongly affected by government regulations, licensing, or permit requirements, seek professional advice so that you dot all the i's and cross all the t's. Making mistakes here could have a negative impact on your business and be quite costly.

You may also choose to hire someone to assist you in securing investment monies for your business. Working with investment capital firms is not an easy task, and an expert in this area can provide invaluable guidance.

Additionally, anticipate hiring an expert in contract law to review agreements between you and vendors or suppliers. You want to be sure your interests are protected, and a contract attorney can definitely help you on this front.

The Least You Need to Know

- Be realistic in your business plan. Don't just include the good stuff. Include the risks and show how you plan to handle them.
- Create a realistic budget for your business. Be practical about what you really need to do now and what can wait until later.
- Don't shortchange the planning process.
- Get the support and advice you need from experts.
- Research the various options for funding your business.

Developing Your Strategy

In This Chapter

- Evaluating the strength of your value proposition, mission, and vision statement
- Aligning your business with your customers' needs
- Developing goals and benchmarks
- Reaching your business's goals with SMART objectives
- Developing, managing, and refining the strategy for your business

What are your business objectives, and what is the guiding strategy you will use to meet those objectives? Without a strategy, you really have nothing to move toward— no end goal in sight. What is that goal? How will you convey what your business is all about to employees and to the rest of the world? What is the purpose of your business?

Businesses succeed only when they are focused on the customer. The customer makes or breaks your business. To that end, your *value proposition*, vision statement, and mission should be focused on your customers and what you can do for them rather than on your business per se. This chapter helps you to get started in creating these important components.

Your Value Proposition

Your value proposition must tell your customers the value (benefits) you bring to them based on what they want and need. A value proposition is not a list of the services and products you offer your customers. Rather, it concisely summarizes the problems you can solve for your customers and how you will solve them.

DEFINITION

A **value proposition** should be no more than three to five sentences conveying to your customers the value and benefits that you bring to them. It should prompt potential customers to purchase your products and services over your competitor.

For example, if your business provides meals to go for busy professionals, the problem you solve for customers is lack of time for cooking good, healthy meals. Your value proposition might sound like this: Healthy-Meals-To-Go, Inc. provides healthy, affordable, quality home-cooked meals for your family without the "having to cook at home" part.

Your value proposition should help you to differentiate yourself from your competitors by communicating to your customers how you will meet their needs (solve their problems). Henry Gregor, Founder and CEO of StrategicVisions, a small consulting company based on the West Coast (www.strategicvisions.com) has developed the following value proposition:

> StrategicVisions cost effectively helps growth-oriented technology companies grow their annual revenues by at least 20 to 30 percent by extending their business base with new products, new markets, and strategic alliances.

In this example, if you were a customer of StrategicVisions, you would know exactly how the company can help your business.

BEST PRACTICE

Ask your employees to help you develop your value proposition. Use brainstorming techniques to determine the needs of your customers (problems to be solved) and various approaches to satisfy those needs (how to solve those problems).

What's the Value You Deliver?

The value proposition is part of a discovery process and should involve multiple people in your organization. The better you understand your customers' needs and the various ways your organization meets those needs, the clearer you will be about your value proposition. Developing it is the responsibility of the entire business.

A value proposition that is clear and concise provides your customers with an obvious differentiator between you and the competition. A strong value proposition is also useful in selecting the right partners, vendors, and suppliers for your business. You might also use your value proposition to educate new hires about the benefit you provide to the customers so they can better serve those customers.

Start developing your value proposition by focusing on the unique benefits you deliver to the customer. If your business designs and sells jewelry, your value may be providing jewelry that is unique in design and uses a variety of semi-precious and precious stones and metals. Additionally, you allow your customers to bring you their designs that you will recreate in a piece of jewelry. The overall value to the customer is unique jewelry that they will find nowhere else, designed to their specifications, at a price they can afford. This differentiates you from your competitors, who may sell the same jewelry that the next shop sells. Your value proposition might start to take this shape:

> Unique jewelry for everyday wear and special occasions that you will find nowhere else, at a price that doesn't break the bank—designed specifically for you.

As a best practice, take these steps to understand the value you bring to the customer:

1. Survey or interview your customers. Why do they purchase your product or service? What are the benefits they receive? Listen carefully to your customers. What do they like or not like about your business?

2. Ask your employees. What do they hear from customers about the product or service and what do they think would be of value to offer those customers? If they ran the business, what would they do?

3. Pull all of this information together and begin to develop your value proposition with the assistance of all employees in your business.

Until you understand your customers—what they want, what they need, why they buy from you rather than the business down the street—you cannot develop your value proposition. Don't rush this process.

And now, a reality check. If you are in the process of starting your business, you will not be able to fully develop your value proposition. You should certainly think about the value you will bring your customers since you know what your product or service will be and you have an idea why you are starting your business. But until you begin to secure customers, you can't finalize your value proposition.

For instance, let's say you have just started a bakery in your town. You sell freshly baked breads, pastries, and cookies. You started this bakery because you like freshly baked items and the closest bakery was 10 miles away. As you start to get to know your customers, you learn what they find valuable in a bakery—in other words, what services you can bring to them to increase the value you provide them. You learn this through conversations with them as they come into your bakery and through a survey you conduct via e-mail.

PRACTICE MAKES PERFECT

Talk with your customers to understand them better. The better you understand how your service or product meets the customers' needs, the better you are able to serve them.

Here is what you add to your bakery business based on the needs and wants of your customers:

- Provide the ability to special order pastries and cookies for parties and other events so they don't have to do the work.

- Increase your regular offerings to include zucchini bread, pumpkin loaf, and banana-nut bread for variety.

You are beginning to learn the value you bring to your customers based on their needs and wants. Use this data to begin to develop your value proposition which, in the preceding bakery example, might begin to take shape as follows:

Neighborhood Bakery lets you select your own ingredients for customized, quality products that taste homemade but take only minutes to order.

You have solved a problem!

What Is Your Differentiator?

Think of the value proposition as your differentiator. What do you bring to the customer that your competitors do not? What makes you so special?

Many businesses mention excellent customer service in their value propositions. But because everyone claims to offer excellent customer service, this doesn't differentiate your business from the rest of the pack. Break it down further: what kind of customer service makes you unique to your customers?

Suppose you own a bookstore in New Hampshire that sells books written by New England–based authors. You want to provide your customers with a reason to keep coming in to your bookstore that differentiates you from the big chain bookstores. You decide to offer the following excellent customer service options to your customers—all at no charge—to distinguish yourself from the chain bookstores:

- An evening of wine and cheese with an author

- Free creative writing classes

- Newsletters with announcements of upcoming new releases to preorder on discount

- Children's hour once a week with storytelling, reading from children's books, and cookies and milk

All of these ideas provide a benefit to your customers and give them a reason to come to your store other than to just shop for books, although they will likely buy when they are there—and that is exactly what you are trying to accomplish!

PRACTICE MAKES PERFECT

Determine your differentiators with the assistance of your customers. Ask them what they would like to see from your business that would be of value to them that they are not getting anywhere else.

Some businesses are more difficult to differentiate than others. For instance, most day spas and salons offer the same services, so simply telling customers that you provide massages, facials, and manicures isn't going to do the job. You need to be more creative in your approach.

Let's look at the day spa and salon example. There are already numerous day spas and salons in your immediate area (within 10 miles), so you need to come up with value-added services that make you stand out from the crowd. You might consider offering the following value-added benefits for your customers:

- Child-care services

- Wine and cheese night with free makeup sessions

- Couples' massages with champagne, chocolates, and strawberries

- Product samples

- Free touch-ups for manicures or pedicures

- Last minute squeeze-ins for longtime customers

- Mother/daughter events

All of these are options for enhancing the value you deliver to your customers—in addition to a great haircut or manicure! As you build your business and begin to know your customers, you'll learn what products or services to add to increase the value you bring to them—thereby making your business the one they purchase from and the one they recommend to others!

Your Company Direction and Scope

Often, entrepreneurs have many wonderful ideas of what they want to do for their business and the variety of customers they will serve. But to be successful, it is important to stay focused. Find what you do well and do it better than any of your competitors. Don't try to be all things to all people. You can't serve every customer well. Some customers are just not good for your business because you can't solve their problems.

We know of an ice cream shop that was doing quite well. However, a deli moved in next door and the ice cream shop owner felt the need to compete with it. The ice cream shop began to offer pastries and sandwiches to his customers. He lost focus. That part of the business didn't do well. Customers wanted ice cream from him—that is why they come to his shop. He soon realized the sandwiches and pastries added no value to his business and actually detracted from the ice cream component of his business because he stopped concentrating on developing new and different ice cream flavors. Within a few months, he stopped providing pastries and sandwiches and went back to his core strength—ice cream.

The Vision and the Mission

Every business benefits from vision and mission statements. Your vision statement is your long-term view of your business—where you want to be in the future. It is the reason for your business's existence. The vision and mission statements enable you to keep sight of what is and is not your business as you grow. Vision statements focus on far-reaching goals with the intent of showing the ideal future state of your business. James Collins and Jerry Porras first introduced the term BHAG—Big Hairy Audacious Goal—in the late 1990s. Many vision statements incorporate such goals.

For example, if your business rescues animals that are hurt or in need, your vision statement may be:

> A world where all animals are safe and happy.

This would be considered a BHAG vision statement given its scope of the entire world. It's certainly a Big Hairy Audacious Goal, but a good goal to strive toward.

Google's vision statement is:

> To organize the world's information and make it universally accessible and useful.

That's a big job!

Your vision statement is the reason you wanted to start your business in the first place. It describes, in just a few words, what you want your business to be, and achieve, in the future. It should be positive and inspire others to want to be a part of your business—either as an employee or a customer.

Without a vision for your business, you really don't know where you want it to go in the future. You have no direction.

Another great example for a vision statement comes from Ben & Jerry's Ice Cream, which sets out a three-part vision that has outlasted the company's founders, who sold their interest in the firm years ago. This triple vision statement reads:

> Product: To make, distribute, and sell the finest quality all natural ice cream and related products in a wide variety of innovative flavors made from Vermont dairy products.

> Economic: To operate the Company on a sound financial basis of profitable growth, increasing value for our shareholders, and creating career opportunities and financial rewards for our employees.

Social: To operate the Company in a way that actively recognizes the central role that business plays in the structure of society by initiating innovative ways to improve the quality of life of a broad community: local, national, and international.

Your vision statement also should provide the foundation for developing your mission statement. The vision statement is the future; the longer mission statement is what you are going to do in the present to meet the goals of the vision statement. Your mission statement helps you to determine how to run your business—what employees to hire, what to produce, and how to market and sell to your customers.

PRACTICE MAKES PERFECT

While the main ideas behind your vision and mission statements may come from you as the owner of the business, it is beneficial to get your employees involved, especially in the development of the mission statement. Your employees can provide invaluable insights, and by including them you gain support of that mission.

Your business mission statement is the purpose for your business, and it should clearly convey ...

- What your business does.

- How your business does it.

- Who are you doing it for.

Looking back at our bakery example from earlier in this chapter, your mission statement might be:

To create fresh-from-the-oven baked goods using only high-quality organic ingredients to provide our customers with home-baked goodness for their families without having to bake themselves.

Breaking down the example, you can see this mission statement conveys the three primary points:

- What the business does: it fulfills the need for home-baked goods.

- How the business does it: by using only high-quality organic ingredients.

- For whom the business does it: for customers who want home-baked goodness without having to bake themselves.

The mission statement is clear and concise and lets the customer know what the bakery does for them and why they should buy from that bakery.

It's also a good idea to include in your mission statement information about your values and beliefs about your customers and employees. For customers, these might be:

- We will treat our customers as we want to be treated ourselves.

- We will never cut back on quality and will always provide our customers the very best ingredients in our baked goods.

- We will provide our customers the very highest level of personalized service.

And for your employees:

- We will treat our employees as if they are part of our own family.

- We will provide professional and personal development opportunities for our employees.

The mission statement enables customers to understand how you work with those around you and what they should expect from you. Most larger organizations post their mission statement on their websites and in public areas for all to see. You should do the same.

As a best practice, take the following steps in developing the vision and mission statements for your business.

For your vision statement:

1. Think about the future of your business. What do you want the business to be in the future? What are your goals for your business at a very high, lofty level?

2. Put it down in writing and then read it aloud. How does it sound? Share it with others. Are they excited by the possibilities of your business? If you aren't excited by what you have written and the possibilities of what your business can contribute, start over.

For the mission statement:

1. Use your vision statement as a guide in developing your mission statement, and have your employees help!

2. Answer the questions: What does the business do? How does the business do it? Who are we doing it for? How will your business meet the mission statement?

3. Test it out on your customers and with your friends and family. How does it sound to them? Do they understand the purpose of your business—what you do, how you do it, and whom you do it for?

While your vision and mission statements should help to guide your business and its direction and growth, they should not be written in stone. Changes in the economy, in the customer base that you serve, and in your competitors may require you to re-evaluate your business vision and mission.

Use the vision and mission statements as a guide to how you will make decisions about your business, including the kinds of products and services you will offer and the kinds of customers to whom you will offer those products and services.

Setting the Right Timeline

You'll also need to start setting some goals for your business in the following key areas:

- Revenue and profitability
- Sales and marketing
- Product development and manufacturing
- Human resources

As a best practice for your business, set specific major goals and supporting goals in each of these areas. Pick shorter timelines for the supporting goals to help keep you moving your business forward in both the short and long term. For example, set quarterly goals and then measure against those goals on a monthly basis.

BEST PRACTICE

Don't set such lofty goals that you are not going to be able to achieve them. Make the goals achievable. Breaking down your goals into bite-size pieces that are easier to accomplish will help your business build momentum.

Let's look at an example. Suppose you just started your business, which is focused on producing door mats made of organic materials. Your goal is to start marketing your business via the Internet using social media outlets. Let's break the goal down into smaller objectives and then into strategies to meet those objectives.

Overall goal: Market business via social media channels

Objective #1: Learn about options for social media marketing

Strategies:

- Read books on social media marketing

- Attend webinars on how businesses use social media

- Ask local Chamber of Commerce members about use of social media accounts

Objective #2: Set up accounts on Twitter and Facebook

Strategies:

- Set up Twitter account for business

- Set up Facebook business page

Objective #3: Use Twitter and Facebook to build brand and promote products

Strategies:

- Put links to Twitter account and Facebook page on website, promote with current customers, and include in marketing materials

- Ask employees, current customers, friends, and family to "like" your Facebook business page and to "follow" the business on Twitter

- Set up plan to "tweet" and post to Facebook three times a week, recruiting others to help

Set benchmarks to evaluate how you are doing. Your benchmarks, for this example, may be as shown in the following figure.

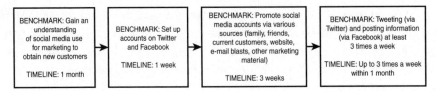

Four benchmarks to measure against to determine if you are meeting your ultimate goal of using social media to market and promote your business. Timelines are associated with each benchmark.

Since you know nothing about using social media, your first benchmark is learning about it. You give yourself one month to accomplish this goal.

You probably have lots of goals you want to accomplish running through your head. Make a list of all those goals for each of the key areas of your business, then start to pare down the list by prioritizing what should be done within 3 months, 6 months, 9 months, and 12 months. Determine what is required in terms of resources (internal and external), amount of money, and time to accomplish the goal.

Certainly one important set of goals will relate to bringing in revenue. After all, you need to pay your bills!

Let's assume you are starting off your consulting business with two customers who are purchasing your services already. You need to gain more customers in a short time in order to continue to develop your business and bring in revenue. You may set a goal to obtain one new customer per month. Set objectives to meet that goal of obtaining one new customer a month, with written strategies for each of the objectives and weekly benchmarks to measure your progress against the goal.

Develop SMART Objectives

Let's get into a bit more detail about best practices around goal-setting. When setting objectives around the goals to be achieved, set objectives that are SMART:

- **S**pecific: clear, concise, and well-defined
- **M**easurable: able to be measured
- **A**chievable: reasonably achievable goals that are not too lofty
- **R**elevant: aligned to business strategy
- **T**imely: able to be completed in a specified time frame

Ensure that all objectives you set to reach your business goals follow the SMART formula above. Well-written, SMART objectives increase your chances of reaching your business goals. SMART objectives are easily shared with your employees and provide them with specifics on how to reach the ultimate goal.

Let's look at an example. Your goal is to increase your revenue for your business. An objective to do that is to find new customers. Here is the objective written as a SMART objective:

> Increase revenue by 15 percent in one year by obtaining through referrals from existing customers five new customers who each purchase $10,000 worth of services.

Now, let's look at what makes this a SMART objective:

- Is it specific? Yes—you want to obtain 5 new customers in a year through referrals by current customers at a value of $10,000 each to increase revenue by 15 percent.

- Is it measurable? Yes—you want to achieve a 15 percent increase in revenue, and you can easily measure that.

- Is it achievable? Yes—five new customers is not a significant amount to obtain in a one-year time period.

- Is it relevant? Yes—your goal is to increase revenues for your business and this is a way to do so.

- Is it timely? Your timeline of one year to accomplish this meets your revenue goals.

When writing SMART objectives, include in the process the employee(s) who will be necessary to carry out the tasks involved in meeting that objective. If they are not comfortable with the objective and the timeline for meeting it, they will be unlikely to complete the task.

Refining Your Strategy Over Time

Your strategy is going to change over time. Changes in the economy, changes in your customers' needs and wants, new competitors entering the marketplace, and competitors leaving the marketplace will cause you to change your strategy for doing business with your customers.

BEST PRACTICE

Even if you believe there are no major changes that would affect your strategy, review your strategy for doing business annually. This is a great way to ensure you are always a step ahead of your competition and that your business remains fresh and relevant to your customers. It also keeps your employees engaged in the growth of the business.

Suppose you own an IT recruiting business and your current mission statement is as follows:

> To recruit the most qualified full-time Information Technology employees for our customers at affordable prices.

However, you find the current economic environment challenging, and you notice that your customers are hiring far more part-time contractors than full-time employees, and when they do hire personnel, they want your company to handle the entire hiring process. Additionally, you are expanding your company to service application development and desktop support personnel. In response to these changing conditions, you revise your mission statement to more accurately reflect your current business:

> To provide assistance creating job descriptions, recruiting, assessing, and hiring support of the most qualified part-time contractors and full-time employees for our customers in the areas of information technology, desktop support, and application development, at affordable prices.

You have used what you learned from conversations with customers and employees as well as indications in the economic marketplace to change your business's strategy in how it supports customers' needs.

The Least You Need to Know

- Create a vision for your business and use that vision to develop your value proposition and mission statement with the help of your employees.
- Use SMART objectives and benchmarks to measure progress against your business goals.

- Learn your customers' needs and wants so that you can develop products and services that are focused on them.
- Business strategies cannot remain static; change your strategy to meet changes in your environment and customer needs.

Best Practices for the First Two Years

What can you expect during the first two years your business is in operation? What must you, as an entrepreneur, be ready to do during that critical period? How do you move beyond the broad strokes of your business plan? What should your strategic plan look like? How do you put together, motivate, and retain the right initial team? What should your sales and marketing goals be, and how should you measure your progress toward those goals? How can you lay the foundation for a great customer service culture?

In this part, you'll get the answers to these and other important questions you will face during the early phases of your business's life.

Beyond the Initial Business Plan

In This Chapter

- Effective planning for your business
- How your personality type affects your planning style
- The benefits of using SWOT analysis techniques

Running a business is not about mindlessly copying your competitors and simply aping whatever they are doing. That's usually a reliable path to failure. You must plan for your business to stay ahead of the competition. Aim for your business to be the trailblazer—the leader of the pack. At the same time, you have to make sure that the path you take is the path your customers want you to take. In other words, your business's objectives must be aligned to your customers' needs and wants.

This chapter helps you take control of the planning for your business beyond your business plan.

Real World Planning Basics

Planning for your business should be a regular part of your role as a business owner and should involve your employees—especially those in leadership or management roles. Prior to beginning any planning sessions, gather the following information:

- Your value proposition and vision and mission statements
- Your business plan
- Information on your current products and services
- Information on revenue and profitability, broken down by product and service categories

- Recent SWOT analyses you have conducted (you'll learn about this later in this chapter)

- Information on how you are currently marketing your products and services, and samples of your advertising and marketing materials

As a best practice, consider setting aside an entire day or two for your planning sessions, ensuring that all key individuals are available to participate.

Planning is an intense process and is best done away from interruptions. Get out of the office—away from the phones, the computers, and the other everyday stuff that will interrupt your session and distract you and the team.

To run your business effectively, you'll need a variety of plans, all of which should be created in conjunction with each other and in support of the comprehensive *strategic plan* (see Chapter 7 for details on creating a strategic plan).

DEFINITION

A **strategic plan** is a long-range plan that serves as your roadmap for the future. It encompasses the product lines and services you will offer, the number of employees you will have, your technology requirements, industry trends, competitor analysis, your revenue and profitability goals, the types of customers you will have, and your long-range marketing plans.

Think of the plans outlined in this chapter as precursors to your strategic plan. You can use them to help measure your progress against your goals and objectives. They can also be helpful when it comes to securing investments or partners for your business. As such, they are similar to your business plan and will probably draw on the work you did there.

You will want to develop the following plans:

- Marketing plan

- Technology plan

- Product development plan (or services offering plan)

- Sales plan

- Human resources plan

- Disaster recovery plan

All of these plans should be incorporated within your strategic plan. They should all include current resources and plans for future resource needs based on growth strategies.

Let's look more closely at each of these plans.

Marketing Plan

A marketing plan should include information on how your business will market products and services. This plan should be tied to your product development plan. As you develop and release new products or services, they should be included in the marketing plan. For each product and service offered by the business, your marketing plan should include the following information:

- Target customers
- Revenue goals
- Marketing budget
- Marketing promotional activities/campaigns/tactics (e-mail, direct mail, events)
- Competitor landscape/analysis
- Plans for increasing the customer base (new market opportunities)
- Ways to measure success of marketing campaigns

Technology Plan

The technology plan needs to include information about current technology use as well as future needs based on growth strategies. The plan should include the following information:

- Current network diagrams
- Current hardware and software configurations
- Data security
- Hardware and software upgrade plans
- Group policies (user access policies)

- Communications (phones)
- Information on lease and maintenance agreements
- Information technology budget

Product Development Plan

Your product development plan should look at your current product line, the life cycle of the products, and new product development based on customer needs. This plan will be closely tied to your marketing and sales plans as these groups—sales, marketing, and product development—must work very closely together. It should include the following information:

- Details of the current product line and life cycle of each product in the line
- Distribution channels for products
- New products planned for development along with a timeline, resource needs, quality checks, and prototype and final product rollout/release dates

BEST PRACTICE

If you offer services rather than products, you'll want to develop a Services Development Plan rather than a Product Development Plan. This will include similar information but will be focused on services you offer.

Sales Plan

Your sales plan should have sales goals broken down by each product line or service offered by the business. This plan is tied to the marketing and product development plans. The sales plan should include the following details:

- Sales forecasts: sales activity plans (trade shows, conferences, sales calls) and revenue and profitability goals per month/quarter/year
- Sales strategies: current target markets/customers (renewal business), new markets/customers (new business opportunities), average sales orders, and order value expectations

Human Resources Plan

Your human resources plan will delineate both current and planned employee needs. It will include your organizational chart along with the following information:

- Workforce analysis: a breakdown of current employees by function, years of service, etc.

- Workforce analysis: future employee resource needs (based on data from other plans)

- Professional development and training plans (career development)

- Compensation and benefit information

- Performance review plans

- Employee relations information (especially if you are a union shop)

- Succession planning

Disaster Recovery Plan

Your disaster recovery plan should be focused on how you'll get your business back up and running after a disaster. (Chapter 16 looks more closely at disaster recovery plans.) This plan should include the following information:

- How to restore website and phone service functionality.

- How to account for employees and their families (employee contact information and a calling tree).

- How to ensure your data is secure and accessible (customer information, financial information, etc.).

- Plans for alternative workspace for employees, or the ability to work virtually.

- Plans for alternative suppliers in the event your current suppliers are affected by a disaster. In such cases, your alternative suppliers should be prepared to step in immediately to support your business.

You might have other plans for your business, but these are the standard plans used by most successful businesses.

Which Planning Style?

Some business owners prefer a rigorous planning regimen that's rooted in spreadsheets and detailed regression analyses while others prefer a cocktail napkin, short and sweet, bare-bones approach; many are somewhere in the middle. One style is not necessarily better than the other—it all depends on what works for your business and your personality. Don't try to adopt a style that doesn't work for you.

David Merrill and Roger Reid, in their book *Personal Styles & Effective Performance* (CRC Press, 1981), discuss four personality styles: driver, expressive, amiable, and analytical. Each style has its own approach to business and requires a different spin on planning.

BEST PRACTICE

The dynamics of the various personality styles are not only relevant to the strategic planning process but to any number of interactions with your team. By knowing your own personality style, you can call on others in your business to help fill in the gaps where needed. For example, if you are not detail-oriented, you can include someone on the planning team who likes the details and delegate appropriate tasks to that person.

Let's take a closer look at each of these styles so that you can understand where you might fit:

- **Driver:** Business owners with this style are goal-oriented and want to see results. They are decisive individuals who tend to make decisions quickly. They will likely take control of the planning sessions and make all decisions related to the business.

- **Expressive:** Business owners who have this style are more social and want to involve others; they are outgoing and people-oriented. They are motivators and will want to have others involved in the planning process. They will not rely on data as much as emotions to make decisions.

- **Amiable:** Business owners with this style work well in a team environment and prefer to make team decisions. They are also people-oriented and will use opinions—including input from those around them—rather than data to make decisions.

- **Analytical:** Business owners who display this style are more data-driven. They are not comfortable making decisions unless they have all the data in front of them. They are much more methodical than the other styles and will take a longer time to make a decision to ensure they have considered all possibilities.

PRACTICE MAKES PERFECT

What better way to understand how you work with your employees than to do a team activity that involves learning each other's personality type? Once you and your employees understand how you work together—what drives you, how you make decisions, how you interact with others—you'll find planning sessions (and other undertakings!) to be much more productive.

Another way to learn how you prefer to work with others and make decisions is to use the Myers-Briggs Type Indicator (MBTI). The MBTI theorizes that an individual's personality is structured by four preferences: extraversion or introversion, sensing or intuition, thinking or feeling, and judgment or perception.

As with any personality inventory, no individual fits perfectly into any single type. However, understanding how you work best with others and how you think through making decisions enables you to be more successful in your business.

Determine how you work best—what methods are most comfortable for you—to determine how to plan for your business. Again, there is no right or wrong way; your personal style will be most effective for you.

Performing a SWOT Analysis

A *SWOT analysis* helps you to better understand how your business is positioned to achieve your objectives. By understanding your business's strengths, weaknesses, opportunities, and threats, you better understand how to position your products and services against your competitors and can plan for potential future threats to your business.

DEFINITION

A **SWOT analysis** is a planning method used to evaluate the strengths, weaknesses, opportunities, and threats involved in a particular strategic direction for your business.

Let's look at an example. You are considering developing a new product for your business. It will require an investment of $100,000. You want to figure out if the investment will be worth it—in other words, if the product will meet your customers' needs. You use a SWOT analysis to determine whether to move forward with the investment in the new product by asking the following questions:

- **Strengths:** What is the customers' perception of your products? What do your products offer that the competition does not? Why do customers buy from you?

- **Weaknesses:** What could your business be doing better to meet customers' needs? Where do your products fall short?

- **Opportunities:** What are the opportunities to meet customers' needs through new products? What is the market for a new product from your business? Will releasing a new product into the marketplace offer additional revenue for your business?

- **Threats:** What are your competitors doing? Are there any new products coming out from competitors—or already released into the marketplace—that will affect your market share?

By performing a SWOT analysis on the new product opportunity, you are better prepared to make a decision to invest in the new product or to consider other avenues to increase revenue if this particular idea poses too many threats to your business.

Why Conduct a SWOT Analysis?

A SWOT analysis is considered one of the most important tools for business planning. This analysis provides a variety of benefits, including …

- Understanding how your business is positioned in the marketplace as compared to your competitors.

- A thorough review of challenges you are facing in your business and how you are positioned to meet those challenges.

- An analysis of your opportunities to help you choose the most appropriate opportunity to drive revenue and profitability.

A SWOT analysis is a great brainstorming activity, and you should always involve your key employees in the process. Use it as a precursor to developing your strategic plan. You may even choose to include customers, vendors, suppliers, and other partners in this activity, as they can provide quite a bit of insight to help you in developing products and services to grow your business.

When analyzing your strengths, weaknesses, opportunities, and threats, keep in mind that strengths, weaknesses, and opportunities can be internal or external to your business, while threats are almost always external to your business.

Let's look at an example. Your business focuses on delivering team-building activities for other businesses. You are contemplating expanding your product line by developing team-building activities specifically for certain industry groups. You perform a SWOT analysis to determine if an additional program geared toward industry groups is a smart investment for your company.

You look first at the quality of your current product as compared to your competitors' since you'll be using this as a base to build the new product:

- **Strengths:** High-quality product easily customized and priced right in the marketplace; individuals who train customers on how to use product are well-respected in the industry

- **Weaknesses:** Demand is increasing and difficult to keep up with; individuals who train customers on products are not employees but rather contractors, and you fear you may lose them to larger organizations that would be able to pay them more

- **Opportunities:** No one has yet concentrated on team-building activities specifically for industry groups; team building is becoming more popular and has been written up in many research papers as a key component of an organization's success; you already have a successful product with your current team-building program

- **Threats:** Larger organizations are beginning to come out with similar programs and offering them at reduced rates; you haven't changed your current program in a few years and it needs to be updated to address current best practices in team building

Your SWOT analysis should also take into account other areas of your business, such as your market share, customer service, marketing effectiveness, and financial strength. A SWOT analysis in each of these areas will help you to better plan your strategy and make a decision on whether to expand your product line.

Using Your SWOT Analysis

Use your SWOT analysis to determine what you can leverage for your business's success—either strengths or opportunities you can build upon. The SWOT analysis results will also help you to plan for threats to your business and address weaknesses, allowing you to continue your path of success. Use your SWOT analysis results to …

- Determine the components of your strategic plan for the upcoming year.

- Prioritize projects that will have the most impact on meeting your business objectives.

Let's look back at our example. After completing the SWOT analysis, you will have the information you need in order to decide whether to expand your product line specifically to provide team-building programs for industry groups. If you decide not to move forward, you'll have a solid set of reasons why it is not the right move for your business.

As you can see, a SWOT analysis enables you to make the best decisions for your company—provided you use the analysis appropriately and spend the necessary time to complete it. The SWOT analysis, when done right, will highlight aspects of your business to focus on now and will tell you whether certain decisions really make sense.

Evaluating SWOT Analysis Results

Simply conducting a SWOT analysis is not enough—you must do something with it. Use the SWOT analysis both as a regular part of your planning process as well as to make ongoing improvements in real time in your business.

The actions you take (or don't take) as a result of conducting your SWOT analysis will have a major impact on your business's ability to achieve important goals. For example, your goal is to offer three new training courses to your customers within the next six months, but the SWOT analysis you conducted shows you that you are weak in the areas of resource development (i.e., creating the courses) and quality control procedures. Thus it should be clear that you are not going to reach your goal of offering three new training courses within six months unless you are willing to make some changes in your process. Use the SWOT analysis to focus on the areas you need to improve upon to get back on track with your goals.

You can and should use a SWOT analysis as part of any major decision facing your business. For example, let's assume that you are considering adding another location to your restaurant this quarter. This time period appears to be a perfect opportunity for you to do so, as the restaurant business has been picking up and people are eating out more frequently, both nationwide and in your area. Prior to making such a large decision—an initiative that will require sourcing a location, hiring additional staff, purchasing or leasing equipment, obtaining a license to operate the restaurant and a liquor license, and so on—you will want to conduct an in-depth SWOT analysis on your current restaurant.

That analysis might show that you are not competing effectively against your competition in your existing restaurant. Suppose that it shows your competition's latest menu offerings to be a major threat, one that is causing a steady decline in your profits. This is definitely something you want to take into account. You might also learn that your customer service is not up to par—in fact, customer service shows up as a major weakness in your current operation.

If you evaluate the results of that SWOT analysis carefully, you would probably make the decision not to open another restaurant, regardless of events in the larger economy, because your current restaurant needs some attention first. There are clear problems on the horizon, and you must address them before expanding. You don't want to be saddled with two problem investments!

Update SWOT analysis at least annually. The only thing worse than relying on an outdated SWOT analysis is to make decisions about your business without any SWOT analysis at all!

The Least You Need to Know

- Determine the plans you need to effectively run your business.
- Decide what your planning style is and work with that style, calling on others to help in areas where you are not as strong.
- Perform a SWOT analysis for any major changes in your business and to understand whether you are working in the right direction toward meeting your objectives.
- Update your SWOT analysis at least annually.

Creating Your Strategic Plan

In This Chapter

- Strategic planning for success
- Balancing short- and long-term planning
- Identifying your performance indicators

This chapter shows you how to look at your business strategically, both in the short term and the long term, and how to determine what you need to do to be profitable today and still have enough money left over to plan for tomorrow.

Short-Term Planning

While it's important to look at your business over the long term, you'll first need to consider planning for the short term—no more than a year down the road—in order to continue to support your business today. In short-term planning, you'll want to do an analysis of your current status.

Specifically, you'll want to know where your business currently stands in the following areas:

- Your position in the marketplace and reputation
- Your current product or service offerings
- The strength of the industry of which you are a part
- Your cash flow and access to capital
- The strengths of your employees and their ability to meet customer needs

- Your ability to produce new products and services

- Your sales and marketing capabilities

PRACTICE MAKES PERFECT

Take baby steps when moving toward your ultimate business goals. Short-term plans provide milestones to measure your progress against and, when accomplished, provide a morale-boosting sense of accomplishment for you and your employees.

By analyzing how your business is currently positioned, you will be able to understand where improvements or changes need to be made. Once you have that data, compare it to your business objectives. Are you heading in the right direction? Your planning tells you how you are going to get there.

Identifying Profitability Needs

A major priority in any short-term planning initiative is confirming how you'll pay the bills. How will you bring in the revenue needed to keep your business moving in the right direction?

Your profitability needs are based on a variety of factors, including the cost of producing products and offering your services, marketing and sales costs, overhead costs such as facilities and utilities, and employees' salaries and benefits. Additionally, you'll need to consider cash reserves should you hit a bump in the road as well as having some profit left over to invest back into your business for expansion, research and development, and innovation.

What do you need for the future to remain a viable company? Let's look at an example. You sell customized products for businesses. Let's look at the profitability of one of your product lines—customized mugs. The formula is a simple one: Sales – Costs = Profit.

Sales of Customized Mugs from January Through December

Per Unit Sales	Per Unit Costs	Profit Per Unit
$10 per unit	$6.50 per unit	$3.50 per unit

15,000 customized mugs were sold from January through December at a cost of $10 per mug, leaving you with the following numbers:

Total Revenue	Total Costs	Profit for Year
$150,000	$97,500	$52,500

Average discount to customers is 5 percent; taking that into account, your numbers are as follows:

Total Revenue	Total Costs	Profit for Year
$142,500	$97,500	$45,000

The preceding calculations indicate that your profitability per mug sold is $3.50; your overall profitability, taking into account an average discount of 5 percent, is $45,000 for the year, given a sale of 15,000 customized mugs. However, you know the following is true for this particular product for the upcoming year:

- Cost of production per mug is increasing by $0.10.

- Cost of shipping per mug is increasing by $0.50.

- Cost of materials per mug is increasing by $0.15.

Therefore, your costs are now $7.25 per mug. If you retain the current price of $10 per customized mug, your profit per mug is now at $2.75, or a 27.5 percent profit per mug.

BEST PRACTICE

Regularly evaluate the profitability of your products and service offerings. Changes throughout the year—increases in salaries paid to employees, marketing cost increases, increases in shipping costs, increases in the price of raw materials, and changes in the marketplace overall—all affect your profitability.

The profit you retain from the sale of customized mugs provides you with a cushion to hold in reserve and leaves you with some money left over to reinvest in your business for innovation. You may take the 27.5 percent profit from each mug and distribute as follows: sales commissions 5 percent, cash reserve 15 percent, innovation (research and development) 7.5 percent.

Here is one small example. As a business owner, you should have a clear understanding of the profitability of each of your products and services. This information helps you to determine what products to continue to market or what products to remove from the line, where price increases are necessary to cover increased costs, and where savings may be generated to reduce your costs.

Failure to break down your profitability per product line or service offering makes it very difficult to truly assess your business's profitability overall. This is certainly a path to failure of your business.

Setting the Go-to-Market Plan

When planning your *go-to-market plan*, you'll need to consider what channels you will use for delivering your product to the marketplace. For example, will you use your own sales team to sell the product to customers, or will you sell to other businesses who will then sell your product (resellers), or some combination? And how will you get information about that product out in the marketplace? Will you use direct mail marketing, e-mail blasts, advertising in magazines, social media channels, or a combination of methods?

DEFINITION

A **go-to-market plan** is a plan for introducing a product or service into the marketplace and for selling and delivering that product or service to your customers.

As an example, Avon Products, Inc., sells its products (which include cosmetics, fragrances, and jewelry) through independent sales representatives. They market their product through these sales representatives, who use brochures, samples, and websites to sell the product.

You should have a go-to-market plan for each product and service that you sell, or for a group of products that have similar characteristics. For example, if you sell training courses in project management, business analysis, and management and leadership, you may have one go-to-market plan for the entire training courses category. Your go-to-market plan will also vary depending on the sources for selling your product to the customer. For example, your go-to-market plan for your in-house sales folks will look different than your go-to-market plan for resellers of your product. Determine the best, most appropriate paths to reach your customer base, which may include the following:

- Website and e-commerce
- Sales personnel
- Storefront locations

Your go-to-market plan should include information on the value you offer to your customers, a strategy and timeline for new product and service rollout, and the costs involved.

Developing Tactical Objectives

Part of any strong plan is developing your *tactical objectives*. What will you do in order to meet your goals—what tactics, or steps, will you take? Your tactical objectives should be mapped to your long-term strategic goals. What will you do now to meet those longer-term goals? You should break your longer-term goals into smaller milestones. In this way, you can easily measure your progress toward meeting those goals. Your tactical objectives help you to achieve your long-term strategic goals.

DEFINITION

Tactical objectives (also called *operational objectives*) are short-term goals that help a business move closer to achieving its strategic, or long-term, goals.

Let's look at an example. Your business does event photography. Your long-term goal is to be the primary source of photographs for all major events in your geographic area. This is a two-year goal. One of your shorter-term goals toward reaching that ultimate long-term goal is to be the photographer at smaller local events.

You plan to achieve the short-term goal of photographing local events by reaching out to hosts of local events to offer your services as a photographer. You will do that through tasks such as …

- E-mail marketing about your services to local businesses.
- Advertising in the local newspapers about your services.
- Visiting local hotels, halls, and restaurants to talk about events held at their venue.
- Reaching out to local groups such as the Chamber of Commerce and various clubs.

You should assign these tactical objectives to employees along with deadlines for carrying them out. So your employee in charge of marketing would place an advertisement in the local newspapers about your services—this would be done on a monthly basis over a one-year time period. Your goal would be to secure one new photography gig a month based on the newspaper ads. You will measure your progress against that goal.

BEST PRACTICE

Make sure the tactical objectives you develop are SMART objectives (see Chapter 5) and that employees assigned to the tasks know how those objectives fit into the big picture.

By breaking down strategic goals into smaller tactical objectives, you are able to assign the tasks to others and measure their progress in those tasks.

Long-Term Planning

In any business, you should have a strategic plan that outlines how your business will operate and what it will strive to accomplish. Strategic planning is a major project for your business.

Don't confuse your strategic business plan with your business plan (see Chapter 4). The business plan is the document that delineates the objectives of your business and explains why you believe your business will be a success and how you plan to make it a success.

During your strategic business planning sessions, you won't just plan for the sake of planning; instead, you will plan with specific end goals in sight. For example, maybe you need to develop a plan to introduce three new products within five years. Your planning should be focused on what types of products you want to introduce, how those products will meet customers' needs, what you need in the way of resources and budget, how much revenue you expect to generate from the products, and at what point you'll recoup your costs for development.

BEST PRACTICE

Consider holding annual strategic planning sessions for your business. Use your last strategic plan as your base document. Review the plan, discuss progress against it, and make adjustments to it based on new information. Don't create your strategic plan and then stash it in a desk drawer—use it!

The whole point of your strategic planning sessions is to assess the current state of your business—what its strengths and weaknesses are and where you fit in the competitive landscape. It's only after you've established this baseline that you can determine where the gaps are and can plan for the future.

You will use this plan to convey your business's strategic goals to employees and others. It should say exactly where you will be going in the future and how you will get there. And that should excite you and anyone who works for you!

In the past, long-term planning was done 10- or 20-plus years out into the future. Today—given the constant changes we see in the economy, the marketplace, and in how business is done in general—planning is best suited for no more than five years out. In fact, you hear more today about setting a *strategic direction* for periods longer than five years rather than developing a strategic plan.

DEFINITION

A **strategic direction** provides flexibility in reaching your goals. With a strategic plan, many businesses are focused on sticking to that plan; with a strategic direction, you have a path to move forward on—a direction to follow—but with a lot of flexibility in how you reach that ultimate goal, so that you can easily maneuver to meet changing market conditions and customer demands.

Long-term planning is becoming increasingly important, especially in today's ever-changing economy. Changes in technology, increased global competition, and changing demands of the consumer require long-term strategic planning to ensure a successful business.

Developing a Strong Strategic Plan

Strategic planning is all about determining the path your business will take to reach a specific point in the future. It addresses the customers your business will focus on, the products and services it will offer, and the resources it will need.

BEST PRACTICE

Plan your strategic planning session as you would any other important project. Have key information on hand prior to the start of the session so you, and others involved, are well prepared.

You should have a goal in mind for doing strategic planning. What are you trying to do within a five-year time period? Your goals might include any of the following:

- Increase your market share
- Introduce new products into the marketplace
- Expand globally
- Develop a distribution channel

Take these steps to ensure a successful strategic planning session:

1. Gather together information to be used in the planning session: value proposition, vision and mission statements, SWOT analysis, financial statements, operating plans, current marketing plans, and customer information.

2. Gather the right people to participate in the session. You shouldn't be doing this yourself as the business owner. Include others in your business who will make valuable contributions to the session.

3. Set aside at least four hours of uninterrupted time. Many businesses have found it easier to go off-site where the phone is not ringing and e-mail is not a distraction.

Your Strategic Long-Term Objectives

Strategic long-term objectives should be measurable and aligned with your vision for your business. This isn't a matter of throwing a dart at a dartboard and choosing what you'll be working on over the next few years. Be strategic! What will you need to do to expand your business? Increase your profits? Pull ahead of the competition?

Strategic objectives should be focused on key areas of your business, such as profits, customers, and your operations.

Let's assume that you are developing a strategic plan to go from an in-house sales force today to a sales force in conjunction with distribution channels to enable nation-wide expansion.

BUSINESS BUSTER

Overlooking the need for continuous strategic planning can cost your business growth and market share. Plan for an annual strategic planning session and measure your progress toward achieving your objectives on a quarterly basis.

You'll need to develop a plan to achieve your overarching goal of developing 10 distribution channels to sell your product nationwide. Break down your strategic objective—in this case, developing distribution channels—into shorter-term tactical objectives (or tasks) to achieve the outcome. Those tasks should be measurable and able to be completed within the time period you set. These tasks might include selecting geographic locations, sourcing distribution channels in those areas, contracting with the distributors, and training in the product line.

Too often, small business owners get caught up in the day-to-day operations of running the business and let strategic planning fall by the wayside. To be successful, you must have a strategic plan to work toward, and you must continuously measure your progress against it.

Your Future Capital Needs

Strategic planning will enable you to determine the future capital needs for your business. As you develop your strategic plan, you'll need to consider how much money you'll need to achieve those goals. For example, if one of your strategic goals is to release three new products to the marketplace within three years, you'll need to set aside monies to invest in research and development efforts. You'll also need money to market the new products once they are released.

Strategic planning enables you to determine how much money you need to set aside in order to fund strategic objectives. Earlier in this chapter we discussed setting aside some of your profits to reinvest in your business. Here is where that money gets put into play. You can use the money you set aside to fund your future business activities, such as new product development or geographic expansion.

BEST PRACTICE

In a tough economic environment, it's a good idea to set aside a bit more cash than you otherwise might for future investment, especially if business loans are difficult to obtain.

Reality Check

We have talked about the importance of understanding the purpose of your business and communicating that purpose to others. We also talked about business planning and developing short-term and long-term objectives. To bring all of this work to fruition, you must also understand what the relevant *key performance indicators* (*KPIs*) are for your business.

Performance indicators are not necessarily static; they may change frequently. Certainly they must be evaluated on a regular basis. For performance indicators to be successful, they must be tied to *critical success factors* (*CSFs*).

DEFINITION

Key performance indicators (KPIs) are quantifiable measurements that connect to the critical success factors of a given business, and that can be monitored over time. For example, a consulting company may have as a KPI the percentage of revenue gained from repeat customers. **Critical success factors (CSFs)** are activities that your business performs in order to meet strategic long-term goals. You measure CSFs with performance indicators.

Let's look at a quick example. You have a KPI to improve your company's customer service response time. Your target is to reduce the time it takes your help desk to answer phone calls to two rings from four rings. A CSF that is necessary for the KPI to be reached is to install new call center software that provides routing of customer service phone calls.

While the scope of this book does not permit a full discussion of CSFs and KPIs, the following sections look at bit more closely at the topic to get you started. We re-examine KPIs from a marketing perspective in Chapter 9.

What Are Your Performance Indicators?

In many industries CSFs and KPIs are published by trade associations or industry groups. Visit www.SmartKPIs.com for examples of standard KPIs for the finance industry and many other industries. You might also try the KPI library database, which allows you to search more than 5,900 KPIs for a variety of industries. You can find it at http://kpilibrary.com.

BEST PRACTICE

Limit the number of KPIs for your business to no more than 10, and ideally less than that, for each functional area of your business. Research has shown that more than 10 are unmanageable.

As a best practice, set performance indicators for the following areas of your business:

- Customer acquisition and retention/customer service
- Finance/operations
- Product development
- Marketing and sales
- Human resources

Keep in mind that KPIs can be either financial or nonfinancial measures, and they must be linked to your overall business long-term strategy.

Much like with developing mission statements and business plans, determining the KPIs for your business should not be done in a bubble. Involve other key players—employees, vendors, suppliers, customers—in the process.

Let's look at an example. Your business is growing and you want to be sure you are focusing on employee development. Effective employee development is a key component of meeting your customers' needs. You notice that in a recent survey, customers are satisfied only 80 percent of the time. One of your KPI-related goals is to increase satisfaction to 100 percent. You'll measure this through observing employees interacting with customers and through customer surveys. In order to implement that KPI, you'll need a CSF. Your CSF is to develop and implement a training program in effective customer service for your employees.

Measuring Business Performance

Use KPIs to measure the performance of your business on a regular basis. Some KPIs may be measured quarterly, others monthly, and some even weekly or daily. Your timeline for measuring KPIs must be based on what you are trying to accomplish and what you are measuring.

Let's look at another example. One of your strategic business goals is to increase profitability. This affects both marketing (which generates leads for sales) and sales (which works directly with the customer). Your CSF is to generate $5,000 in profits each month through purchases from new customers. Your KPI is to acquire at least two new customers each month at a profit of at least $2,500 per customer. You will measure this on a monthly basis.

> **BUSINESS BUSTER**
>
> Failure to monitor progress against your KPIs can have a negative impact on your business overall. Even the smallest businesses need to have KPIs in place to evaluate the success and key components of the business. Additionally, tasking your employees with activities to meet business goals and then never measuring their progress against those activities serves to disengage your employees from the business.

By measuring your progress regularly, you'll be able to identify issues before they bloom into major problems for your business. Monitor changes in your KPIs early to determine if it is a short-term issue or if you are on the wrong track entirely. Continuing with the preceding example, if you find that for the first five months you are gaining two to three new customers a month at a profit of at least $2,500 per customer, you are on the right track. However, during the sixth month, you don't gain any new customers, and then in the seventh month you gain only one new customer at a profit of $1,500. What's going on? When you notice this decline, you get together with the individuals responsible for meeting this CSF—your marketing and sales folks—to determine what might be happening. Maybe it's a short-term issue and by month eight you will be back on track. Maybe there's an issue with your products or services, or maybe you have tapped out the market. You'll need to gather data to determine the problem. No matter what the source of the problem is, by implementing, measuring, and evaluating your KPIs regularly, you'll keep your business moving in the right direction to meet the long-term strategic goals for your business.

> **PRACTICE MAKES PERFECT**
>
> When analyzing how you are progressing against your KPIs, look for common issues such as employee turnover, breakdown in processes and procedures, changes in the economy, and cash flow issues.

What Do You Do with the Information?

Don't just gather the data of how you are performing against your KPIs—use it! This information should be used for a variety of purposes, including …

- Strengthening your customer relationships.
- Improving the quality of your products or services.
- Improving the marketing practices of your business.
- Improving employee retention and engagement.
- Expanding your geographic reach.

At annual strategy meetings, take time to review your current KPIs to be sure they are still meeting your needs. Your KPIs will not remain static year after year. As your business grows, you develop new products and services, and your customer base changes, your KPIs will need to change to keep you moving in the right direction.

The Least You Need to Know

- Both short- and long-term planning is essential for a successful business; don't shortchange the process.
- Involve others—employees, customers, vendors, and suppliers—in your strategic planning efforts; they have valuable information about your business.
- Regularly evaluate the profitability of your products and service offerings.
- Use performance indicators to measure and track the success of your business.

The Right Team

In This Chapter

- Finding the best people for your business
- Interviewing effectively
- Building the best team
- Kicking off your sales initiatives with the right salespeople

In the first few years of getting your business off the ground, having the right team will be critical to your success, yet your resources will likely be scarce. You'll need team players—individuals who can pitch in to do whatever it takes to get the job done. You're looking for flexible, energetic folks who are willing to wear lots of different hats, not card-carrying members of the "it's not my job" club.

This chapter will talk you through the best practices of getting the right team in place for those crucial early years.

How to Select the Best People

As a new business—and a small business—you'll face unique challenges to getting the best people. You probably won't be able to compete with the big guys when it comes to salaries and benefits, but you will be able to offer something else they may not: the ability to get involved in many aspects of the business from the ground up. The learning opportunities working in a small business are great and varied, which is a terrific selling point to candidates!

The best people for your business are those who treat the business and the customers as if they are their own. They are committed to the business's success and do what needs to be done to ensure that success. They are engaged in their work and excited about new opportunities.

The best people to select for your business are those individuals who ...

- Are willing to take on many responsibilities and play a variety of roles.
- Put the customer first.
- Can make decisions.
- Are team players.
- Have an entrepreneurial spirit.
- Can work autonomously.

The best people are those who can think outside of the box and therefore can help you in building your business.

Identifying Your Needs

The first step in hiring these kinds of employees involves writing a good job description, which you'll need to revise regularly as your business grows. We'll look at job descriptions in much more detail in Chapter 13, but let's discuss them briefly here.

The responsibilities you define for your employees should clearly focus on skills needed to help you in growing the business. Make sure the job description you develop broadly covers the goals and responsibilities of the particular role but also emphasizes that the individual needs to play many roles.

Selecting the best people requires an analysis of who you need in your business right now to accomplish your goals. Think about the behavior and attitude you need from your employees. In doing a job analysis for the role for which you wish to hire, think about the following issues:

- Responsibilities of the individual in that role
- Skills and experience they will need to be successful

- The goals they will need to meet in that role and tasks required to accomplish those goals

- Long-term expectations for that role

Don't discount contract, or temporary, employees to help out during particularly busy times or just as a stopgap measure. And certainly don't discount family members and friends. Often small businesses get their start by calling on friends and family to help. Gina, one of the authors of this book, remembers when her brother opened a small deli in New Jersey many years ago. She took time off from work to help him get started—clearing and cleaning the counters, serving the customers, shopping for suppliers, washing dishes when the dishwasher broke—while he did all the cooking. Once he got the business off the ground and saved a bit of money, he was able to hire his first couple of real employees to help out.

Winning Interview Strategies

When interviewing candidates for a job with your business, keep in mind two essential characteristics of anyone you hire:

- Must fit with the business culture

- Must have the skills necessary to do the job

Many hiring experts argue that a good fit with your organization's culture is, as a general rule, at least as important as the skills the applicant brings to the table. Most skills, after all, can be learned. We don't disagree with this advice but would recommend a balance, with a slant toward culture fit.

When thinking about whether someone is a fit for your business culture, consider the values of your business. What is most important to you and your business? Is it fantastic customer service? Is it a family feel among your staff? Is it a team environment? Look for individuals whose outlook matches these values.

Interviewing effectively requires preparation. The goal during the interviewing process is to determine if the person you are interviewing will be a good fit for your business—someone you can work with and who can help you reach your goals. *Behavioral interviewing* techniques are more difficult than regular interviewing but provide a much better picture of the candidate's ability to get the job done.

DEFINITION

Behavioral interviewing (also called *competency-based interviewing* and *scenario-based interviewing*) looks at a candidate's past experiences to determine his ability to perform a role. Past experience is often a good predictor of how the candidate will perform in the job for which he is being considered.

Behavior-based interview questions provide you with the opportunity to understand the behavior of the individual you are interviewing when they are in specific real-life situations. You will learn how a candidate solves problems, handles stress, works with difficult customers, handles adversity, and whether they have been successful in their past roles. Probing, detailed questions asked of the candidate make it difficult for her to cover up her past and lie about her capabilities.

Frame your questions of candidates to get to the following information:

- The situation or circumstances that occurred that caused the individual to behave as he or she did, or caused the individual to take a particular course of action

- What the candidate actually did in that situation—ask for specifics

- The result or outcome of the action the candidate took or the behavior he or she displayed

- What the candidate learned and what they would do differently today

Effective behavioral interviewing questions might include the following:

- Can you give me a specific example of a time when you had to abide by a policy you thought was wrong?

- Tell me about a time when you persuaded someone to take a certain course of action they were initially skeptical about taking.

- Give me an example of a time when you used your problem-solving skills to resolve a stressful situation.

Take the following best practice steps to ensure an interview with a candidate will get you the information you need to make a decision:

1. Prepare the questions you will ask beforehand based on the candidate's resumé and experience and the role to be filled.

2. Set aside a quiet place for the interview where you will not be interrupted or distracted.

3. Welcome the candidate and make him feel comfortable. Introduce yourself; make a bit of small talk.

4. Let the candidate know you'll take notes during the interview and you'll be asking questions designed to understand if there is a match between the needs of the position and the candidate's background and goals. Also let the candidate know that he will have the opportunity to share information about his past experiences and to ask questions about the position and the business culture. The point of the interview is so you both can determine if there is a fit within the business for this candidate.

5. Allocate about 50 minutes for you to ask scenario-based questions and about 10 minutes for the candidate to ask questions.

6. Close the interview, thank the candidate for his time, and discuss next steps. Ask if there are any additional questions from the candidate or if there was something that was not covered during the interview that they would like to share relevant to the position and their ability to do the job.

Have other people interview the candidate, too; don't feel like you have to make the decision alone. It is nice to have another perspective, and other interviewers might pick up on things you did not.

PRACTICE MAKES PERFECT

Practice your interviewing skills on family members and friends. Write out the questions you will ask and have someone play the role of the interviewee. Especially when using behavioral-based interviewing questions, practice makes perfect!

No Lone Wolves Need Apply

When pulling together your initial team for your business, do not hire lone wolves—those individuals who do not work well with others and prefer to do their own thing. Given that in the first few years you won't be able to hire vast numbers of employees, it's essential that the individuals you do hire are team players.

When interviewing candidates, specifically look for instances where they have worked as a member of a team. Candidates simply saying to you they are team players is not sufficient; you'll want proof. Ask questions to learn about how well the person can work in a team environment.

Hire Slow, Fire Fast

Don't feel rushed to make a decision on a candidate; take time to explore options and ensure that the candidate you hire is the best fit for the role. Many business owners don't have the time to be experts at hiring and interviewing, but you should not shortchange this process. Learn how to do it well!

Avoid these common mistakes business owners make:

- Skipping the interview process when the candidate is family, a friend, or referred by someone

- Not preparing for the interview with behavior-based questions

- Not having a formal hiring process to ensure consistency and that the best individuals are selected for the business

- Asking inappropriate questions during the interview process

Avoiding these common pitfalls will reduce the chances of you making a bad hiring decision; however, you should probably accept that some mistakes are inevitable. If you find that you have made a bad hiring decision, make a commitment to fix the problem quickly. Smaller businesses tend to find it difficult to let go of employees who are not working out. Often this is due to the close "family" environment that many small businesses have. You may feel a sense of guilt that you made a bad decision, or may not feel comfortable making someone else "pay" for your mistake. Bear in mind, however, that keeping the wrong person employed is simply bad for business—which means that you are letting the whole "family" down when you hold on to someone who is not working out.

Generalists Needed

There is a considerable amount of discussion lately among organizations as to whether it's better to hire generalists or specialists. Much of this conversation is among the big players—the Ciscos, Googles, and Microsofts of the world. In the case of smaller businesses, and especially in their early years, generalists are the way to go. The benefits of hiring generalists are that they …

- Can wear many hats in the business.
- Generally learn quicker and adapt to changes in the business and environment more easily.
- Bring a variety of skills and experiences to the table.
- Can fit into multiple areas within the business as it expands.
- Can play an internal consultant role within the business.

As your business grows, you may need individuals with certain specialties, such as a marketing specialist or someone to manage human resources. But in the early stages, individuals who have a generalist background and experience in a variety of areas enable you to launch your business successfully without having to hire too many employees to meet all your varied needs.

Hire Self-Directed Individuals

It's important to hire individuals who do not need to be micromanaged. Instead, find people who take the initiative to do what needs to get done. During the interview process, ask pointed questions to determine if the individual is self-motivated and has the initiative you need for your business. Here are some questions you might ask:

- What do you do when there is downtime or a slow period at work?
- Tell me about a time when you had to learn a new task in a very short time period. How did you go about learning the task?
- Tell me about a time when you needed to solve a particularly thorny problem and no one was available to assist you. What did you do?

You are looking to determine if the candidate has the wherewithal to manage herself and tasks assigned to her.

BUSINESS BUSTER

You can't expect to be able to micromanage employees and run your business at the same time. To ensure you can focus on building your business, hire individuals who are self-sufficient, self-motivated, team players, learn quickly, and need very little direction.

Lots of Hats ... Few Heads

Just as you are wearing multiple hats in your business, your employees will need to do the same! You'll be looking for folks who can transition smoothly from task to task. You'll also need individuals who are able to multitask. Any business will need people who can do marketing, sales, product development, finances, administration, operations, human resources, and training. As a small business you can't afford to hire someone for each area, and it's unlikely you need full-time employees in each area.

One small business owner, a magazine publisher, hired individuals whom she had worked with when she headed up the marketing department at a large organization. The problem was that the people were not used to a smaller business, were used to working from 9 to 5, and had gotten used to concentrating on one project at a time. Additionally, in their previous jobs they had assistants to help them out. They were unprepared for the hectic schedule and were not a good fit for a small business. The owner learned quickly that interviewing for fit was more important than anything else for her business!

Roles and Responsibilities

As you are getting your business up and running, it is not easy to have a clearly defined set of roles and responsibilities for every job. In fact, it likely isn't possible! The authors know of one small business that hired two employees to help out in the office. The employees had a variety of responsibilities: sales, marketing, administrative work, special projects, and following up with clients. When the business owner tried to develop job descriptions, she was at a loss for where to begin. The staff of three was doing everything for the business. She ended up not worrying about formal job descriptions for the two employees and instead used the mission statement and strategic plan for her business as a guide for her employees.

BEST PRACTICE

While you want to develop job descriptions for your employees as a best practice, don't feel pressured to have the perfect description in the early stages of your business. Consider a brief job description that includes an overall description and essential responsibilities of the position. Keep it flexible in the early years.

The Right Starter Sales Team

Chapter 18 focuses on how to hire the best sales team for your business. Here, we take a look at the *kinds* of salespeople you need when you are in the early years of your business.

As your business develops and you bring salespeople on board, you will likely have clients that you can pass on to them—customers they can contact who have already done business with you. Certainly, you'll expect them to bring in new business, but you may already have some customers or prospects you can assign to them to get them started. In the early years, it is unlikely that you will have a pool of customers for your salesperson to call upon; rather, you expect them to get out there and find customers for your business! In other words, you need hunters—individuals who can seek out business rather than sit back and wait for business to find them.

Look for sales applicants who have already proven their ability to launch brand-new business relationships and manage a sales process from beginning to end—then give them all the support you can.

Of particular importance for new salespeople is to have an *onboarding* process in place to support them in those first few crucial days. One important best practice is to team a new sales hire with a more experienced mentor during this onboarding process.

DEFINITION

Onboarding is the process of assimilating new employees into your business in the shortest time frame possible. It includes helping them to understand the culture of the business and providing them training on products and services you offer and on your processes, policies, and procedures.

Send newly hired sales personnel information about your products and services prior to their actual start date; once they start, train them in your sales process and spend time helping them understand the products and services you offer, the types of customers you are seeking, and your overall business approach. You want them to hit the ground running.

Spotting the Perfect Salesperson

One very effective best practice is to provide the sales candidate with a mini scenario describing a specific problem to solve, such as a call from a customer who is unhappy with an order that has shipped. Give the candidate some time to read the case study and then ask him or her to respond to it. Ask what he or she would do in the situation. Much as with behavioral-based interviewing questions, you are trying to determine how the candidate thinks through problems.

The perfect candidate will have a resumé and references that show that she has experience …

- Developing business where none existed.
- Building strong customer relationships.
- Finding creative ways to position products and services to meet the customers' needs.

While many businesses separate marketing and sales functions, as a business just starting off, it may not be practical to have both marketing people and salespeople. Your salespeople in the early years should have experience in marketing products through social media, business connections, networking events, and at conferences.

BEST PRACTICE

Look for candidates with connections in the community and a solid reputation, as they will be the face of your company.

Where's the Proof?

When evaluating candidates for a sales role, do not take their resumés or what they tell you in an interview at face value. Do your homework. Ask for specific examples of their ability to source new customers and close the deal. Get all the details.

PRACTICE MAKES PERFECT

When checking references of potential employees, have a list of questions to ask before picking up the phone. In addition, plug the candidate's name into search engines and see what comes up about them. Check your own connections on LinkedIn to see if you know anyone who might have worked where the candidate last worked. Come up with your own list of references for the candidate; don't just rely on the list they provide you.

A best practice proven in countless industries is to hire a salesperson on a temporary contract basis to confirm whether he or she can really do the job. For instance, you might offer a candidate a 90-day temporary contract with a promise to move the person to a full-time position if he or she meets certain clearly outlined goals. During those 90 days, the salesperson will be expected to secure new customers for the business and generate a certain amount in revenue. This approach is a low-risk way to try out the salesperson to see whether he or she presents a good fit with your business. One business we know of that sells clothing customized with company logos requires all new salespeople to bring on at least one new customer within the first 90 days at a value of $500, and to sell $1,000 worth of product to a minimum of three current customers during the same period.

Assign all new salespeople short-term goals for customer and revenue generation. Evaluate them against those goals within the first three months and then again within six months.

The Least You Need to Know

- Plan for the interview session; be well prepared and take the time necessary to make the best decision for your business.
- Remember that the individuals who are best for your business in the early years are those who are willing to wear many hats and take on a variety of roles.
- If you hire the wrong person for the job, fix the mistake! Terminate the person and start looking for the right person.
- Be sure that the sales team you hire are hunters who can go out and secure customers for your business. Look for individuals who can start with no customer base and grow it quickly.

Sales and Marketing Goals

In This Chapter

- Focusing on sales and marketing in the early years
- Getting started when you have no leads
- Determining the appropriate KPIs for the first few years
- Narrowing your market focus

Unless you are lucky enough to have started your business with an ample supply of customers who are already eager to purchase from you, you will have to face a fateful question: where do you find new business?

You will need to invest a significant amount of time getting your business recognized and spreading the word about your products and services. Truth be told, even a reliable base of core customers should not relieve you of the ongoing responsibility of marketing your business. Reliable accounts have been known to vanish without warning.

The very best sales and marketing person for your business is *you*. While you will no doubt have others helping you, you are likely to be the key player in this area, at least in the early years.

Later on in this book, we look at best practices for sales and marketing as long-term responsibilities (see Part 5). In this chapter we focus on best practices for kick-starting your sales and marketing processes.

Setting Goals for Sales

In the early years, your goals for sales will likely be more fluid than later on, when you have your business moving along smoothly.

Customers or no customers, you have a product or service to sell, and you are confident it will do well in the marketplace given the research you put into the idea before launching your business. You need to set revenue goals for those first couple of years, keeping in mind that you are starting from scratch.

The first, simplest, and perhaps most important best practice is to set revenue goals that are aggressive but achievable. Don't build your first year or two around assumptions that your company will instantly be a national (or global) phenomenon. Assume that building a vast customer base is going to take some time.

Depending on your business, it's quite possible that for the first few months there will be no sales at all. You may be spending a significant amount of time meeting with potential customers and telling them about your products and services. That sales activity will pay off in the long run; you just don't know when. For the purposes of establishing your cash flow requirements (see Chapter 12), you're probably going to want to make a conservative estimate.

Initial goals you set may not be built around income at all, but instead around generating activity toward future sales. For example, you might establish the following goals:

- Make a set number of daily sales cold calls.
- Schedule a set number of weekly meetings with potential customers.
- Attend conferences or other events to promote the products or services.

These kinds of goals will introduce customers to your products and services and begin to build your database of potential customers. They will also help you get a clearer sense of the average amount of time it actually takes to close a sale and the size of the average deal. Once you know that, you can begin to set goals for actual revenue amounts on a monthly basis.

Lead Generation from Zero

As a business with no customers lined up, you'll need to generate customer leads from scratch. Certainly some of the goals listed in the previous section will begin to generate leads; however, you may also want to consider the following options:

- Purchasing marketing lists of individuals or businesses who would buy your products

- Making connections through industry groups and Chambers of Commerce

- Drawing on personal connections, such as online networks, groups and organizations to which you belong, and friends and family

As a best practice, establish daily and weekly routines for generating leads. The best way to do this will vary, but some proven approaches include making a set number of calls a day to brand-new contacts; reaching out to family or friends to tell them about your products and services and ask them to refer business to you; attending networking events on a weekly basis; and talking daily to the owner of at least one new business that complements yours and offering to share leads.

BEST PRACTICE

For ideas for creating and executing good sales call scripts, check out Brad Massey's excellent, and provocative, online article "Stop Cold Calling," available at www.sandlerblog.com/?p=155#more-155.

It takes time to build a base of customers for your business. As you begin to develop your customer base, you'll begin to see patterns. For example, you will learn that for every x number of leads you generate, only a certain number close business with you and buy your product. Use this information to determine what kinds of ratios emerge.

Through researching your industry, you'll learn some important facts about which metrics are necessary to track to be successful in generating revenue and becoming profitable.

You will also learn that some customers are simply not worth the time and effort necessary to keep them happy. Some customer relationships that generate short-term cash flow simply do not justify the effort, energy, and resources necessary to sustain them.

Let's look at an example. You have one client who purchases from you each month. His purchases average around $5,000 to $10,000 a month. However, he is constantly contacting your sales team to complain about products and demand discounts, and he frequently threatens to take his business elsewhere. All in all, he is a drain on your resources.

As your business grows and prospers, you'll get better at recognizing desirable and undesirable customers. In Chapter 19, we share some more thoughts on what makes a customer good or bad for your business.

The Entrepreneurial Edge

Your goal, of course, is to recruit and retain people with a proactive, "go for it" attitude. You can't afford to have people on board who are content to sit on the sidelines simply waiting for things to happen. Instead, you want individuals with an *entrepreneurial edge*—those individuals who have the gumption, self-direction, and drive to get the job done.

DEFINITION

An individual with an **entrepreneurial edge** has the spirit and drive to identify and create opportunities that result in sales that generate revenue and profits for the business.

You started this business because you wanted to control your destiny and be the determining factor in how much money you make. That spirit is essential in the early years of your business.

Your initial sales and marketing team will need this same edge to be successful in helping you grow your business. We talked about the skills and experience these individuals need in Chapter 8. Not only do these individuals need to be innovative, they also need to be able to execute. Innovation alone isn't a recipe for a successful business; the ability to implement ideas is also required.

The individuals you need to help jump-start marketing and sales in those first crucial years of your business should have the following qualities:

- Independent thinker
- Goal-oriented
- Driven to succeed
- Able to deal with ambiguity
- Able to change direction quickly
- Willing to take on challenges and tolerate stressful conditions

Hunters Take the Lead

For those first few years you will need hunters—those individuals who know how to go after business and secure customers.

> **BUSINESS BUSTER**
>
> If you hire salespeople without a demonstrated record of tracking down and closing their own deals, you are gambling with your organization's revenue stream—and, possibly, its very survival. For these first few years, consider hiring only individuals with experience sourcing their own leads and generating sales quickly.

Expect to spend time with your salespeople generating leads, visiting potential clients, and generating sales. You may find that many hunters are successful at finding customers and closing the deal but not so skilled at keeping the relationship going. That's fine—at this stage, you need people who can seek out those individuals and businesses that will buy from you and close the deal to bring in that revenue. However, don't discard the need to keep customers engaged with your business. This may be the role that you play with your customers. You are, after all, the face of that business, and you want your customers to get to know you.

Focus on Key Performance Indicators

Your key performance indicators (KPIs) for revenue generation will change over time. The KPIs you need now in the early years may not be the same KPIs you have two, three, or five years down the road.

In the early years you want to focus on the right KPIs for your business and measure against those KPIs regularly. Make adjustments as necessary to keep moving in the right direction. Don't expect to get it right the first time, but be prepared to make the changes necessary as you learn what works and what doesn't. Early on, it's important to be able to turn on a dime.

> **BEST PRACTICE**
>
> Collaborate with others on the appropriate KPIs for your business. Reach out to some of the executives at SCORE who can help you in focusing on the right KPIs at the right time. Many of them have already been down the road you are traveling and have sage advice.

If you are starting at zero (meaning no customers), your KPIs will almost certainly be focused on generating leads of potential customers for your business. If, on the other hand, you are starting out on your own full time after having done some consulting work while employed at another company, your KPIs may be focused on generating additional revenue from current customers and also on developing leads of new customers for your business. Perhaps you are just starting to expand your business out of your local area. In that case, your KPIs might be focused on geographical expansion through Chambers of Commerce, at industry events, or through a network of business allies.

Identifying the Right KPIs

For any new business, identifying specific KPIs for revenue generation is a critical best practice. These KPIs may be focused on early marketing and sales goals, such as …

- Making 20 cold calls each week.

- Generating three inquiries a week from the website.

- Setting up five meetings a week with potential customers.

You need to identify the critical success factors (CSFs) for your business and determine KPIs to support those CSFs. Let's look at an example.

Assume you have a small business focused on selling and repairing antique clocks and watches. This was a side business for about two years, and you launched it full time about six months ago. You have 10 regular customers who collect grandfather clocks and antique watches and are frequent visitors to your business for both repairs and purchases. You need to expand that customer base in order to succeed full time in this endeavor. You set a CSF to generate new customers for your business, and specifically to generate 30 new customers over the next year, at a value of $5,000 per customer. To achieve this goal, you decide on the following actions:

- Develop a website within two months.

- Write a monthly article for antique magazines on collecting and repairing clocks to highlight your expertise.

- Display products at antique shows twice a year.

- Contact jewelry stores to handle repairs for their customers with the goal of partnering with five jewelry stores within six months.

- Ask for referrals from current customers with a goal of each current customer referring one potential new customer.

- Purchase mailing lists of potential customers and introduce your business via e-mail blasts or cold calls.

- Obtain testimonials from your current customers to use for marketing.

These are your KPIs toward meeting your CSF of generating 30 new customers in a one-year time frame, at a value of $5,000 per customer.

Monitoring and Adjusting

Now you need to monitor your progress against those KPIs. You may find that what you have proposed is not sufficient for generating 30 new customers within one year. If so, make adjustments to your KPIs.

Continuing our example: if you find that by displaying your products at antique shows twice a year you are able to generate at least two profitable customers per show, you might want to consider increasing your attendance at antique shows. Or if you find that the lists you purchase generate no new customers, you need to determine what the problem is: Are you marketing incorrectly to these folks? Is the list you purchased not valid for your business? Or does this form of identifying potential customers just not work for you? Maybe you are better off investing in showing your products at antique shows and building your customer lists there.

In these first few crucial years of getting your business off the ground, monitor your KPIs frequently—even as frequently as weekly. Look for indicators that adjustments need to be made to the KPI, or wholesale changes in the KPIs you are measuring, to keep moving in the right direction for your business.

PRACTICE MAKES PERFECT

One good source of information on KPIs in the area of marketing and sales is *Key Performance Indicators: Developing, Implementing and Using Winning KPIs* by David Parmenter (John Wiley & Sons, Inc., 2007).

Who's Your Market?

You've done all the research up front, yet determining who the market really is for your products and services may not be an easy task. A certain amount of trial and error, and then revising your assumptions, is inevitable during the first few years of a business.

Certainly if you are a retail shop selling baby products and baby clothes, you have an easy time determining your market base. However, what if you offer event planning services? Who's your market? Is it small businesses or larger businesses? Does it focus specifically on small inns or B&Bs who want to get event business but can't manage it? Is it for organizations that need to plan customer appreciation events? What if market conditions change the operating assumptions of all of these prospective buyers? As you can see, determining your market isn't always easy.

> **BEST PRACTICE**
>
> In determining the target market for your business's products and services, determine those individuals and businesses that will most benefit from what you have to offer. By identifying a target market for your business, you know exactly where to focus your marketing and sales efforts to generate revenue for your business. One great best practice is to take a few current or prospective customers out to lunch on a regular basis.
>
> These meetings will enable you to get a better understanding of your customers' needs and insights. You should also consider sending out a semi-annual survey to customers who do business with you as well as those who have stopped doing business with you. You want to understand as much as you possibly can about the perceptions and choices of both current and former customers.

If you have a store that sells organic produce, your target market may be local families who want a healthy alternative to what's available in larger supermarkets in your area. Your target market for a consulting services business may be small businesses just starting out that need guidance to ensure they are successful.

You'll also need to consider segmenting your market for better results. For example, if your target market includes both individuals and businesses, segment your target market into those two groups. Your marketing efforts will be different for each group to focus on each segment's unique needs.

What's the Demand?

After you determine your target market, you must address a critical question: what's the strength of the demand in that market?

Let's look back at one of our examples. You own a small grocery that sells organic produce. Lately, you've seen a lot of news stories about the importance of eating healthier, consuming more fruits and vegetables, and, specifically, eating products free of chemicals. This should increase demand for organic produce, which should translate into increased business for your organic produce.

You need to understand why individuals or businesses want to buy from your business. Is it that your product is unique? Do you have a strong customer service focus? Once you understand why people buy from you, it is much easier to gauge the demand for your product and focus your efforts on meeting that demand.

As a best practice, perform this exercise for each of your products and services: write down the *benefits* and *features* of your products and services.

DEFINITION

Benefits are what the product does for the customer—what problem it solves or what need it fulfills. **Features** are the attributes of your product.

Features of products—chrome finish, 11-inch screen, rubber safety guards—are generally fairly simple to identify, but identifying a product's benefits usually isn't so easy. Why should someone purchase your product or service over someone else's?

It's easy to mistake features for benefits, and it takes some practice to distinguish between the two. One classic marketing exercise is to draw a line down the middle of a sheet of paper, and to write as many product features as you can on the left side. That's the easy part. The harder part comes when you try to establish the benefit by completing the sentence, "My customer would pay for this because …" Once you come up with a compelling enough answer, enter it on the right-hand side as a benefit. Here are some examples:

- Feature: 10 megabytes per second download speed.

- Benefit: You get to listen to more music and spend less time waiting for songs to show up on your computer.

- Feature: Automatic call forwarding with caller ID displayed.

- Benefit: Important calls from clients will never go to voicemail again (unless you want them to).

- Feature: Timer that synchronizes seamlessly with your existing automobile computer interface.

- Benefit: Your car will be warm—and warmed up—when you enter it on cold winter mornings.

To help identify benefits, send a survey to your customers asking them why they purchase from you. Be sure to provide them a list of options to choose from.

Some small business owners are unable to identify the competitive advantage of their business. Consider this example: You offer consulting services around establishing policies and procedures for small businesses, including providing customers with the following products:

- A policy and procedures manual

- Templates for creating policies and procedures

- Software to help in the development of policies and procedures

Benefits of the service you offer would include:

- Peace of mind—your customers know that there are consistent policies and procedures to protect the customer's business

- Time saved in the creation of policies and procedures

- An easier path to growth when a business decides to expand

When thinking about benefits, the most essential best practice of all is to think constantly, and even obsessively, about what your customer wants most. Doing so will help you to spot and take action on all kinds of new opportunities.

BEST PRACTICE

Interview and survey your best customers regularly about why they purchase your products and services. What benefits do they currently realize? What new benefits would they be most interested in learning more about? This information will help you delineate the benefits of your products and services from the customer's point of view. Use this information to enrich your marketing initiatives!

Once you can successfully delineate features and benefits of your products and services, you have taken a step toward determining the demand in the marketplace. You know what kind of customers to reach out to. Search for those customers that need the benefits your products and services offer.

The Least You Need to Know

- Set sales goals that are aggressive but achievable for those first couple of years.
- Focus on generating leads for your business to build up your database of potential customers.
- You are the best marketing and salesperson for your business—focus your efforts in these areas.
- Determine the KPIs necessary now to bring in revenue.
- Understand who you best serve in the marketplace; that is where your opportunities will be.

Best Practices for Customer Service

In This Chapter

- Making the connection between engaged, happy employees and engaged, happy customers
- Using customer service to give you a competitive edge
- Learning from your customers
- Creating position statements to help you with your sales and marketing strategies

True or false: good customer service starts with how you treat your employees.

It's true. Engaged, mission-driven, motivated employees are the key to providing outstanding customer service. This fact assumes tremendous importance when you realize that, for many small businesses, the quality of the customer service is all they have to compete on!

Today, we see huge companies such as Comcast using Twitter to improve relationships with customers. Using the Twitter handle @ComcastCares, a team of employees at Comcast monitor Twitter for all conversations about Comcast. The minute a complaint or problem arises, a Comcast rep jumps in to help resolve the problem. Comcast—and countless other companies—also join in the general conversation using Twitter and other social media tools, thereby creating a personal connection with their followers.

In this chapter, you will learn that best practices in customer service are not just about managing individual problems when they arise but also and most importantly, building a team that truly cares about maintaining good relationships with your customers.

Treat the Team Right

Herb Keller, the former CEO of Southwest Airlines, knew all about the importance of the team. He once commented:

> Years ago, business gurus used to apply the business school conundrum to me: "Who comes first? Your shareholders, your employees, or your customers?" I said, "Well, that's easy," but my response was heresy at the time. I said employees come first and if employees are treated right, they treat the outside world right, the outside world uses the company's product again, and that makes the shareholders happy. That really is the way that it works and it's not a conundrum at all.

Too often, businesses lose sight of the fact that an unhappy employee eventually transfers that unhappiness to everyone he or she comes in contact with—including customers. When customers call or walk in the door, they expect to be treated with consideration and respect and encounter a polite and friendly person on the other end of the phone or across the counter. Whether we realize it or not, the most meaningful customer service training our employees receive for these interactions comes from their own interactions with us.

If you do not treat your employees well, how can you expect them to treat your customers well? If you take care of your employees, they will take care of your customers. If you don't, they won't. It's really that simple.

Great Service Starts at Home

Your employees are a direct connection to your customers. If you have not made and followed through on meaningful commitments to them, they will not be committed to your customers. It follows that you must treat your employees in exactly the same attentive and respectful way you want them to treat your customers.

Above all, you must be ethical, honest, and aboveboard in your interactions with your employees. The ability of your employees to interact ethically (and legally!) with customers is directly tied to your own personal character and to the way you handle the various judgment calls that arise within your team. Whatever issues arise internally, once your team learns that you will address those issues fairly, ethically, and honestly, that standard will carry over to your employees and to your company's relationships with customers.

> **BEST PRACTICE**
>
> In his book, *First Things First,* business author Stephen Covey says he once had a boss who told him: "I see my role as one of being a source of help to you, so I would like you to think of me in this way and let me know what I can do to help you." His boss made good on that statement. Imagine how powerful this approach could be to your employees! By being available to support (not overwhelm) your employees, you can create an environment of outstanding service—one that will inevitably be conveyed to your customers.

Establish a vision of customer service for your employees. Your vision of how you treat your employees—how you will serve them—should include the following elements:

- A commitment to provide them with what they need to do their jobs, including training, resources, and support

- Opportunities for professional development

- Regular, timely feedback on performance

- A safe environment to try new ideas and make mistakes, because mistakes are great learning opportunities

As a best practice, survey your employees regularly to ensure that you (and other managers in your organization) are meeting their needs. If an employee brings a problem to you, treat it as seriously as you would if you heard about a problem from an external customer.

As a small business owner, it is much easier for you to keep your employees engaged and to recognize issues that could turn into major problems for your business than it is for larger businesses. Keep that personal connection with your employees, regardless of how large you grow your business.

Starting an Internal Service Revolution

We know of one small business owner who treated his employees poorly. He denied vacation requests, talked about employees to other employees, bullied employees who weren't working to his satisfaction, and generally took every opportunity to display disdain for the people who worked for him. Needless to say, this attitude carried over to his employees' interactions with customers.

On one occasion, the business owner cut back on the quality of a product. He then told employees that, if a question came from a customer on product quality, they should tell the customer no changes had been made! We know of at least one employee who specifically told a customer he wouldn't buy the product himself because the quality was poor. The company eventually went out of business.

That business's failure was, before anything else, a failure to serve the company's internal customers: its employees. Don't let that happen to your organization!

As a best practice, consider brainstorming with your team to draft a written agreement. This should be an agreement between you and your employees that identifies exactly what employees can expect from you and what you expect from them.

Good customer service in any given situation is not instinctive. It must be learned and practiced. Provide your employees with training on how to interact with customers and handle stressful customer situations. Empower your employees to make decisions for the benefit of the customer. When employees can make some decisions on their own, they will become more confident in dealing with customers.

One best practice you can adapt from the hospitality industry is to give each frontline employee a certain dollar limit within which he or she can operate autonomously to make good decisions on behalf of the customer. You and your team must identify what that limit is, but for the sake of argument, let's say it's $300. That means that your employee has the discretion to improvise a solution to solve any customer issue, as long as doing so costs less than $300. Solutions with higher price tags must be approved by the employee's manager.

PRACTICE MAKES PERFECT

Expect hiccups and course corrections when employees are empowered to make decisions in support of customer service; create a safe environment where mistakes are treated as learning opportunities. By providing good policy guidelines and improving those guidelines over time, you can limit the impact of a mistake and still empower your employees to support the customer in the best way possible.

Working with the Customer

Your vision of customer service must be the same as the customer's vision. By working with customers directly and understanding their needs and their expectations in working with your business, you and your employees will be better able to determine expectations around customer service and align your organization with those expectations.

Your company's stated mission must emphasize the values that support your customers. The more customer-service focused your business, the more likely you are to step ahead of the competition.

Let's look at an example. The online retailer Zappos is well regarded as having excellent customer service. They provide a 365-day return policy and offer free shipping for returns. On its website, the firm talks about Zappos Family Core Values (http://about.zappos.com/our-unique-culture/zappos-core-values) which includes "Deliver WOW Through Service."

Zappos regularly trains its employees in customer service and rewards them publicly for a job well done. The company empowers employees to resolve as many customer problems as possible on the spot without going to a higher level.

The result: Zappos continues to grow and prosper, and their customers are loyal, often referring other customers. Nothing Zappos is doing or has done is exclusive to larger businesses. You can build the same core values into your business regardless of its size. It's all a question of relationships, internal values, and your own willingness to communicate.

Talk with your customers regularly to determine how well you are doing at serving them. Whenever possible, hold in-depth discussions with them, either in person or over the phone. If you have a storefront location, ask your customers at the point of sale (POS) if they received the assistance they needed. Ask if you can contact them later to inquire about their experience—and get their e-mail address or phone number.

BEST PRACTICE

There is no magic number for how often you should survey your customers; it is based on how much you interact with them. For example, if you sell Christmas trees, wreaths, and other seasonal items, customers only buy from you once a year—so you only need to survey them once a year. However, if you own a small gift shop and customers come in a number of times a year to purchase gifts for birthdays, anniversaries, and other special occasions, you might want to survey your customers a couple of times a year. Choose a time frame that works for your business and stick to it!

Consider sending a customer satisfaction survey to your customers on a regular basis. Include questions asking how satisfied they are with …

- Your business's products and services.
- The individual who helped them make the purchase.
- Their interactions with the business.
- The quality of your products and services.

In addition to finding out whether your customers are satisfied, you want to determine how loyal they are to your business. Loyal customers translate into increased profits. It requires a bigger investment to get a new customer than to sell to returning customers. That doesn't mean you don't need new customers, but don't forget about your current customers. Additionally, customers who are happy with you and repeatedly purchase your products and services are more likely to refer you to someone else and are less likely to be enticed by special offers made by your competitors.

To determine customer loyalty, ask your customers in the satisfaction survey if they would buy from you again and why or why not. Also ask if they would recommend your products and services to others and whether they enjoyed the experience of working with your business.

Remember that just because a customer is satisfied does not mean the customer is loyal to your business. Satisfaction and loyalty is not the same thing. Remember the Zappos core value mentioned earlier: "Deliver WOW Through Service." What are you doing in your business to stand out from other businesses offering similar products and services; what is the WOW you provide your customers?

BUSINESS BUSTER

Don't just survey your customers and put the results in a desk drawer. Follow up with customers who have had a negative experience (ask on the survey if you may contact the customer to discuss a particular situation further). Track the data you receive from customer satisfaction surveys so you can see trends in your customer service. Use the data from surveys in training events with your employees.

Customer surveys, when done properly, provide you with a wealth of information, including the following:

- Ideas on new products and services to offer based on customer needs
- Areas where you need to improve your interactions with customers or the quality of your products or service offerings

- Information on your strengths

- The effectiveness of your marketing and sales efforts

- Customer concerns that may have an impact on your business

We talk more about customer surveys in Chapter 19.

Consider creating a customer council consisting of a cross-section of your best customers and meeting with them at least twice a year. Use these meetings to learn what's going on in your customer's world, what new products or services they would like to see from you, and what processes need improving from their point of view. You can also use this time with your customers to tell them about what's on the horizon for your organization. As with any good advisory group, you will want to ensure that what is discussed in your office stays in your office; you might want to have members of your council sign confidentiality agreements.

We look more closely at how to create and run such councils in Chapter 17.

Developing Customer Service Policies

Your formal customer service policies should include the following information:

- Return or exchange policies

- Privacy policies

- How complaints will be handled or problems resolved

On your business website, include a "Frequently Asked Questions" section that the customer can refer to. If possible, include a variety of ways for people to reach customer service representatives, including e-mail, phone, fax, or other methods.

Avoid outsourcing customer service functions to people who don't understand or buy into your company's mission or share its values. The person who answers your service line or responds to a customer e-mail can be located in Mumbai or Minnetonka, but he or she must be part of your team and share the same core values you are using to create a positive service experience, both internally and externally.

BEST PRACTICE

When you talk with your customers—either in person or through surveys—ask them what you can do to provide them a better customer service experience. Strive to make the best suggestions part of your formal policy.

As part of your formal customer service policy, let your customers know they can expect easy access; respectful, courteous treatment; and a speedy resolution of issues.

Your customer service policy should be focused on ensuring that your customers' needs are met in the most friendly, professional, efficient, and effective way possible. The better your customer service, the more likely you are to retain customers and get leads to other customers.

Hiring a Customer Relationship Manager

Consider having a customer relationship manager on your staff. Individuals in these roles need to be customer-focused people who are personable, friendly, helpful, and always have a good attitude. They should be employees who genuinely like other people and can handle stressful situations and upset customers.

A customer relationship manager may have the following responsibilities:

- Ensuring that customer's needs and concerns are addressed quickly and to the customer's satisfaction
- Following up with customers after they have made purchases to ensure the experience was a good one
- Surveying customers on a regular basis
- Using data gathered from customers to improve how the business interacts with customers

The customer relationship manager should be the main point of contact for your customers. The individual in this role should establish a close working relationship with customers. In this way, customers feel comfortable working with that person. When problems arise, customers will be more likely to bring them to the individual's attention immediately (rather than letting the situation get worse) because they have established a relationship. Your best customer service person should be assigned this role.

Offering Introductory Deals

You may want to offer special deals that help your customers to get to know you by trying out your product or service at a special first-time rate. However, be careful with such special deals so you don't set any unwanted precedents on pricing or on discounting in general.

Let's look at two situations based on real companies. Both are small training firms. In the first company, when the owner meets with a potential customer for the first time, he spends time learning about that customer and her challenges to determine if he can assist her in addressing those challenges. If he sees possibilities, he offers his services at a heavy discount for her to try without having a significant impact on her budget. For example, a potential new customer was considering offering some additional professional development workshops for employees. The owner of the training firm offered to run one of his professional development workshops—a three-day course of the customer's choosing—at a 65 percent discount for up to 15 employees so they could try it out.

This business owner spends time with potential customers beforehand to ensure he understands what they want to get out of the workshop, thereby effectively customizing it for them. He makes it clear that this is a one-time offer to enable them to see how he works with his customers relatively risk-free. He has been very successful with this approach.

The other business does things a bit differently. This owner frequently feels pressure from competitors. Rather than selling new customers on the value of his professional development workshops and determining how he can best meet customers' needs, he competes on price alone and will make customers an offer to run a workshop at a significant discount (sometimes up to 50 percent) if they will select his workshop over a competitor.

A few things happen regularly to this owner. One, the customer simply says no because they don't see the value of his programs (he never talked about the value!); or two, they run the program and then never run another training program with him because it did not address their needs; or three, they run the program and then demand that same discount going forward to continue to do business. This is not a successful approach.

BUSINESS BUSTER

Use discounting sparingly and strategically; otherwise, your customers will come to expect regular discounts.

Measuring Up Against the Competition

In Chapters 3 and 5 we discussed the need to understand your competition so that you effectively differentiate yourself and stand out from the crowd. This is not a one-time task.

As your business continues to grow, you'll need to continue to monitor the competition and determine where you stand in relation to your competitors. In running their own small businesses, the authors have found that they frequently learn about competitors from current customers.

For example, in one situation, one of us was talking to a prospect about his needs and asked about the details of the challenges he was facing. He remarked, "Wow—I feel confident already since XYZ Company [a competitor] never asked anything about my challenges. They just assumed they knew the answer to my problem!"

BUSINESS BUSTER

Don't bad-mouth the competition to current or potential customers. This only makes you look bad.

Learn as much as you can about your competitors' customer service practices. You'll find information on their website about their policies, but also be sure to keep your ears open for what you hear from customers and others. Additionally, set up Google Alerts or scan press releases for information about your competitors and what they are up to. When you survey your customers, ask them if there is anything else you can do to make their experience better; you'll likely hear what others are doing that they appreciate.

The New Kid in Town

New businesses need to prove themselves. It's difficult to get customers to take a risk on a new business, and you need to get them to do that so they can see the value and benefits you bring with your products and services. Offering a trial of some sort—whether it is free samples or a heavy discount—helps to get others to try you out. Depending on your business, however, this may not be easy.

For instance, an information technology consulting firm may not be able to offer a free consulting job or a heavy discount; however, they may be able to prove themselves through writing case studies of work with their customers and by demonstrating their expertise by writing white papers and posting them on their website. They might also offer free one-hour planning sessions for potential customers.

Another option for any business to attract new customers is to use the knowledge you have about your competitors to position yourself as a better choice. For example, let's say that you want to open a fast-food restaurant franchise in an area where a couple already exist. Don't let that sway you from your plans. Eat at the other restaurants and learn about how they treat their customers—what's working and what isn't—and use that information to find a way to stand out when you open your restaurant. Maybe you notice that at the other restaurants the parents seem to feel hurried (and other customers annoyed) when kids start running around the restaurant. So for your restaurant, you decide to set aside an area for kids to gather (within the sight of their parents) to watch videos, play games, and otherwise be entertained; you might even hire a clown to entertain them!

Being the new kid on the block involves a lot of work, but with a bit of preparation you will find that you can make an impact with your business.

Established Competitors

Don't be afraid of established competitors who have a few years or more on your business. Every other business was once where you are today. Look at Facebook as an example. When it entered the market, one of its major entrenched competitors was MySpace. Facebook came in strong and offered features and benefits not offered by MySpace. Today, Facebook is the dominant social networking site.

BEST PRACTICE

Use outstanding customer service to differentiate yourself from established competitors. For many customers, customer service—and specifically the feeling of truly being listened to by a supplier—ranks higher in importance than factors such as price or product selection.

Small businesses frequently need to compete against much larger companies. Your organization's ability to deliver personalized customer service may be your best, and perhaps only, differentiator.

As a smaller business you can learn about your customers more easily and be on a first-name basis with them. Suppose you're a retailer. The next time Mrs. Smith walks through the door to make a purchase, ask her about her grandchildren or whether she had a nice holiday. You really are building customer loyalty with such exchanges! If you can build strong enough relationships, you won't need to compete on price.

Respond to your customers' requests to carry certain items or place special orders for them and you will find you have a customer who will keep coming back. For example, if you run a specialty food store and you know that one of your customers likes to purchase fresh figs and olives, e-mail that customer as soon as you get some in and set aside some for him or her to pick up.

By being creative and innovative in your customer service and the products and services you offer your customers, you will find that you can hold your own against established competitors. Smaller businesses should consider a niche market to compete with the big chains. You may offer fewer, more unique products. For example, a small gift boutique may compete by offering handmade crafts from local artists and even courses taught by those artists.

By gaining customer loyalty, you can ensure your competitive positioning in the marketplace even if you are surrounded by competitors. While pricing may seem to be a big driver for many customers, as long as pricing is competitive, customers will factor in the quality of your and your competitions' customer service when deciding where to spend their money.

Positioning Statements That Work

Develop a *positioning statement* for your products and services that helps you to market, sell, and support your offerings to customers. You should create positioning statements for each new product or service you introduce into the marketplace.

DEFINITION

Positioning statements include information on what your business does (products and services it offers), who the target customers are for those products and services, how you bring value to your customers (what needs do you fulfill or problems do you solve), and why you are different from your competitors.

Positioning statements are used to develop sales and marketing strategies, but they must also be well understood by everyone with front-line customer service responsibility. In essence, they represent your company's promise to the customer. Keeping that promise must be a critical priority for your customer service people.

A position statement for an organic pet food store might sound like this:

> Our pet products are made from the highest quality, all natural, organic ingredients; they surpass all other commercial pet food products in quality and purity. We understand that your pet is a part of your family, and we believe that he or she should be treated with the same respect, care, and love you would show to any other family member for whom you were planning a meal.

Many people prefer positioning statements that are considerably shorter. For instance:

Not "pet food"—food you would actually serve your pet.

Some famous one-sentence positioning statements that have stuck in the minds of consumers include Timex's "It takes a licking and keeps on ticking" and Ivory Soap's "99$^{44}/_{100}$ percent pure." Use these examples as inspiration for developing a catchy, concise positioning statement for your product or service.

When creating your positioning statement, call on employees to help in the process. Those employees who work with customers on a daily basis will be able to help you position a product to best meet your customers' needs.

Positioning statements must be grounded in reality; they aren't based on what you'd like to see but rather what actually is the case. Take these best practice steps to develop your positioning statement:

1. Gather together those employees who have the most contact with your customers on a daily basis.

2. Set aside one to two hours for brainstorming in a quiet area where you won't be interrupted or distracted and compile the data needed to create the positioning statement. Have handy the mission and vision statements to reference.

3. List your target customers—who they are, what their needs are, and what, if any, challenges they face. Gather this information from customer survey data and customer meetings.

4. List your products and services and map them to how they meet the customers' needs or address their challenges/problems. You might be able to identify opportunities for new products and services to fill in the gaps.

5. List your competitors and the similar products and services they offer and how those products and services compare to yours; list their strengths and weaknesses.

6. Use this information to create a concise positioning statement. Keep it short and sweet—no more than two to three sentences, but one sentence is even better!

Remember that positioning statements are not static. As you update your products and services, move into new markets, and serve new customers, you'll need to update and refresh your positioning statement. Southwest Airlines, for instance, has gone through many such statements. One was, "You are now free to move about the country." FedEx is still generating a market advantage from a positioning statement that now applies only to one dimension of its multi-tiered business model: "When it absolutely, positively has to be there overnight."

The Least You Need to Know

- Treat your employees as you want them to treat your customers and as you want to be treated yourself.
- Develop customer service policies that are aligned with the customers' expectations.
- Survey your customers to ensure they are satisfied.
- Outstanding customer service is frequently a small business's key to success.
- Use your positioning statement(s) to develop your sales and marketing strategy. Positioning statements must also be well-understood by everyone with front-line customer service responsibility.

Best Practices for Running Your Business

How do you assess and manage the risks your business will face as it grows and changes? What must you do to set up adequate budgeting and money management systems for your company? How can you keep your employees feeling fulfilled and satisfied—and keep them from defecting to the competition? What human resource processes will you need to put into place? How can you keep your company on the right side of the law? What kinds of investments should you make in information technology?

In this part, you learn about best long-term practices that will help you to maintain a flexible, intelligent approach to supporting and growing your business over time.

Risk Management

In This Chapter

- Determining your business's insurance needs
- Paying attention to regulatory issues that concern you
- Growing your business the right way
- Choosing an advisory board

Risk management is a key component of any business. By doing your homework upfront, calling on help when needed, and taking action when you know it's necessary, you can ensure that your business is both operating legally and protected to the very best of your ability.

Too often, small businesses don't consider risk management planning as a need for their business. But isn't it better to be prepared than not?

As a small business owner, you won't have expertise in every area of your business. You may be great with sales but not have a head for finances; maybe you excel in operations but aren't so great with strategy. That's why you need this chapter and its primary best practice: assemble a group of advisors to provide you with the guidance and support you need as your business grows and the risks you face multiply.

Securing the Right Advisors

As your business grows and changes, you will face many different kinds of risks. You'll want a group of advisors you can call on to assist you with operations risk assessment, strategic planning sessions, problem solving, and decision making. This group can take the form of an *advisory board*.

DEFINITION

An **advisory board** is an informal group of individuals who help you make strategic decisions about your business by providing guidance, acting as a sounding board, and offering their own expertise.

Although advisory boards tend to be informal groups of individuals, you can make the process and the advisory board structure more formal by implementing the following best practices:

- Set regular meeting dates. Consider quarterly meetings that run between two and three hours in duration. (For smaller businesses, you may want to consider meeting twice a year initially.)

- Compensate members for their time and commitment with a small stipend on an annual basis.

- Have a staggered term of office of two years for advisory board members. By staggering the terms of office, you are not replacing your entire advisory board at the same exact time.

- Have a process in place to remove advisory board members who do not fulfill their responsibilities.

Choosing the Inner Circle

Advisory boards can provide you with valuable expertise that nobody else in your business has. To get the most out of your board of advisors, include individuals with a variety of backgrounds, including your particular industry, financial, strategic planning, human resources, and sales and marketing expertise.

Also include as part of your advisory board your accountant, legal counsel, insurance agent, banker, and any other professionals you hire for your business.

Many smaller businesses have seen the value of having an advisory board to help them to meet their goals. Sometimes you just need a push in the right direction—and the advisory board can do that for you!

Do Your Own Homework

Of course, having an advisory board doesn't exempt you from doing the hard work of running your business. Specifically, you are in charge of running the advisory board meeting and setting the agenda. For every meeting, develop a formal agenda of what you would like to cover during that time. For instance, you might cover the following topics:

- New product-development initiatives
- New service offerings
- Expansion opportunities
- Partnerships
- Customer challenges
- General strategy planning

Let the advisory board members know what you need from them via the agenda. For example, maybe you want input on new products you are considering developing.

Take the advice you receive from the advisory board and combine it with your own experience and the experience of others to help you evaluate all the risks and make the very best decisions for your company.

The authors know of one small business—a magazine publishing company—that has been using an advisory board since inception. Members include an attorney, a marketing expert, a director of urban development, a publisher, and corporate and nonprofit executives. The board has assisted in directing the path of the magazine, helped with strategic growth plans, and served as a sounding board for the publisher/editor.

Managing risk effectively is a vitally important job but one that is virtually impossible to do well without the insights and advice of experienced people. All of the advice that follows in this chapter assumes that you will take the first step of forming and consulting regularly with your advisory board.

Protecting Your Business

Regardless of the current size of your business, you need to take steps to protect yourself and the business. Certainly part of protecting your business is incorporating or setting up a similar legal structure (see Chapter 3).

You can also protect yourself and your business by following some commonsense best practices: purchase the appropriate insurances; make sure that you meet all state and federal regulations appropriate for your business; and track and document your responses to relevant incidents, such as a customer who trips over boxes stacked in an aisle of your store or an employee who gets injured on the job. If you operate a shop that works with caustic materials, you would be required to have eye wash stations throughout the shop floor in the event of chemicals splashing into an employee's eyes.

As your business grows, it becomes even more necessary to ensure you have taken these steps. Failing to follow regulations or have the right protections in place can be a serious hindrance to your growth.

Handling Insurance Needs

Insurance needs vary widely depending on your particular business, the industry as a whole, and your location.

Protecting Small and Home-Based Businesses

If you're running your business out of your home, do not assume that your homeowner's policy will cover any business losses; likely it will not. Talk with your homeowner's insurance agent to find out what you need to do to be protected if you run a business out of your home. They may offer Home-Based Business Insurance policies. However, some agents will advise you that you cannot run certain businesses out of your home because of the risk involved. While they aren't necessarily prohibiting you from doing so, they will not insure you.

PRACTICE MAKES PERFECT

According to Nick Dager of Gagne & Dager Insurance Agency in Merrimack, New Hampshire, you should spend some time with your insurance agent describing your business and what you are doing—the products and services you offer, the number of employees you have, their roles and responsibilities, and your future goals. The more you share with your agent, the better able he will be to help you in protecting you and your business.

In fact, if something happens to your home business, you may find your insurance does not protect you and you are effectively uninsured. The complications from such a possibility are not even something you want to think about! Additionally, some states and cities require you to register a business you are running out of your home, which may entail paying fees. Do your research!

One policy common for small businesses is called a *business owner's policy* (*BOP*). BOPs can cover businesses that make up to $10 million in revenue. It is a very reasonable insurance for small businesses and costs between \$500 and \$1,000 per year for coverage.

DEFINITION

A **business owner's policy (BOP)** is similar to a homeowner's policy in that it is a package policy. A BOP combines property, liability, and business interruption insurance for small to medium-size businesses. Retail and office services (such as medical offices, real estate firms, and so on) can be covered under a BOP.

A BOP covers incidents such as damage or destruction of business property and actions (or nonactions) taken by employees of the business that result in injury or property damage to others. Additionally, depending on your policy, you may have coverage for burglary or theft, protection if your product causes harm to someone, and coverage for vehicles registered to the business. Your agent can help you to select the BOP most suited for your business needs.

BOPs are not available for restaurants and bars. These businesses will need other types of insurance policies to cover them effectively.

Often, business owners are unsure of what coverage they actually need. For example, did you know that any employee you hire, even if he or she only works for your business one or two days a month, must be covered under a *workers' compensation* policy? If something happens while they are on the job, you will be held personally responsible for the incident. These are the types of things you'll learn from an insurance agent.

DEFINITION

Workers' compensation is an insurance policy that is provided by the employer to ensure medical compensation for employees injured on the job. All employers should have workers' compensation insurance on their employees, even if they are part-time employees.

Protecting Larger Businesses

Larger businesses may have to purchase insurances separately (rather than in a package such as a BOP). You should look into purchasing the following types of insurance for your business:

- General liability insurance
- Property insurance

- Loss of income insurance

- Disability insurance

- Product liability

- Criminal insurance

- Business interruption insurance

- Malpractice insurance

- Terrorism protection

Some of these insurance policies may not apply to you and your business. A conversation with your insurance agent will clear up many issues regarding insurance and ensure you are getting the appropriate level of protection for your business.

Dealing with Regulatory Concerns

Many industries have local, state, and federal regulations that must be followed. If your business—even if it is home-based—is part of one of those industries, you need to be sure you are in compliance with those regulations.

Employment laws may vary from state to state. Check out federal government and state websites, along with the U.S. Chamber of Commerce site, to help you determine which laws are applicable to your business. Additionally, many states require licenses to operate businesses within the state. This information can also be found on state websites.

Additional federal and state regulations that may be applicable to your business include the following:

- Patent, copyright, and trademark information (see Chapter 15)

- Tax laws (see Chapter 15)

- Certificate of Occupancy for buildings

- Laws relating to employees, including labor laws, wages and overtime, family and medical leave, jury duty leave, unemployment insurance, unionization, immigration, health and safety, workers' compensation, termination, and sexual harassment protections

BEST PRACTICE

Two key resources are the Service Corps of Retired Executives (SCORE) and the U.S. Small Business Administration (SBA). Visit the SCORE website (www. score.org) and consider meeting with volunteers from SCORE to help you think through requirements for your business in your state. This is also perhaps the easiest and most effective way to assemble an advisory board. SCORE provides a wide variety of resources for businesses and also includes links to additional information. Many SCORE Business Counselors will serve as a personal mentor. Don't discount the importance of this valuable resource for your business! You should also visit the SBA's website (www.sba.gov) for free and low-cost help and support from a team of experts who can help you make sense of the regulatory requirements relevant to your business. The SBA offers business guidance and support in a wide range of areas and can connect you with counseling, training, and business development specialists providing free and low-cost services in your area.

Key Employee Insurance

For many small businesses, one or two individuals are absolutely key to the business. If you own a small business, you are a key employee of that business as well!

Key employee insurance ensures continuation of the business operations if a key person passes away, becomes seriously ill, or otherwise cannot participate in the business. This insurance policy is something like a life insurance policy on your key employees. Banks might require that you have this type of insurance before they will lend you money. Additionally, some key employee insurance policies provide financing meant to help you find a replacement for a business owner and to compensate you for loss of profits in the business.

Growth Risks

A big challenge for smaller businesses is managing growth. Common challenges relating to growth include managing new customers, retaining loyal customers, introducing new products and services, and figuring out when and how to hire people to support all those efforts.

For example, when is the right time to expand your inventory, take over more space, hire new staff, and address pressing infrastructure needs? How do you balance those initiatives against the fact that you are just starting to see more activity with your customer acquisition efforts? Shouldn't you devote your limited resources to ensuring that those customers come back? You want to keep customer satisfaction high, but you also want to expand. By the same token, you don't want to hire prematurely or invest in infrastructure you don't actually need.

You face big choices, and every one of those choices affects multiple areas of your business. A poor decision about how to address growth could cause significant problems for your business, up to and including the need to lay off employees.

Let's be frank: your competitors are probably hoping you don't make the right calls here. The best way to disappoint them? Surround yourself with experienced advisors—paid or unpaid—who have faced similar growth issues in the past. These are the members of your advisory board.

We know of a situation where a small business decided that since they were doing so well, it was time to hire more employees to support that business and take over some additional space (at the time when the real estate market prices were sky high) in various areas throughout the state. Here's the problem: they had only just started growing, and they had no idea whether it would continue.

Rather than getting advice, keeping track of what was happening in their industry, and developing sound strategic plans for growth, they embarked on the following course:

- Increased staff by 20 percent
- Signed multi-year leases for three new locations in office buildings
- Agreed to lease clauses that mandated significant investments in build-outs and other improvements

The business did no analysis of their plans. In one situation, they chose an area because a competitor was there. This is emotionally driven decision-making at its most dangerous.

They ended up in serious financial trouble when the market changed, and it changed quickly. Bottom line: they had no sound strategic plan for growth, no guidance, and no backup plan.

When you are ready to expand (or believe you are ready), develop a business plan for the expansion of your business and then discuss it with your advisory board. Remember all that planning we talked about as being critical to starting your business? Well, it is just as important when planning for your company's growth.

Dealing with Rapid Growth

When you start to see rapid growth, try to avoid making snap decisions. You want to be sure the growth you see is actually sustainable growth and not just a spurt that you need to get through.

PRACTICE MAKES PERFECT

Monitor what is happening in your industry. You'll see growth patterns there that will help you understand and plan for what is happening in your own business.

The biggest challenge is determining how much growth you can handle before you start investing in that growth. Don't invest any money in growth before examining whether it makes good strategic sense for you to do so.

When you begin to see rapid growth in your business, try to identify the cause of that growth. Ask yourself the following questions:

- Has your marketing strategy improved?
- Is the growth due to the release of a new product or service?
- Has something occurred in your industry to create growth?
- Has your customer profile changed?
- Has the competitive situation changed?

Don't assume that, just because you're busier than you used to be, your business is growing. It may be that you are catering to the wrong customers and that this new group of customers simply takes more work. Maybe your pricing could be increased because demand for the product or service has increased. Maybe processes in place need to be reworked to be effective for your business, or you need to improve your systems in general. Analyze the situation—and create a realistic plan for dealing with it!

Balancing Innovation with Efficiency

One major challenge for small businesses is balancing innovation with efficiency. How do you balance the objective of making profits now to support the business and the objective of building for the future to sustain your business?

One best practice that can help you achieve this balance is to set aside time for being innovative. By this we mean calendar slots for both you and your employees. By scheduling specific time periods devoted exclusively to innovation, you engage your employees in brainstorming sessions that may turn up some fantastic business ideas. You create a culture of sharing ideas and being creative that can benefit your business in the long run.

> **BEST PRACTICE**
>
> Schedule idea development sessions on a quarterly basis with your employees and partners. These brainstorming sessions will enable your employees to participate in growing the business and will encourage them to think of creative, innovative ideas for the business.

Part of running your business effectively and efficiently means to have processes and procedures in place to ensure that orders are fulfilled, services are delivered, customers are invoiced, and inventory is managed. Employees who work in these areas may have ideas for changing processes and procedures to be more cost effective, efficient, or more in line with customers' needs. Setting aside some time to catch up with those doing the work to learn their ideas for improvements will garner you some great ideas on how to be more innovative.

As you grow, you might want to give employees time off from their daily responsibilities by allowing them to be part of an innovation team. You don't need a large team—even a handful of key employees can come up with great ideas. Find a way to invest the time, even if it means taking a few hours out of the day each month to work together as a team and brainstorm.

The Least You Need to Know

- Choose an advisory board to guide you in strategic decision-making and provide advice for you and your business.
- Work with an insurance agent to determine your business's insurance needs.
- Ensure you understand regulatory issues that apply to your business based on the state and industry in which you work.
- Manage growth by planning for it.
- Find a way to balance innovation with efficiency in your business.

Managing the Money

In This Chapter

- Working with budgets and managing cash flow
- Setting up an accounting system that works for you
- Monitoring progress with regular reports
- Handling accounts receivable and accounts payable

This chapter provides you with the information you need to master the sometimes foreign-sounding language of finance and take control of the finances of your business.

Relax. It's easier than you think.

Budgeting to Ensure Success

Budgeting is the core financial best practice for small businesses.

Budgets are essential for any business but are especially important for smaller businesses. Of necessity, you'll be running a tighter ship than larger companies because you'll have less access to money. That's why it is essential that you learn how to manage the money you do have with maximum efficiency.

There are, of course, various best practices that support the budgeting process. To plan effectively, you'll need to develop the following financial documents for your business:

- **Balance sheet**   Shows a snapshot of the business's assets and liabilities for a particular time period

- **Income (profit and loss) statement** Shows revenue and expenses for your business for a period of time—a week, month, quarter, or year

- **Cash flow statement** Shows you how the cash of your business moved (both in and out of the business) for a specified time period

- **Budget** Delineates revenue and expenses expected over a specified time period, such as a calendar or fiscal year

Being able to understand and use all of these documents will enable you to monitor and run your business. Understanding all four is essential if you hope to master budgeting.

Let's look briefly at the first three documents just mentioned before moving on to budgets.

Balance Sheets

Balance sheets summarize the assets, liabilities, and equity of your business for a particular period of time using the following formula:

Equity = Assets – Liabilities

Your assets include cash you receive from your customers, outstanding accounts receivable, inventory (products yet to be sold), and capital assets (such as manufacturing equipment you own). Your liabilities include both short- and long-term liabilities.

Short-term liabilities may include lines of credit you are paying off and money you owe to suppliers (accounts payable); long-term liabilities include loans you have on equipment or machinery, leases on capital equipment or office space, and mortgages on your office building or your manufacturing facility.

Your equity includes any past profits that you have put back into the business and have not spent (such as monies held for future research and development efforts) as well as capital that you or other business owners have invested into the business.

Thus your balance sheet shows what your business owns (assets) and what is owed by your business (liabilities).

Income Statements

Income statements show the revenue you have received and the expenses you have for a given period of time, based on this formula:

Net Income = Total Revenue – Total Expenses

Your income statement for a month period may look like this:

Income Statement for Gift Shop for the Month Ending June 30

Revenue	$30,000
Expenses	
Supplies	$3,000
Rent	$2,500
Utilities	$900
Salaries paid	$4,250
Cost of goods sold	$8,500
Total Expenses	$19,150
Net Income	$10,850

Income statements provide the information you need to manage your business operations to ensure that expenses do not get ahead of revenue and that you have enough profit left over to invest back in your business or pay yourself (as the business owner and an investor in the business) a dividend.

DEFINITION

Cost of goods sold (COGS) is the direct costs associated with producing and offering your products or services.

Cash Flow Statements

Cash flow statements are meant to show you where your money is going and how fast it's going there. Information from balance sheets and income statements help you to determine your cash flow statement.

Cash flows from three main sources:

- **Operations**   Current assets and liabilities of your business
- **Investments**   Investments made in buildings or equipment
- **Financing**   Long-term bank loans or any dividends paid to business owners

Managing cash flow is a big challenge for many small businesses. This is a challenge you must meet. After all, you don't know how well your business is doing unless you know your cash flow!

Budgets

When creating a budget, be sure that you cover what is necessary for salaries and investment back in your business. It's always good to have something tucked away for emergencies or unexpected opportunities that are too good to pass up.

BEST PRACTICE

Many tools are available for budgeting. Certainly you can use a simple spreadsheet such as Microsoft Excel; more advanced tools include Quicken or QuickBooks. Select the software that you find easiest to use on a regular basis— that's the one that's best for your business.

Budgeting enables you to see and respond to important trends in your business. Consider this example: you sell consulting services. You notice your expenses are increasing each month. When you review the budget you created earlier in the year, you notice that your revenue has not changed significantly month after month but that the expenses associated with that revenue—such as the cost of contract consultants and marketing—has increased. In further analysis, you make the following observations:

- Rates for contract consultants have increased to about $200 more per day. Given this increase, on average it now costs the business $1,000 more for contract consultant fees each month.
- Marketing costs have increased an additional $800 a month.

You need to answer an important question: what is going on with your expenses?

You do some investigating, and here is what you find (actual amounts shown only for illustrative purposes):

Partial Monthly Budget Report (Four Months)

Account	May	June	July	Aug	Sept
Revenue	$20,000	$20,000	$20,000	$20,000	$20,000
Marketing	$2,000	$2,800	$2,800	$2,800	$2,800
Prof Fees	$8,000	$8,000	$9,000	$9,000	$9,000

This partial table shows you that marketing costs began to increase in June and have held at the higher amount since that time and professional fees (contract consultants) began to increase in July and are holding at the higher amount. Your budgeted amounts look like this:

Partial Monthly Budget Report (Four Months)

Account	May	June	July	Aug	Sept
Revenue	$20,000	$20,000	$20,000	$20,000	$20,000
Marketing	$2,000	$2,000	$2,000	$2,000	$2,000
Prof Fees	$8,000	$8,000	$8,000	$8,000	$8,000

You are seeing an increase in costs from June to September as follows:

- An $800-per-month increase in marketing expenses from June to September, bringing you $3,200 over budget to date

- A $1,000-per-month increase in professional fees expenses from July to September, bringing you $3,000 over budget to date

Why have marketing costs changed from what was budgeted in the beginning of the year? Are you doing more marketing than you planned (even though you don't see an increase in the number of new customers and revenue)? Or has the cost of marketing—such as spending on direct mail campaigns—increased? Has postage increased? Are you mailing to more customers than you assumed in the budget?

Why are your contract consultants charging you more money per day for their time? Was it part of a contract increase that you neglected to include in your budget, or have they increased their rates without telling you?

You'll need to make some adjustments to your budget for the balance of the year based on your findings and the solutions you develop. Without a budget, you might not even have realized that your expenses were increasing, or, if you did, you might have had a more difficult time determining where the increases were coming from.

PRACTICE MAKES PERFECT

As a regular part of managing your business, set aside time on a monthly basis (or more frequently if necessary) to review your finances to see how you are tracking against your budget. Consider including select employees in these budgeting review sessions. Giving employees a clearer understanding of how money flows in and out of your business may enable them to make smarter choices on the front lines.

Beating Budget Fatigue

A lot of small business owners think of budgeting as a stressful process. Actually, poor budgeting is a stressful process, and not having any budget is perhaps the most stressful financial situation of all.

For example, consider a small convenience store that does not use any budgeting system. Its owners rely on a point of sale (POS) system to keep track of inventory needs, but have no real understanding of cash flow needs or budgeting for certain "busy" times of the year or for future investment. While this may seem to work in a very small business, ultimately it is not sustainable and could actually cause the demise of the business due to poor budgeting and forecasting.

A business that sells training courses could use budgeting techniques to get a better understanding of the cost associated with delivery of each individual training course the business offers and could establish exactly how many seats must be sold to ensure a profit. Without using a budget, this business would be unable to track the success of any training product or shift its strategy to ensure the profitability of a particular program. Such businesses often find out they are in deep trouble, and barely profitable, only when it is too late to fix the problem.

By effectively using money management tools, such as a cash flow statement, income statement, and balance sheet, and monitoring your monthly budget to see trends in your business, you can reduce stress and fatigue—and be in a better position to control your business's future.

Managing Finances and Cash Flow

When you understand how cash comes into your business, you are better able to manage your cash flow. For example, if you know that a customer takes, on average, 45 days to pay his invoice, you know you need to have cash available to cover expenses until that payment is made.

Similarly, if you know that you are busiest during certain times of the year, you'll want to manage your expenses and outlay of money to ensure that you can still meet your commitments during the nonbusy months. Review your cash flow on a regular basis to stay ahead of the game. Remember cash is king, especially in a tight economy.

In Chapter 4, we discussed getting started in your business by creating a budget to cover the first couple of years. As your business gets underway, you have a much firmer grasp on that budget, plus years of historical data. This enables you to develop a trends analysis, which makes the development of the budget easier to manage and more accurate.

Setting Revenue Goals

When setting revenue goals, the most critical best practice is to be realistic. If you have never brought in $1 million in revenue in previous years, don't assume you can do so this year! If you want to see an increase in your revenue goals from last year, you need a plan to get there. For example, you can't assume you will increase your revenue by an additional $100,000 in a new year without increasing expenses such as marketing, sales costs, and development of new product or service offerings that will help you gain that extra revenue.

When setting revenue goals, consider the following:

- How many customers do you have currently, and how much does each customer spend with your business each year?

- How many new customers do you believe you will secure in the coming year and what is the average amount they will spend with your business in that year? (Remember to have a plan in place to obtain new customers; they won't just come out of the woodwork.)

- How much do you have in cash to invest back in the business to gain more revenue? (You have to invest to increase your sales.)

- What core expenses must you cover each month without fail?

Determining Your Profitability

Conducting a *break-even analysis* assists you in determining how many sales you need to break even (no net loss or gain) and to begin to make a profit for your business.

DEFINITION

A **break-even analysis** is a technique used to analyze how much you need to generate in sales in order to achieve enough revenue to pay expenses and generate a profit.

By using a simple spreadsheet, you can determine how many sales you need to make of each product and service to offset your variable and fixed costs. This is your break-even point. Once you understand how many sales you need to make to cover all of your expenses, you can then determine how many additional sales are required to begin to make the desired profit for the business.

Let's look at an example. Assume your break-even analysis shows that for you to cover your expenses you need to sell 25 widgets in a month. If you sell more, you begin to make a profit. You would like a profit of at least $5,000 each month to invest in research and development. To gain this much profit, you will need to sell 100 additional widgets each month. If you do not believe you will be able to sell 125 widgets in a month, you need to find other ways to make your profit of $5,000. This might include reducing your costs of producing widgets by negotiating with suppliers of your material or increasing the price of your widgets in the marketplace.

Determining your profitability requires you to have an understanding of two types of costs for your business: fixed costs (costs that remain the same no matter how much of a product you sell, such as costs for rent for your storefront—these costs must be covered even if you don't sell anything) and variable costs (costs that change depending on the number of products you sell, such as material costs or sales commissions).

Use this formula for your break-even analysis:

Break-Even Point = Fixed Costs ÷ (Revenue Per Unit Sold – Variable Costs Per Unit)

Let's look at an example using this formula to determine how many units of a product you must sell to cover your fixed costs.

Your business makes handmade photo frames. Your fixed costs are $20,000 a year. Your variable costs total $10 per photo frame. You are considering selling the hand-made photo frames for $25 each. Simply plug the numbers into the formula:

$$\$20,000 \div (\$25 - \$10) = 1,333$$

Now you know that 1,333 frames must be sold each year before a profit is made.

The Right Accounting System

When setting up an accounting system for your business—regardless of whether it is an off-the-shelf small business accounting software system, a simple spreadsheet, or even a simple ledger book—it is important to ensure it is set up accurately right from the start. For storefronts, a POS system integrated with accounting software is readily available at a reasonable price to help you better track inventory and finances.

Just hiring an accountant is not enough. One of our accountants noted sadly that she has many small business clients who walk in to meet with her around tax time with a shoebox full of receipts, invoices, and cancelled checks, imagining that this is the information needed to complete the taxes for their business for that year.

Her questions to such clients include: Where's the audit trail? How will you know where your business stands from a cash-flow perspective? You are doing such a poor job of tracking the finances for your business—are you even sure you have been paid for all your work, or all your orders?

BEST PRACTICE

Some kind of relationship with a qualified accountant is a must. Even if cash is tight, consider hiring an accountant for at least a couple of hours a month to explain financial accounting to you and help you set up and monitor a system that works for you and your particular business. This is well worth the minimal investment. Be sure you get started off right!

Consider purchasing a system that will grow with your business. Don't start out with a simple spreadsheet now if you know you'll need a more advanced system in a few years. Starting with the advanced system now provides you growth expansion and continuity in your business. Most systems have modules (additional functionality) you can purchase as needed.

BEST PRACTICE

Consider investing in an enterprise resource planning (ERP) system. This is an integrated software application that serves as a business management tool, helping you to track resources, tangible assets, materials, finances, suppliers, vendors, customers, and employees. You are able to share information from the ERP system with your accountant via accounting reports. An ERP system can easily grow with your business.

There are two basic ways to track your business's finances: the cash basis accounting method and accrual basis accounting method.

With cash basis accounting, income and the expenses are recorded when the income is received and the expenses are paid out. With accrual basis accounting, income is reported in the fiscal period in which it was earned regardless of when it is received, and expenses are recorded in the fiscal period in which they occur, whether they are paid at that time or not. The simpler of the two is the cash basis accounting method.

Cash basis accounting is frequently used by smaller firms or by cash-only businesses. For instance, a convenience store owner would likely use cash basis accounting as they mainly deal with cash or credit cards and receive immediate payment.

On the other hand, if you are a project consulting business, you may have longer-term projects for customers, contracts associated with those projects, and invoice payment terms of 30 days. Your costs may be incurred in one fiscal year and not paid until the following fiscal year. In this case, the accrual basis method might give you a more accurate picture of your finances.

Your Reporting Needs

There are a variety of reports that help you to manage your business. These include the following:

- Cash flow statement
- Balance sheet
- Income statement
- Inventory tracking report

- Accounts payable report

- Accounts receivable report

- Aged accounts receivable report

- General ledger

These reports provide insight into how your business is performing and provides historical data to track progress. Smart business owners regularly review reports on how their business is performing to enable quick course corrections when necessary to get back on track.

Frequent reports on your business's health may be required by bankers (if you have outstanding loans), investors, and your accountant. Select those reports you need to best manage your particular businesses and the challenges you face.

The Right Dashboard

Dashboards are visual representations of where you are at a particular point in time. They are designed to be easy to read and give you all the information you need to run your business. Components of a dashboard may include the following:

- Sales metrics

- Revenue numbers

- Budget

- Marketing metrics

You may have multiple dashboards covering key performance indicators (KPIs) for the different areas of your business such as marketing, sales, finance, and production. Alternatively, you may have one dashboard that displays all of this information.

If dashboards are connected to an enterprise resource planning (ERP) system, you can have access to real-time metrics. You can define KPIs that are pulled from your ERP system to display on the dashboard. For example, you might pull revenue, expense, cash flow, and any other data you want to see to regularly monitor your business. Dashboards are useful for keeping your finger on the pulse of your business.

The term "dashboard" describes any reporting mechanism that presents you with a concise visual summary of your finances or other relevant business information. You might have multiple dashboards for each department in your business, or one dashboard for the overall business. Dashboards can be based on a spreadsheet or accessed as part of an ERP system.

Processing Payments and Receivables

Certainly a key component of your business is receiving money for your products and services in time to make payments to your creditors and suppliers. Delays in getting money in from your customers can cause a cash flow crunch and delay payments, which may cost you more in interest payments and other fees.

It is becoming increasingly common for larger organizations to increase the amount of time before they pay on invoices. Where 30 days may have been the norm at one point, you now see larger organizations pushing that to 45 or even 60 days. This becomes a real problem for smaller businesses that rely on this money to keep cash flow positive.

Setting Up a Payments System

When setting up accounts with your suppliers and vendors, you want to establish terms of payment that benefit both of you. While you may be tempted to pay suppliers and vendors when you get paid by the customer, it's unlikely you'll be able to make this arrangement.

PRACTICE MAKES PERFECT

Be sure to have contracts or agreements in place with all of your suppliers and vendors that specifically outline payment terms, shipping commitments, quality of product, return policies, and any other relevant information. As a best practice, evaluate all these contracts and agreements on an annual basis.

Follow these best practices to ensure an accounts payable system that works for your business:

- Use purchase orders for all purchases you make.

- Create a record for each supplier and record all purchases made from this supplier in this ledger.

By keeping this simple system in place, you can track materials received against what was ordered and avoid overpaying your suppliers. Additionally, you'll easily see those suppliers and vendors with whom you purchase the most and might be able to use this information to negotiate more favorable terms or better pricing when the contract comes up for renewal.

If a supplier provides for a discount for early payment, consider taking advantage of those discounts to save costs if your cash flow allows.

Streamlining Collections

There are many things you can do to help speed the collection process. Having an agreement in place for all of your customers will certainly help; however, you may find that some customers simply will not abide by any agreement.

Consider these best practices:

Have milestone payments. Where appropriate, especially for longer-term consulting engagements, invoice the client in thirds—one third up front, one third in the middle, and the final third due upon completion—or when specific milestones are met on a project. Specify such payment terms in your contracts with customers.

Follow up with customers. If customers are late on a payment, follow up with them immediately about that overdue amount via telephone; don't let it wait.

Invoice immediately. Invoice customers as quickly as possible. Delaying invoicing only delays payments to you. As a best practice, try to get invoices out to customers within 5 to 10 days of project completion.

Offer early payment discounts. Offer a discount of 2.5 percent to 5 percent for early payment to some or all of your customers. For example, if a customer will pay an invoice within 10 days, give them a 5 percent discount; in 20 days, give them a 2.5 percent discount.

Set up late payment fees. Even though you will be unlikely to get additional money when a customer pays you late, it makes sense to include late payment fee terms should you ever have to go to collections on an account.

Make sure your customer information is accurate. Don't discount the importance of ensuring that the information on the invoice is accurate. If you need to reference purchase order numbers, make sure the number is correct and reflected on the invoice, and that the "bill to" information is accurate. Too often late payments are the result of inaccurate invoices.

Should you decide to extend credit to your customers, do your homework first. Only extend credit to long-term, good customers of your business. Be sure to check their credit history and ask for references from their other suppliers of credit. Use Dun & Bradstreet (www.dbn.com), Experian (www.Experian.com), or a similar service to check on your customers' credit history and financial standing.

Cost-Cutting

As part of cost management best practices, businesses should review and manage their costs on a regular basis. Certainly in difficult economic times, cost-cutting measures may become necessary to keep your business moving forward.

BEST PRACTICE

Involve your employees in conversations about cost-cutting. They may have great ideas on saving money for the business. Additionally, bring up the topic in your advisory board meetings and ask for your advisor's ideas on how to reduce expenses in the business.

Consider these steps to regularly monitor and control your costs:

Review your budget. Compare your actual expenses against your budgeted expenses on at least a monthly basis.

Have processes in place for purchases outside of budgeted items. Go through a formal process before making large purchases that were not previously budgeted for; if there isn't an ROI tied to the purchase, don't make the purchase.

Look for efficiencies. There may be efficiencies you can take advantage of that will save costs over the long run for your business.

Ask employees for help. Ask your employees to help keep an eye on expenses along with you. They are on the front line and may see ways to save costs that you haven't yet seen.

Keep your cash flow statement updated. Keep your cash flow statement updated, and keep an eye on it.

Do the basics. Do the simple stuff—turn off lights that aren't needed, reduce the air-conditioning setting, turn off computers and other electronics that don't need to be left on. Small things add up!

Internal Cost-Cutting Options

Internal cost-cutting options are focused within your business. Here are some suggestions for cutting costs internally:

Manufacturing and production: For manufacturing businesses, consider leasing rather than purchasing equipment, or look into the feasibility of purchasing major pieces of equipment from the used market to save money. Additionally, review your manufacturing processes to look for ways to increase their efficiencies.

Overall process and procedure review: Fine-tuning processes and procedures enables for efficiencies in productivity that save costs. As you make adjustments, you may find that you can get products out the door faster, find ways to customize services for your customer for less cost, and close the deal more quickly with new accounts.

Sales and marketing: By utilizing technologies such as WebEx, Skype, and other web-conferencing software, you may be able to reduce travel costs for your sales team. Consider restructuring sales commissions to reward salespeople more for bringing in new customers or for closing deals over a certain amount of revenue. For marketing, rather than mailing out postcards or brochures to your customers, consider e-mail marketing that routes potential customers to your website, where they can download brochures.

Human resources: As you begin to experience growth, don't immediately jump to hiring full-time employees. Consider hiring part-time or temporary staff or contractors as a stopgap measure while you determine the need for additional full-time resources. Rather than using a recruiting firm to source new hires, ask your employees for referrals. They know your business better anyway, and you might offer them a referral fee—it will be less costly than hiring a recruiting firm! Consider savings in benefits offered to your employees by reducing the amount you contribute and increasing the contributions from the employees toward health-care costs, or reduce contributions to 401(k) accounts until things improve in your business. You might also ask your employees to take a temporary cut in pay while the business gets back on its feet.

Office supplies: Buy less costly pens and pads of paper, use recycled toner cartridges, and make cuts in your office supplies. While this may seem minimal, it all adds up in the long run.

Electronic banking: Consider using online banking services to make payments to suppliers and send invoices and receive payments from customers. You'll save on mailing costs.

External Cost-Cutting Options

External cost-cutting measures are focused outside of your business, and there are a variety of options for you to consider here.

Suppliers and vendors: Consider renegotiating with your suppliers and vendors for better terms and lower costs. Consider also sourcing other vendors—a little competition goes a long way toward getting you some concessions from your suppliers.

> **BEST PRACTICE**
>
> Consider renegotiating agreements with your suppliers and vendors on a yearly basis. By asking your suppliers to respond to a Request for Proposal (RFP) to handle your needs, you will find you are getting some of the best deals because they don't want to lose your business to a competitor.

Shipping: Negotiate for better shipping rates for your products. You may find that by putting all your business with one shipping company you are able to secure better rates. Alternatively, you may choose to pass some of these costs on to your customer.

Health care: Look into alternatives for health-care coverage for your employees. By changing providers or the type of coverage you offer (PPO or HMO), you may find that you are able to provide the same level of service and coverage to your employees but at reduced rates. Look at all your options and consider talking with your local Chamber of Commerce, business associations, or industry groups for lower-cost options.

Internet/telecommunications provider: Consider alternatives to sources for your Internet and phone services. Depending on your need and criticality for "up time" and bandwidth requirements, prices can vary dramatically from one vendor to another. Similarly, check in with your cellular phone service provider to see if they have any lower-cost plans that will work for you.

Printers: Look at your options for printing marketing and sales collateral and business cards. Consider printing your own business cards and brochures.

Leases/rent: Try to renegotiate rental costs, especially during a depressed real estate market. If there are lots of options in your area for space, your landlord may be willing to negotiate with you to reduce your costs.

The Least You Need to Know

- Track your finances regularly via a balance sheet, income statement, cash flow statement, and your budget.
- Hire an accountant to help get your accounts set up to ensure accuracy and ease of reporting.
- Consider using a dashboard to help you easily see metrics of your business.
- Develop processes and procedures for accounts receivable and accounts payable.
- Monitor costs associated with your business frequently to look for potential savings.

Investing in Your Employees

Chapter 13

In This Chapter

- Providing employees with opportunities for professional development
- Establishing clear roles and responsibilities
- Acknowledging and rewarding excellent performance
- Managing employee compensation

Investing in your employees is important regardless of your size—and it isn't difficult!

The need for growth and development is deeply imbedded in the human species. When employees feel they have opportunities to develop personally and professionally, they are more likely to become engaged in the business—which means you have more loyal, hard-working employees dedicated to the success of your enterprise. Employees who feel as if their contributions really matter and have opportunities for personal growth work more effectively for your team and are less likely to leave or be wooed away by your competitors.

As a small business owner, you may think that there are few or no opportunities for advancement for your employees—and you may be right. But there are opportunities within the business for your employees to continue to develop their skills and expand their knowledge. In this chapter, we show you how to exploit those opportunities.

Establishing Clear Goals and Objectives

Establishing clear goals and objectives for each of your employees is the critical first step. This requires, certainly, developing job descriptions, which we talked about briefly in Chapter 8 and will discuss in more detail in Chapter 14. Outside of the job description, it is essential that employees understand their specific role within the organization, the responsibilities of that role, and the goals and objectives they must work toward.

Let's look at an example. You have hired a receptionist for your business. The goals and objectives for that role may be as follows:

- Answer telephone calls within two rings.

- Greet all customers immediately upon entry with a smile and an offer of coffee, tea, or water.

- Learn customers' names and greet them personally.

- Be the face of the business.

In addition, you expect the individual to be friendly, professional, courteous, and helpful at all times. By establishing these goals and objectives, you have something to measure the employee's performance against.

Setting Roles and Responsibilities

You should define roles for every employee working for your business and clearly delineate the responsibilities for each of those roles. Although you can draw from a variety of resources for a list of the typical responsibilities associated with particular roles, we encourage you to focus more on the role as it pertains to your company and the responsibilities you believe are most important for that role.

BEST PRACTICE

Provide employees with training needed to fulfill the responsibilities of their role. In our preceding example, you'll want to train your receptionist to use your phone system so he or she can answer telephone calls within two rings in a friendly, professional, and courteous manner.

Take these steps to develop the roles and responsibilities for employees:

1. Determine the role title—such as receptionist, administrative assistant, or marketing director. This is an essential first step.

2. Determine the actual tasks involved in each role. What are the responsibilities of the individuals in those roles? For example, the administrative assistant

may be responsible for typing all correspondence, answering phones, and setting appointments.

3. Include for each task defined the expectations of completion. For example, you expect all the administrative assistant's correspondence to be error-free and accurate in all respects. One of the expectations for a marketing director would be that all marketing collateral be accurate and have a consistent look and feel. This is how you'll measure the performance of the employee in completing their tasks.

Employees should understand your expectations and how they will be measured on their performance. We talk more about performance later in this chapter.

For some roles, you may choose to add additional responsibilities, such as assisting others when necessary. You often see on job descriptions, "Additional responsibilities as assigned." These additional responsibilities may include working on special projects or assisting in other areas of the business during busy periods.

As a best practice, review roles and responsibilities of employees on a regular basis to update them. You'll likely find that their roles and responsibilities have changed over time.

Aligning Personal and Organizational Goals

Setting goals for employees to strive toward is essential for meeting your business's objectives, but you need to ensure those goals are aligned with their personal goals. You may think aligning personal goals to business goals is the responsibility of the employee, but that's not entirely the case.

BEST PRACTICE

In 1968, Edwin A. Locke developed a goal-setting theory that stated that setting performance goals is essential to motivating employees; additionally, he noted that goals set must be challenging for the employee, enabling them to further develop their skills and knowledge.

Suppose you have a key employee who helps you to run your manufacturing operations. Lately, he has shown considerable interest in marketing, has been taking classes at the local college, and has been popping by the marketing department frequently throughout the day to learn about what they have going on. He is spending less time in the manufacturing area. He has been with your business for 10 years and is one of your best employees.

What do you do? If you can't help him align his personal goals (getting more involved with marketing) with the business goals (ensuring a well-run manufacturing operation) you risk losing him to another business that will give him that opportunity.

You might consider dividing his time between both areas of the business, which will enable him to learn more about marketing and continue to perform his regular role. To support this, and not have him feel overwhelmed, you'll need to hire another resource to help him out in manufacturing. You may find that he becomes one of your best marketing employees, and he can train the new employee to take over his manufacturing role. Alternatively, if hiring another resource is not possible due to budget constraints, work with him to balance his personal goals with the business goals. There is a happy medium; you just have to find it!

And don't forget the importance of aligning your own personal goals to the goals of your business. We know this sounds obvious, but here's a story to consider. The authors know of a business owner who had an opportunity to expand his business into other geographic locations. It meant working more hours and increasing his travel time. However, he and his wife recently had a child and he wanted to spend more time at home. His personal goal: reduce time at the office and spend more time at home. The business goal: increase time at the office and on the road to expand the business. He had three options to resolve this conflict:

- **Option 1:** Push aside the business goal: don't expand the business and instead spend time at home.

- **Option 2:** Push aside the personal goal: expand the business and spend more hours in the office.

- **Option 3:** Promote a key employee to help expand the business *and* spend more time at home.

He chose option 3.

On a regular basis—for yourself and your employees—set aside time during the workday to review personal and business goals. Are the goals still in alignment? If not, what can you do? What are the options? Don't let employees get to the point where they are completely frustrated and ready to walk out the door to another opportunity or to work for your competitor. Rather, see what you can do to help them meet their personal goals while still meeting the business goals. You'll find a bit of brainstorming goes a long way toward finding a solution that works for both of you.

Professional Development

Developing your employees is essential—regardless of the size of your business, how many employees you have, and their roles and responsibilities within the business. This doesn't have to cost you a lot of money or time. There are a variety of options to consider for providing *professional development* opportunities for your employees.

> **DEFINITION**
>
> **Professional development** includes providing opportunities for your employees to help them further develop their skills and knowledge and grow both personally and professionally.

Mentoring: Mentoring programs help you, as the business owner, get new employees or those moving into new roles up to speed quickly by pairing them with another employee who provides guidance and answers questions about responsibilities of the role and the business culture. Basically, mentors show them the ropes. We discuss this topic in more detail in the following section.

Training: Options for training include sending your employees to workshops, providing in-house training opportunities, and providing e-learning and virtual training courses. Too often smaller businesses don't even consider training for their employees because they believe it's too expensive or haven't budgeted for it. Offering your employees training to strengthen their skills is an excellent way to help them develop and grow in their roles. It's also a great way to build loyalty among your staff; when you focus on their professional and personal development, they are more likely to be committed to you and your business. Consider providing training in skills related to their specific roles—such as negotiating skills for those working with vendors or in new technologies for IT folks—as well as general skills training such as listening skills, communicating with others, and time management, which will help anyone in any role.

Job rotation: Taking on additional roles within the business, even for short periods of time, is a great learning opportunity. For example, if you have a large marketing initiative coming up, why not assign some employees from other areas of the business to marketing to help with the project. Job rotation is a great way to enable employees to experience all of the operations of the business, and for those employees who have the potential to take on a senior leadership role at some point in the future, it's a great way to learn about the business as a whole.

Tuition reimbursement: If you can afford it, consider reimbursing your employees for part or all of their tuition for college classes they take toward a degree program. You don't have to cover the entire tuition—even a small amount offered to employees goes a long way. You might consider a flat amount each year, or a percentage based on the grade received. A tuition reimbursement program requires some planning on your part to ensure it is fair and equitable for employees and well-managed. There may be tax implications, so talk with your accountant about the best way to implement such a program.

Time off for external activities: If your employees are actively involved in volunteer organizations—or if you'd like them to be—provide them time off to engage in those activities without reductions in vacation time.

Conferences: By providing your employees opportunities to attend conferences relevant to their role, you are giving them a chance to expand their knowledge in their field, network with people in the same field, and learn industry best practices. There are conferences for IT professionals, manufacturing, project management, process management, and marketing and sales—to name just a few.

PRACTICE MAKES PERFECT

Ask employees who attend conferences to report on what they learned to the other employees when they return. It's a great way for them to share their knowledge.

As you can see, there are many ways to help your employees to grow and develop personally and professionally—without breaking the budget!

For all professional development opportunities, have your employees complete an action plan to apply the skills they are learning.

Setting Up a Mentoring Program

Mentoring programs partner a junior employee with a senior employee. Often, these programs end up providing development opportunities for both employees. Mentoring programs provide a variety of benefits for businesses, including the following:

- Increase productivity and efficiency in new hires because they get up to speed more quickly

- Prepare high-potential employees for management or leadership roles

- Improve the rate of application of new skills and knowledge from training programs

- Increase the understanding of different cultures and bridge generational gaps among employees

- Build trust among employees

- Show commitment to employees' growth and development in the business

Mentoring programs build a sense of teamwork and camaraderie among employees, which increases engagement in the business and improves employee retention rates.

Be sure to provide mentors with training on how to mentor others, which is a learning opportunity for them!

BEST PRACTICE

To encourage participation in a mentoring program, promote it within your business and, at the end of a year, host a recognition program for mentors and mentees to celebrate their partnership and accomplishments.

When setting up a mentoring program, think about the purpose of the program for your business. Carefully choose mentors and mentees for the program—it's important that they are a good match. Some businesses enable their employees to select mentors from outside the business. If you permit this, be sure to give them a bit of time during their day—be it an extended lunch period, a later starting time, or an earlier ending time—to meet with their mentors.

Providing Growth Opportunities

Most small businesses are too small to reward employees with more senior roles—there is simply no ladder to climb. But don't discount the value of providing your employees the opportunity to take on new responsibilities within the business or to head up special projects. Horizontal development and growth—lateral moves within the business to continue to develop professionally—are great ways to build skills.

BUSINESS BUSTER

If you have a talented employee who appears to be getting bored in her role, take action! Talk with the employee and see what you can do to help them feel challenged again. You don't want to lose your best employees to the competition simply because you couldn't offer them opportunities for growth.

We know one business owner who offers each of her employees, on a rotating basis, a chance to take the lead in planning the annual holiday event for the business. This person leads a project team to plan for and coordinate the event. Additionally, she sends the individual leading the event to a project management basics training program, where he gains valuable skills for managing the holiday event and future projects. To make sure he has enough time to focus on the event, she gives him time to step away from his regular role and has other employees fill in for him, which provides learning opportunities for others, too.

Employees learn when they are given the chance to take risks and fail without worrying about losing their jobs. Provide a safe environment for your employees to try something new and be creative. Let them know that it's okay to fail. By setting processes and procedures for such situations, you can reduce the impact of a failure on the business. In such situations, let them have some decision-making authority within guidelines you set, and make yourself or your managers available as a sounding board or to provide guidance. Some great ideas have come out of giving employees an opportunity to be creative and take risks.

Don't discount your nonexempt employees (hourly employees, administrative or clerical staff, union employees) from development opportunities. Just like all your other employees, they want opportunities to develop their skills and expand their knowledge. Provide them the same or similar opportunities you provide all your other employees.

Handling Succession Planning

Succession planning is your process for identifying, developing, and retaining individuals to take on key leadership roles within your business. It is a component of overall *talent management*.

DEFINITION

Talent management encompasses such diverse elements as recruiting employees; onboarding them into the business; and then providing them with opportunities for professional development, performance management, career path development, and succession planning.

As you develop your employees and evaluate their work, identify those individuals who can take on even greater roles and responsibilities in the business. Perhaps you have a smart marketing assistant who is a quick learner and a hard worker. Based on what you've seen so far, she has the potential to lead the marketing division of your business in the future. Make sure your managers are trained to identify these kinds of employees and give them the appropriate training and opportunities.

Too often small business owners don't plan for the future of their business. Who is going to take over your business when you are ready to retire? Unless you expect to just shut the doors, someone needs to fill your shoes. Often there are employees in the wings who are capable of taking over. Your job is to manage that talent—identify them and develop their leadership skills. In other words, you need to develop a succession plan.

PRACTICE MAKES PERFECT

Your advisory board can assist in succession planning for your business. For family-owned businesses, get your family involved—whether or not they will be taking over the business at some point. Additional resources include your accountant and legal counsel.

Developing a succession plan includes these steps:

1. Identify those employees who are capable of greater roles and responsibilities. You might use assessments to help determine an individual's capability, strengths, and development areas.

2. Have a development plan in place for these high-potential employees. This should include having them work in different areas of the business, enrolling them in training courses, allowing them to head up new and challenging projects, and providing them with a mentor to help them grow into a leadership role.

3. Create a timetable for when the individual will take on a senior leadership role in the business. Ideally they should be able to spend time with your current senior leaders to learn from them.

While not every employee will be part of your succession planning program, they must all have development plans. Not all employees are headed for the top, but they are all valuable to the business's success and should be given opportunities to grow professionally and personally.

Managing Employee Performance

As we discussed earlier in this chapter, giving your employees clearly defined roles and responsibilities, with clear goals and objectives for fulfilling them, provides you with a way to measure your employees' performance. If employees' roles and responsibilities are not clearly defined, you don't have metrics in place to measure against. Any evaluations will just be guesswork.

Provide your employees feedback about their performance on a regular basis, not just at their annual review. If you nip problems in the bud early on, you have a better chance of getting the employee back on track before larger problems surface. A problem employee becomes a morale issue for all employees. Most employees want to do well in their roles. Don't assume employees just don't care—this is very rarely the case.

BEST PRACTICE

You can improve the performance of your employees simply by having daily conversations with them. Use these conversations to congratulate them on outstanding work they are doing, ask them about problems or issues you can assist with, and generally just catch up with them about what they have going on in their role. Through regular conversations with employees, you'll detect issues before they become performance problems, and you'll learn more about what excites them.

If an otherwise excellent employee is suddenly performing poorly, there is obviously something going on, perhaps outside the work environment. While you can't resolve every employee's personal problem—nor should you attempt to do so—the more you know about your employees, the easier it will be to get them back on track. Suggest outside resources to help them to resolve their personal problems.

Your job is not just to focus on problems. You should regularly encourage your employees and provide them positive feedback. When you hear from one of your managers about what a great job one of the employees did on a particular task, seek out that employee to congratulate him. It's impossible to overestimate the value of recognizing employees for a job well done. A pat on the back by the boss is a wonderful thing.

Handling Performance Reviews

Develop a plan and a process for formally evaluating employee performance. At a minimum, consider formally evaluating performance twice a year. Keep in mind that this doesn't need to be an extensive process.

During the performance review process, nothing should come as a surprise to the employee being evaluated. If you are having regular conversations about performance, employees should already know what to expect in the review. Don't wait to talk to them about performance during the formal performance review sessions. That isn't effective (or fair) for either side.

BEST PRACTICE

Use a simple, consistent, performance evaluation form for all of your employees. Microsoft has a good free sample of such a form available at http://office. microsoft.com/en-us/templates/employee-performance-review-form-short-TC006088952.aspx.

Your performance reviews should measure the employees against their performance of their assigned tasks and responsibilities. Are they meeting the goals and objectives of the assigned role? You might consider using the following ratings: Outstanding, Exceeds Expectations, Meets Expectations, Below Expectations, and Unsatisfactory. Whatever words (or numbers) you choose for ratings, make sure that it is very clear what each rating means within the specific position in question.

During the performance review, you should set specific, unique goals and objectives for the individual for the upcoming year. Ask the employees to contribute to those goals and objectives—what do they want to accomplish? What are areas they want to develop? Provide your employees support and opportunities to improve in areas where improvement is needed, and give them opportunities to strengthen their skills.

As your business grows, you may need to make changes to your performance review process. Evaluate your process and its effectiveness on a regular basis. When there are any major changes in your business—such as significant growth or new roles and responsibilities for employees—make changes in the performance review process so it remains effective.

Managing Compensation Issues

Each role in your business should have a salary range with a low, mid, and high point. There are many resources available that show salary guidelines for various positions. Salary.com (www.salary.com/mysalary.asp) and Salary Expert (www.salaryexpert.com) are two online resources for salary guidelines.

As a smaller business, you'll have trouble competing with salaries offered by the big businesses, but don't discount the value many employees place on working for a smaller business. Smaller businesses frequently enable employees to work on a variety of projects and be involved in a wide range of business areas. Getting this kind of experience is more difficult for employees who work in larger organizations, where employees often have very specific roles and are unable to work on projects or assignments outside their area of responsibility.

Be sure to explain exactly what you offer employees when trying to attract good candidates to the job. Total compensation packages include any health-care costs covered by the company, tuition reimbursement, professional development opportunities (conferences or workshops), disability and life insurance, vacation time, sick time, stock options or *profit sharing*, 401(k) plans, year-end bonuses, dependent care or child care benefits, and flexible spending accounts. If you hire salespeople, commissions and bonuses are also part of their packages. The value of these benefits, in addition to the employee's salary, is a component of their compensation package.

DEFINITION

Profit sharing enables employees to share in the profits of a business by receiving a one-time bonus or percentage increase in salary based on how well the company performed that year.

One big challenge business owners face—regardless of the size of their business—is determining how to provide employees with salary increases. Some companies base them on performance reviews, with the percentage of increase tied to ratings; others award salary increases outside of the performance review process, giving employees an across-the-board percentage raise every year regardless of performance. The latter practice, however, can set up some real animosity among employees. Hard workers will be bitter that the slackers in your company receive the same raise.

Some businesses get around this issue by providing a cost of living increase for all employees and adding a bonus for top performers. If you choose this option, delineate clearly what makes a top performer.

Finally, some businesses tie salary increases exclusively to the performance of the business. All employees share in the success of the business through profit sharing.

Tying raises to performance is one way to drive excellent performance in the business. If you decide to tie salary increases to performance reviews, you'll need to ensure that the process is perceived as fair by all employees. As we noted previously, the performance review must evaluate individuals against their assigned roles and responsibilities and must also assess whether they are meeting the goals and objectives of those roles. Anything else is not only unfair to the employee but also sets you up for potential legal challenges. The following table outlines one method of tying salary percentage increases to performance ratings:

Performance Rating and Salary Increase Percentage

Rating	Percentage Increase
Outstanding	10%
Exceeds expectations	8%
Meets expectations	5%
Below expectations	3% (or just cost of living)
Unsatisfactory	0% (or just cost of living)

Based on the performance of your business, the percentages may change year from year. If it is a bad year profit-wise for your business, you may choose lower percentage increases for employees; the percentages may become 5 percent, 4 percent, 2 percent, .5 percent, 0 percent, or whatever works for your business and your financial situation. Make sure employees know the percentages and the factors used in setting them.

Generating Great Front-Line Ideas

As we have mentioned in previous chapters, your employees are very likely to have important ideas for improving how you run your business. They may have ideas for products or services you might offer, ways to generate revenue, cutting costs, or marketing products or services to customers. Your job is to make generating and sharing creative ideas part of the company culture.

For example, if you are trying to find a new way to market your products to customers, hold a contest among your employees and reward the best ideas. If you want your employees to find ways to cut costs in their operational areas, reward employees in the department that show the most savings without affecting the product quality or customer service. Rewards may come in the form of an extra day off from work, a bonus, a gift certificate, or lunch on the boss.

> **BEST PRACTICE**
>
> When employees feel their ideas are valued and appreciated, they are more likely to continue to contribute to the business's success. Acknowledge all employee ideas—there is likely some nugget of greatness in all of them.

Some employees consistently contribute ideas that improve your business. Acknowledge those contributions publicly and via the performance review process.

The Least You Need to Know

- Work with employees to align personal goals to organizational goals.
- Have a development plan in place for all employees, regardless of their role in the business, so they can develop their skills and build their knowledge.
- You must have a succession plan in place for your business no matter how small your business is.
- Develop an effective employee performance review process that measures employees' accomplishments against the goals and objectives of their roles.

Human Resources

In This Chapter

- Finding the best people for your business
- Interviewing techniques to get the best information
- Protecting your business with proper policies and procedures
- Getting acquainted with employment law

Human resources covers a variety of areas, some of which may be relevant to your business from day one and some which will only become important as your business grows. For example, as a start-up business, you'll need to focus on hiring and compensation issues. As your business grows, you'll begin to look more closely at issues such as retention and succession planning.

Human resources will be a component of your business from the very first day and throughout the life of your business.

Recruiting Top Talent

Recruiting the best talent for your business is a key function of human resources. Choosing the best talent starts with understanding what resources you need in your business and developing job descriptions and roles and responsibilities for each of those resources. It also entails understanding the type of behavior—or personal attributes—you want in your employees. For example, if you are customer-service focused (and aren't all businesses?), you need individuals who are outgoing, friendly, and go above and beyond to meet the needs of the customer. You will also need employees with a high degree of *emotional intelligence*.

> **DEFINITION**
>
> **Emotional intelligence** is the ability to control and manage one's own emotions and evaluate and manage the emotions of others. Individuals with high emotional intelligence levels are often good at leading teams, managing others, and working with customers. To learn more about emotional intelligence, visit www. unh.edu/emotional_intelligence.

Think of emotional intelligence as a level of emotional maturity. Some people are absolutely brilliant but aren't capable of working with others. You need individuals who are intelligent *and* make others feel good about working for your company. For instance, a person who shines during a one-on-one interview with you by giving you all the right technical answers but is rude or dismissive to the person working as your receptionist would show a low level of emotional intelligence.

Genuine empathy and concern for others is a trait of people with high levels of emotional intelligence. Many analysts believe that this kind of intelligence plays a far greater role in personal and emotional success than the classic intelligence quotient measured by IQ tests.

The very best way to find top talent for your business is to commit to improving your own hiring and interviewing skills over time, and then to ensure that you, as the business owner, stay involved in the hiring process. We are not suggesting you should be responsible for the entire process of recruiting, interviewing, and hiring, but you want to be sure you put the final stamp of approval on all selections for your business—or delegate this only to your most senior managers.

Recruiting the best talent also requires having a formal process in place to be sure you are selecting the best people for your business. Take the time necessary in the hiring process to do it right. It's better to take your time selecting the best hire rather than jumping at hiring the first or second person through the door for an interview only to have to terminate them later.

Interviewing Techniques That Work

It is important that you provide good training to employees who will be interviewing job candidates. Especially if you will use behavioral (or competency-based) interviewing techniques, you must provide people with some background for interviewing effectively using these skills. Additionally, coordinate the interviewing process so you get the most information from the candidates being interviewed to make a decision.

Let's look at an example. Let's assume that you need to hire a receptionist for your business. You have asked your marketing assistant, your administrative assistant, and one of the sales team members to be part of the interviewing process. In order to ensure that everyone isn't asking the same questions, you focus the interviews as follows:

- Marketing assistant: She will ask the candidate about handling angry or upset callers and to provide examples of how the candidate has handled such callers in previous jobs.

- Administrative assistant: He will ask the candidate about tasks the candidate has performed as a receptionist at other companies to get a feel for how well the candidate can juggle multiple responsibilities.

- Salesperson: He will focus on asking the candidate what she likes most about her role as a receptionist and what she likes least. His goal is to understand what motivates the candidate to do a good job.

You will also be interviewing the candidate and will focus on whether or not she is a fit for the business culture. You should prepare questions for each of the interviewers to ask the interviewee. You should also do some role-playing, with another employee acting as the job candidate, so the employees who are part of the interview can practice their skills.

By taking some time to prep the interviewers, you have a better chance of getting the information you need to make a decision on a candidate. Additionally, teaching your employees interviewing skills also helps them develop professionally (see Chapter 13). You might want to bring in an outside resource to train your employees in effective interviewing skills, but it may not be necessary if you are able to do this yourself. Additionally, the recruiting agency you hire might be willing to offer this service to you as part of the contract.

Making the Offer

Once you have checked references and are ready to make an official offer to a candidate for the job, consider the following:

References: Ask for at least three references from the candidate, including one from their current job. Some candidates may be hesitant to provide a reference from a current job, especially if that employer doesn't know they are looking for a new job.

In this case, ask for three other references and tell the candidate you will check their current employer reference if they choose to accept a position with your company.

Pre-employment screening: If you require pre-employment screening—such as background checks for criminal records, driving records, or drug use—be sure you have a process in place to ensure you are complying with all applicable laws. Remember that some states require background checks for certain roles within a business. Check with your state or your legal counsel to ensure you know the laws. We recommend you hire an agency to do pre-employment background screening for you.

> **BUSINESS BUSTER**
>
> According to Sandy Glover, President of Gold Shield Legal Investigations (www. goldshieldli.com), businesses risk legal liability if the procedures utilized to investigate candidates infringe on legally protected areas of privacy. Laws that protect such inquiries include the Fair Credit Reporting Act (FCRA), the Driver's Privacy Protection Act (DPPA), and the Health Information Portability and Privacy Act (HIPPA). Additionally, the state and county in which the business operates may have additional laws specific to pre-employment screening. Bottom line: be sure any agency you hire is a member of the Consumer Reporting Agency (CRA) and works within the confines of the law.

Make sure all potential candidates know you do pre-employment screening. You'll likely find that those candidates who have something to hide will not proceed with the interview process. You'll need to have the candidate sign a form acknowledging that they are giving you permission to conduct pre-employment screening.

Resumé check: Checks the facts on the individual's resumé, including all past employment, roles they held at those companies, dates of employment, reason for termination, and salary at the time they left the position. Additionally, check educational background and any other relevant information.

Consider hiring the individual on a 90-day trial period during which employment can be terminated if the new hire is not working out satisfactorily. You can check references and do pre-employment screening during that initial 90-day period. Any issues that arise during these checks may be considered grounds for termination.

Your offer letter should include the following items:

- Role for which the candidate is being hired
- Salary for that role

- The name of candidate's immediate supervisor

- Start date of employment

- Benefits they will receive (include a benefits package)

- Any conditions of employment, such as reference checks and pre-employment screening

- Any other relevant information for your business

Ask the candidate to sign and return the letter accepting your offer of employment.

Setting Up Internal Policies

Every business, regardless of its size, needs policies and procedures in place to ensure the effectiveness and efficiency of its business operations. Establishing, documenting, and maintaining policies and procedures helps ensure success by avoiding communication problems, inconsistencies in how employees are treated, or potential lawsuits. You should develop a policy and procedure manual for your business that meets your needs now and can grow with your business. As a best practice, review and update the policy and procedure manual on an annual basis.

Your policies and procedures manual may include information on the following issues:

- The handling of customer data and other information

- Travel expense reimbursement

- The handling of computer files

- Inventory procedures

- Clean desk policies to protect company information

Some policies are required by law and must be posted in a common area for all to see. These include the following federally regulated policies:

- Sexual Harassment

- Family and Medical Leave Act

- Workers' Compensation

- Fair Labor Standards Act
- Job Discrimination
- Equal Employment Opportunity
- Job Safety and Health

See the U.S. Department of Labor's website (www.dol.gov) for information that must be posted in the workplace. Local and state government websites will also provide this information.

We can't possibly discuss all the human resource policies and procedures that you might include for your business—it all depends on your business, the number of employees you have, and the industry in which the business exists. However, some policies and procedures to consider include workplace rules and guidelines (such as breaks and lunch time, vacation time, dress code, filing grievances or complaints, and making personal phone calls), employment policies (such as ethics, handling confidential information, behavior in the workplace, and personnel files and records), and payroll policies (such as employee classifications, pay periods, timesheets, payroll deductions, and advances).

Keeping It Flexible

Be sure to build some flexibility into your policies or procedures. For example, suppose you have a two-week vacation allowance for all your employees and require them to use their vacation time within the calendar year with no carryover into the next year. You include this information in your employee manual. However, one year, during a particularly busy time period, some members of your manufacturing department weren't able to take vacation allocated to them because the business needed them on the job. (Keep in mind that if they insist on taking vacation, you might be legally required to allow them to do so no matter how busy you are. However, let's assume for the purposes of this example that they are willing to forego a week of their vacation time to meet the business's needs in getting product out the door.) Here is where the flexibility comes in. You don't want these employees to lose a week's vacation just because they were loyal to the business. A good policy would permit allowances to be made in special circumstances, such as emergency situations or tight deadlines. The policy would permit the immediate manager to allow the exception and would provide details as to the relevant timelines.

It should go without saying that you need to be consistent about being flexible; in other words, you can't allow an exception in the policy for one employee and then refuse to allow an exception for another employee when the same conditions apply.

The Art of Consultation

Don't feel you need to go it alone in determining the appropriate policies and procedures for your business. The members of your advisory group can help you create appropriate policies and procedures for your business. You may also accept input from a variety of sources, including the following:

- Your accountant
- Your legal counsel
- Industry and other association groups
- SCORE
- Human resource consultants

In addition, groups such as the Society for Human Resource Management (www. shrm.org) provide a variety of resources for human resources professionals.

All of these resources can provide guidance in creating effective policies and procedures for your business.

Know Your Employment Law

Getting into details on employment law is beyond the scope of this book. As a best practice, you should seek legal counsel about state and federal employment laws that affect your business and your industry (see Chapter 15 for a list of major employment laws).

Developing Employee Agreements

Employee agreements are contracts between individual employees and the employer that delineate both the conditions of employment and the rights and obligations of both the employee and the employer. They vary in complexity depending on the status of the employee in your business. For instance, senior-level employees may have stock options and bonus information included in their agreements, along with confidentiality and noncompete clauses.

PRACTICE MAKES PERFECT

Consider hiring an attorney to draft an employment agreement template to use for all employees. An attorney can help ensure that you include pertinent information in the agreement.

A standard letter of agreement may include information such as:

- Job description and responsibilities
- Compensation and bonuses
- Vacation and sick time allowances
- Benefits
- Causes for termination
- Confidentiality expectations

All employees should receive and sign an employee agreement, which is not to be confused with the offer of employment letter.

Full Time? Part Time? Temporary?

When deciding whether to hire someone as a full-time or part-time employee, or as a temporary contractor, you'll need to take the following issues into consideration:

- If the individual will play a key role in your business, such as a salesperson, you'll probably want to hire them as a full-time employee.
- If the individual will have only limited responsibilities, such as a clerical person, you might start out with them on a part-time basis. You can always

transition them to full-time if the workload grows or if you decide to add additional responsibilities.

• If you're looking for help during busy times of the year, such as during holidays, hire a temporary worker.

One option is to hire employees initially in a temporary contractor role as a trial before you hire them as permanent employees for your business.

Be careful in how you classify your employees. Due to the increasing number of companies hiring contractors to work for long periods of time and not providing them benefits, the government has put many new regulations in place to protect workers. When in doubt, check with your legal counsel.

Terminating Employees

Terminating employees is never an easy task. This section focuses on terminating employees for nonperformance or breach of an employment agreement, such as stealing, releasing confidential information, or drug use.

When terminating employees, follow these best practices:

Be specific and stick to the facts. You don't want to get angry or say something inappropriate during a termination interview. For example, you wouldn't want to tell the individual you are terminating that he has "always been difficult to work with" when the stated reason you are terminating the person is that he is not performing up to the standards of the job. The impression you leave by making such a remark may be that you simply don't like the employee, which could very well lay the groundwork for an employee discrimination lawsuit. Be very specific about why he is being terminated. For example, let's say that one of your employees was taking unexcused time off. In the last week, he did not show up for work on two occasions and did not provide a reason for his whereabouts. Your conversation during the termination meeting might go as follows:

"Robert, in the last week you did not show up for work on Tuesday and again on Thursday. When asked, you provided no reason for your absence and got belligerent during the conversation with your manager. As per the employee guidelines, and your employee agreement, unexcused absences from work are grounds for termination. Given the situation, we are terminating your employment effective immediately." Do not feel as if you have to engage in extensive conversation with the employee, especially if he becomes belligerent. Restate the reason for termination and explain that the policy is clear on the matter.

Have a witness. Always have someone else in the room with you when you terminate an employee. If a manager of a department is terminating someone in her department, you or another senior-level employee should also be in attendance in the meeting. If you are a very small business, consider asking someone from your advisory board or your legal counsel to assist in the process.

> **PRACTICE MAKES PERFECT**
>
> If you have never terminated an employee before, seek out the advice of someone who has—such as an attorney or someone in your advisory board—to be sure that you are following proper protocol and are complying with all employment laws.

Be sure that if the termination is due to a performance problem—such as an individual not fulfilling the requirements of the job—you give the employee a chance to improve his or her performance. There is no set amount of time you must provide, but be consistent from employee to employee. Failure to be consistent will leave you exposed to potential wrongful termination lawsuits, which can be costly and damaging to your business's reputation.

Provide the following to an employee upon termination:

- Information on the employee's last payroll check, any severance pay and pay for vacation time that wasn't taken but to which the employee is entitled

- Information on *COBRA* coverage including relevant forms to be completed

- A checklist to ensure the employee returns company property, including laptop computers, cell phones, office keys, and so on

- A reminder of confidentiality agreements that he is bound to honor

> **DEFINITION**
>
> **COBRA** refers to the Consolidated Omnibus Budget Reconciliation Act of 1985 and is a continuation of benefits when employees are terminated or laid off. It basically provides employees with the ability to temporarily continue health coverage at group rates.

In some cases, you may be able to hold the last check or a severance check until the employee returns all company property. Be sure, however, that your state laws allow for this.

The following are the most common termination mistakes made by employers:

- Inconsistency in terminating employees. For example, one employee is allowed unexcused time off from work yet another employee is terminated for the same behavior.

- Lack of sufficient documentation regarding the decision to terminate the employee in the employee's personnel file.

- Not providing the employee an opportunity to improve performance, or not documenting and discussing the poor performance with the employee in a formal performance review process.

- Failing to follow documented policies and procedures in terminating employees.

Any of these mistakes can set you up for a wrongful termination lawsuit. If you are unsure about how to terminate a particular employee, or whether or not you are violating any laws, seek legal advice. Paying for any legal advice in advance will be far less costly than a lawsuit for wrongful termination of employment. For more insights on avoiding legal problems associated with terminations, see http://humanresources.about.com/od/legalissues/a/terminations.htm.

BEST PRACTICE

If you believe an employee will be a problem during a termination process (and you'll likely have an idea of who these employees are), have a security person or a police officer standing by to assist you.

Terminating employees is one of the most difficult tasks you'll face. Be sure you do so fairly, professionally, and after much consideration.

The Least You Need to Know

- Have formal processes and procedures in place for sourcing, interviewing, and hiring the best people for your business.
- Formal policies and procedures protect you and your business and ensure efficient and effective business operations.
- Be sure to know the basics of employment law and seek legal counsel when you have questions or are unsure.
- Document all instances of employee performance or other issues that may be cause for termination.

The Right Side of the Law

In This Chapter

- Knowing the basics of the law
- Understanding the importance of contracts
- Protecting yourself from lawsuits
- Protecting your intellectual property

The best preamble to all that follows is: hire a good lawyer first.

That's because no book can replace a qualified attorney who knows your enterprise well. When it comes to safeguarding your business, its assets, and all its various stakeholders, you really do need a personal legal resource. We're not saying you should keep an attorney on retainer—though many small businesses do—but you will want to have access to a lawyer who knows you, your products, your services, and your customers, so that when you need help you have someone to talk to.

We won't even pretend to cover everything you need to know about the law in this chapter, but we will cover enough to get you started and, perhaps, inspire you to begin a professional relationship with your own attorney if you haven't already done so. You don't want to have to start your search for an attorney at the moment you most desperately need one!

Finding the Right Attorney

Attorneys can help you …

- Understand your insurance needs based on your business type and exposure to risk.

- Determine the best legal formation (LLC, INC, etc.) for your business.

- Develop employee handbooks, policies, and procedures.

- Create and review legal agreements and contracts.

- Handle personnel problems.

- Negotiate with potential partners for your business.

- Protect your intellectual property (IP).

Ask your accountant or people who operate similar businesses for names of attorneys they recommend.

BEST PRACTICE

Among the most important best practices when it comes to legal matters is to get to know an attorney that you trust and who is willing to learn about you and your business. If you don't already have a relationship with a good attorney, one good online resource to help you begin the process of creating this critical alliance is FindLaw's lawyer search engine. You can find it at http://lawyers.findlaw. com. You can also find attorneys through the American Bar Association's website, www.abanet.org.

It's best to meet with an attorney in person before making the final selection. Look for someone who …

- Understands your business and its challenges.

- Has worked with similar businesses in size and type.

- Answers your questions promptly and thoroughly.

- Creates a working environment that you are comfortable with.

You want to know that you are selecting an attorney with whom you can work easily and who will help you to protect both your business assets and your personal assets.

Getting Contracts and Agreements Right

The old saying holds true when it comes to reviewing contracts and agreements: an ounce of prevention really is worth a pound of cure. Too often, small business owners don't think about the need for an attorney; they figure they can handle many matters on their own. Certainly it seems easy enough to handle some legal issues without the aid of an attorney, in part because there are so many resources out on the Internet, and so many templates and forms for contracts and agreements that can be downloaded for free.

Of course, small business owners want to control their costs, and attorneys cost money. Even so, we recommend that you utilize the services of an attorney for developing contracts, reviewing agreements, and other (seemingly minor) legal matters. It's cheaper to seek out an attorney's help up front than to have to call them in later on when you find yourself in hot water.

Seeking legal advice when you're beyond the scope of your experience base is extremely important, especially with something as important as contracts.

Attorneys can help you create numerous agreements and contracts for your business, including nondisclosure agreements, employee agreements, customer contracts, purchase orders, supplier/vendor agreements, lease agreements, purchase agreements, and partner agreements.

In some cases, your attorney may be able to help you create a template that you can adjust for future use. For example, your attorney can create an initial customer contract that you can use for all your customers. You can then edit that base contract for use with other customers by changing certain variables.

Certainly you should ask your attorney to review contracts you receive for signature. You'll find that when you have used an attorney for a while, you begin to know what to look for in the contract and may be able to review some contracts yourself—or at least be able to ask your attorney pointed questions based on your review.

The Most Common Legal Problems

Based on conversations with our own attorneys and other small business owners, the most common reasons small business owners have legal problems are as follows:

- Poorly written contracts (or no contract at all)

- Ignorance of the law, such as the Occupational Safety and Health Administration (OSHA) requirements, licensing and other regulations, employee rights, and tax laws

- Inappropriate questions asked of candidates in interviews

It is worth the investment of a few hours' time and the legal fees to sit with your attorney to educate yourself about the laws that pertain to your business. It may seem expensive upfront, and you may think it is not necessary, but the cost of defending yourself from lawsuits is much higher.

Best Practices: Tax Law

Tax law is the Internal Revenue Code and other state and federal statutes, rules, and regulations that apply to taxation of businesses and individuals. As a business owner, you need to know your tax responsibilities, particularly in the following areas:

Employee taxes: You must withhold taxes from salaries paid to all employees, including Social Security, Medicare, and state and federal taxes. You must also pay Social Security and Medicare taxes for each employee you have (in addition to what the employee has to pay), and you must pay unemployment taxes. Additionally, you'll need to be sure each employee completes a W-4 so you know what taxes to withhold from their paychecks. At the end of a calendar year, you'll need to provide a W-2 for all full-time or part-time permanent employees and a W-9 for all temporary contract employees.

BEST PRACTICE

See the IRS website (www.irs.gov) for more information on tax law, and certainly ask your accountant if you have any questions or are unsure about your responsibilities as a business owner.

Sales taxes for products sold: If you sell a product, you must register with the states in which you sell that product to pay sales tax to the state. It is your responsibility to track all sales for reporting purposes.

You also need to be aware of the due dates for various taxes, such as estimated taxes (due four times a year) and corporate taxes. Pay particular attention to quarterly estimated taxes, which can be a troublesome area for many businesses, especially smaller, home-based businesses. Your accountant will be able to provide information on taxes you must pay for your particular business and when those taxes are due.

Best Practices: Employment Law

As a best practice, seek legal counsel about employment laws that affect your business.

The following list is hardly an all-inclusive list of employment laws that you must abide by, but it does cover some of the major laws:

- **Fair Labor Standards Act (FLSA):** This act sets the federal minimum wages paid to employees and also covers overtime pay.

- **Title VII of the Civil Rights Act:** This act prohibits you from discriminating against employees in hiring, firing, or pay based on their religion, sex, or ethnic background.

- **Occupational Safety and Health Act (OSHA):** This act requires businesses to provide safe and healthy conditions for employees to work in.

- **Family and Medical Leave Act (FMLA):** This act enables eligible employees to get up to 12 weeks of unpaid time off with their job protected to care for a sick child, spouse, or parent or for the birth or adoption of a child.

- **Americans with Disabilities Act (ADA):** This act prohibits discrimination against individuals with disabilities.

Additionally, there are laws regarding the retention of employee records, immigration policies, military leave, jury duty, age discrimination, and even appropriate interview questions.

Some of these laws apply only to businesses with a minimum number of employees; others are for all businesses regardless of the size. See the Department of Labor site (www.dol.gov) or the Equal Employment Opportunity Commission site (www.eeoc.gov) for detailed information on all employment laws and to find out whether they apply to your business.

PRACTICE MAKES PERFECT

Remember that for all employees you hire, you must verify an employee's ability to work within the United States through the use of the Employee Eligibility Verification form (Form I-9).

Keep this information in your employee files; you will want easy access to it if it should ever be required. You can download the form and learn more about it at the U.S. Citizenship & Immigration Services website (www.uscis.gov).

Should You Sue?

In an ideal world, you'll never have to make a decision to sue someone. But let's be honest, you may eventually have to sue. There are a variety of reasons why you may have to initiate a lawsuit, including the following:

- An employee breaches an employment agreement about customer confidentiality or sells trade secrets.

- A vendor or supplier doesn't live up to his agreement with your business or produces products or components of products that cause injury to your customers.

- A competitor (or other person or business) breaches copyright or other IP laws.

- A customer refuses to pay on a contract for services or products purchased and delivered.

- A business partner breaches a partnership agreement.

> **BEST PRACTICE**
>
> If you find yourself in a sticky situation with a customer, partner, or vendor, talk with your attorney to determine if there are options besides suing in a court of law. Lawsuits can be costly and may be disruptive or damaging to your business, even if you are in the right.

All of these are valid reasons to initiate a lawsuit; however, you may want to look at other possible solutions, when it makes sense to do so, prior to suing. For example, do you really want to sue a customer who hasn't paid his invoice? You may win in court, but that's one customer who won't be using your business anymore, and he will also tell others about his negative experience with your company—even if he is at fault.

Using Mediation

Many contracts and agreements allow for *mediation* to resolve disputes between the parties.

> **DEFINITION**
>
> **Mediation** is the process of settling disputes outside of the court system using a third party mediator who is experienced in helping two or more parties resolve their differences. The mediator helps the two parties come to an agreement on resolution, but it is not necessarily a binding process.

Mediation enables the parties to come to resolution themselves, through the assistance of a mediator, without having a court make the decision for the parties. Additionally, both parties can agree to keep the terms of the mediation private, whereas going to court makes the matter one of public record.

One of the benefits of mediation over going to court is that you have a better chance of keeping the relationship with the other party cordial and even continuing the business relationship in the future. The mediator can help each party understand the other's point of view.

If you can't come to agreement at mediation, you can always initiate a lawsuit against the other party.

Getting Sued

At some point you may find yourself in court on the other end of a lawsuit. Businesses often find themselves in court simply because they didn't do their legal homework before starting their business. For example, if you are using a business name that is incorporated by another business or is trademark protected, you may find yourself in court to stop your use of that name. Businesses may also end up in court for terminating employees unfairly or discriminating against them in the hiring process, promotions, or pay.

Similarly, you could end up in court if your product causes harm to someone, or the service you provide interrupts his or her business in some way. For example, suppose you own a computer networking company that begins work on a customer's server—only to find that something you did caused the server to crash and make it impossible for the customer to do business for an entire day!

If you or your business is ever served notice of a suit filed against you, you should immediately seek your attorney's advice on how to proceed. Don't try to handle these matters yourself! This is when you'll thank yourself for having an established relationship with an attorney who knows you and your business.

Errors and omissions insurance for your business is kind of like a "get out of jail (relatively) free" card. Suppose you develop software for companies to run an e-commerce website that accepts credit card information. If somehow the website gets hacked and credit card information gets comprised, certain liability may fall on you as the developer of the software that ran the e-commerce site. If you do not have errors and omissions insurance, you could find your company out of business and owing a lot of money due to the liability of a potential error in the coding of the website that caused the problem. Errors and omissions insurance protects you from such issues.

> **BEST PRACTICE**
>
> Depending on your business, errors and omissions insurance, although quite costly, might be worth it in the long run. Check with your attorney and your insurance agent to determine whether you should carry this insurance, the cost of doing so, and the implications of not carrying it.

Intellectual Property Considerations

Intellectual property (IP) encompasses your ideas, inventions, processes, content, and other materials you have developed. Here's a rundown of the major legal protections available for IP:

Copyrights: Copyrights are exclusive rights granted to the creator of an original work—such as a book, document, or photograph—and provides individuals the right to copy, distribute, and adapt the works for their own purposes. Copyrights actually are automatic when you have completed a work (such as an article or book, a training course, or a photograph); however, in many cases, if you need to fight a breach of copyright, it must have been registered with the U.S. Copyright Office (www.copyright.gov).

Trademarks: Trademarks protect logos and names when use of that logo or name by others might be confusing for the originator. For example, Xerox is a registered trademarked name, and no other company could use that name for their product or service. Trademarks are protected under both state and federal protections. You can learn more about how to trademark logos and names at the U.S. Patent and Trademark Office website (www.uspto.gov).

Patents: Patents are exclusive rights to the inventor of a product or process to prevent others from duplicating the product or using the process without permission. Among Microsoft's 5,000 patents is the technology used in its Xbox 360 games. U.S. patents are protected only in the United States; however, you can apply for patents in other countries.

Trade secrets: Trade secrets can apply to manufacturing processes, information, or ideas that are not publicly known and, if released to the public, could damage the originator. Customer lists can be considered a trade secret, provided the owner of the information has taken steps to prevent the information from being known in the public. This may include requiring a password to access a database of customer information and ensuring all employees with access to the information sign a nondisclosure agreement.

PRACTICE MAKES PERFECT

Because patents and trademarks are specialized areas of law, be sure your attorney has this expertise or can refer you to someone who does. Registering trademarks or patents is a complicated process, and you will need expert guidance to properly protect your IP.

Every business has some IP to protect. For example, if you are a consultant who has developed training programs, those training programs are your IP. If you have a customer database that includes all of your customer data and information, that information is protected under the law. An employee who takes that information with them to a competitor would be considered to be selling trade secrets.

Protecting Your Ideas

Protecting your ideas is crucial to the long-term viability of your business. Depending on what you need to protect, the process ranges from simple things you can do yourself (such as filing for copyright protection for a training course you have developed) to very complex (such as filing for a patent for an invention). Sometimes you can take steps to protect your IP in multiple ways. An attorney can help you decide the best approach.

BEST PRACTICE

If you are unsure whether something can be protected as IP, consult with your attorney.

You should strive to protect your ideas before there is an opportunity for an employee, client, or competitor to walk away with the knowledge and use it themselves. You should make sure everyone involved in the idea you want to protect—even if you are just in the beginning stages of discussion—signs nondisclosure agreements developed with the help of your attorney.

Let's look at an example. Let's assume that you are developing a new manufacturing process that will enable you to produce products more quickly and efficiently. Because you need to finance the process using outside sources, you will be talking to potential investors. You need to make sure those potential investors sign a nondisclosure agreement that prohibits them from disclosing information about the process or stealing the idea. Additionally, all employees working on the project should also sign nondisclosure agreements.

Licensing Intellectual Property

Licensing your IP can bring significant revenue into your business. However, it must be done carefully to ensure that you are protected.

Consider the following issues:

- Will you offer exclusive or nonexclusive licensing? Exclusive licensing provides the licensee with sole rights for distribution of the IP being licensed. Nonexclusive licensing allows the licensor to license the IP to multiple distributors with no restrictions.
- What will you charge for licensing of your IP?
- How long a license will you permit?
- Is the licensing limited in scope?
- How will the licensee protect your IP?
- If the business you are licensing the IP to is sold to another business, will you permit reassignment of the licensing agreement?

It is essential that you work with an attorney to develop licensing agreements that protect you, your business, and your property.

The Least You Need to Know

- Developing a relationship with an attorney can help you avoid legal problems and ease the process if you do find yourself in trouble with the law.
- Be sure you understand the basics of the law as it applies to your business, but seek the assistance of an attorney for working out the details.
- Have an attorney review all contracts and agreements before you sign them.
- Seek the advice of an attorney to protect your intellectual property.

Your Information Technology Infrastructure

In This Chapter

- Determining hardware, software, and data security requirements
- Understanding technology infrastructure needs
- Keeping your data safe and secure
- Planning now for the future

Regardless of the type of business you're in, an information technology (IT) plan is critical to the survival of your business.

Whether you are storing or using customer data, processing invoices, tracking accounts payable and receivable, writing proposals, communicating with customers, or keeping up with the latest news in your industry, you will need to use IT. Choosing the appropriate technology for all of these processes is both a big strategic choice and, potentially, a major investment. And no matter how small your business is, you need, and always will need, some kind of IT infrastructure. That infrastructure will certainly change over time, but that fact should not prevent you from taking action to create a plan that meets your business needs today.

This chapter helps get you started in a key best practice for IT: the ongoing task of setting up and revising the right IT plan—one that serves both you and your customers. If ever there was a best practice that deserves an investment of continued attention over time, this is it.

Hardware Acquisition and Integration

What kind of hardware do you need for your business? Different businesses have different requirements.

Some businesses, such as single-location retail outlets, may require a relatively simple setup: a laptop, a point of sale (POS) terminal bundled with an inventory system, a telephone/fax machine, and the service necessary for that phone line.

If you are running a sales organization with multiple salespeople, you will need to plan for a different level of investment. Such a business could require a customer relationship management (CRM) system, an enterprise resource planning (ERP) system, and all the necessary hardware to support those systems. An ERP system is an integrated software application that serves as a business management tool, helping to track resources, tangible assets, materials, finances, suppliers, vendors, customers, and employees. A CRM system is a software program that enables businesses to track and manage their interactions with their current and prospective customers. It is used by both sales and marketing departments to ensure a coordinated interaction with customers.

You might also require an integrated phone system, such as *Voice over Internet Protocol* (*VoIP*), with a more complex setup than just a single phone line. You could also choose to host a number of servers to support all of these applications, therefore requiring a more business-friendly Internet connection, complete with a firewall to protect all your data.

DEFINITION

Voice over Internet Protocol (VoIP) is a set of technologies and protocols that allows for communication over the Internet. In addition to telephone communications, VoIP allows for multimedia communications, faxing, instant messaging, and video communications.

When it comes to hardware, you can choose between various operating platforms such as Microsoft, Linux, or Apple Macintosh. As of the writing of this book, most businesses use Microsoft-based computers because they are still perceived as being less costly overall, and as offering businesses many more options. Choose hardware that you are most comfortable with and that best meets your needs, including supporting the software necessary for you to run your business.

If you travel frequently, you may opt for laptop computers rather than desktop computers. Similarly, if you have sales folks on staff, they will need laptops since they are likely to be on the road much of the time at customer sites.

The software you need to run your business—word processing, spreadsheets, database, and accounting software—may dictate the hardware and the platform you need. You also need to take into account the need for compatibility with current or projected partners, vendors, or suppliers. To whom will you have to transfer files? With whom will you work to track inventory?

PRACTICE MAKES PERFECT

Consider using ShareFile (www.sharefile.com) as a secure resource for transferring and sharing files over the Internet.

Choose telecommunications equipment (phone system) and services based on your current and projected business needs. If you require an overall networked environment because you have many employees, it is probably more cost-effective to go with a single vendor for telecommunications and Internet services. Alternatively, if it's just you, and maybe one other person, in the business, a simpler phone system may be sufficient. In this situation, a non-business-oriented telecom provider may be the most cost-effective choice.

Your goal should be a flexible, affordable system that allows you to be prepared for growth without going overboard on costs.

The Right IT Investment

We've mentioned more than once that when choosing IT, you need to think about both your current needs as well as your projected future needs. To do this, you need to ask yourself a number of questions.

First, answer these questions to get a good sense of your current needs:

- What are the current needs of your business as it relates to technology?

- Do you or your employees need to travel frequently? If so, you might opt for laptop computers and a means to access your infrastructure from the outside world.

- Do you need any specific software to run your business? What platforms do they run on?

- Will you host your infrastructure yourself on a server in your office, or will your computers be hosted off-site at another location or by a third party?

- Do you need to share data with anyone, such as with suppliers or vendors?

- How much and what kind of customer data will you be storing (e.g., credit card information, customer purchase data)? How will you organize and protect it?

- What other data will you store? How will you protect that data?

- Will you have an online component to your business that enables people to purchase from your website?

- What accounting software will you use, and how will you transfer data to your accountant for tax purposes?

Then think about the future of your business:

- What are your future growth plans for two to three years out?

- How many additional employees will you have, and what kind of technology access are they likely to require? (For example, do your employees need smartphones? Do they need laptops for traveling? Do they need to be able to access certain systems, such as ERP or CRM?)

- Will the type and amount of data you store change in the next few years?

- Will you at some point in the future start to take orders over the web for products?

- Will you have additional partnerships with vendors and suppliers that might require you to share data or inventory numbers with them?

- Will any of your employees work virtually?

PRACTICE MAKES PERFECT

Consider bounding your IT ideas off your advisory board before committing to anything. You want to balance what is reasonable now with your potential future needs. You must treat your IT investment as a strategic decision.

The good news is that when planning for IT needs, you only need to look a few years into the future. There is no need to focus on where you may be in five or more years because technology changes so frequently that you can't plan effectively that far out. Focusing on the next two to three years is a good bet to get the most out of your investment.

Should You Lease or Buy?

Consider the following when deciding whether to lease or purchase technology for your business:

- Do you have the money available to purchase? If not, leasing is a good option since you likely don't have to put any money down on a lease agreement.

- Are you unsure of your technology needs in the future? If so, you may choose to lease for the short term while you determine your future needs.

- Do you just need the basics—a computer, monitor, printer, simple phone system, and Internet connection? If so, purchasing may be a better solution for your needs.

- What are the pros and cons of leasing or purchasing IT from a tax perspective? (Ask your accountant.)

You'll also need to consider whether to purchase maintenance agreements on the technology you lease or buy. If you decide to lease, frequently (although not always—check the lease agreement) maintenance is part of the agreement. Additionally, sometimes you can negotiate for upgrades to equipment you lease. If you decide to purchase your technology, you might want to purchase maintenance and service agreements to protect the equipment.

Software Acquisition and Integration

Depending on your business, software needs will vary. If you are an insurance firm, for example, you'll need word processing, spreadsheets, presentation, and maybe database software for everyday needs. If you are a manufacturer, you may also need inventory control software and ERP software.

You'll purchase software on a per license basis; this means that if you have three people who will be using word processing software, you'll need a three-user license.

> **BUSINESS BUSTER**
>
> The software you have access to will be based on the type of platform you choose for your business. Don't choose a platform before considering your software needs.

Choosing Software

The largest provider of office-related software products (such as spreadsheets and word processing programs) is Microsoft Corporation. A variety of companies have ERP software or accounting software, and your decision on a provider for such software will be based on many factors, including:

- Cost of product

- Functionality of product to meet your needs

- Compatibility with your platform and other technology needs

- Market share and stability of vendor

Just as with hardware, you will want to choose software that will grow with your business, keeping in mind that you will need to purchase upgrades to the software regularly. When selecting accounting software, make sure you can easily share information with your accountant.

Cloud Computing

Many small businesses dispense with purchasing software altogether and instead opt to run much of their IT through the cloud. With cloud computing, the software and data is accessed via the Internet rather than stored on your computers. Instead of purchasing software and hardware for storing data, you simply pay for the capacity you need. Companies such as Microsoft, Google, and Amazon provide cloud computing services.

With cloud computing, rather than investing in IT infrastructure and software, you simply purchase capacity as you need it. With cloud computing technology, you and your employees can access your software applications and data from anywhere as long as you have an Internet connection.

Security and privacy are increasingly important concerns for businesses considering using a cloud computing environment. There are ways to protect your data, of course, but you should consider how much control you want over where your data resides and your access to it prior to choosing a cloud computing environment.

> **PRACTICE MAKES PERFECT**
>
> Using cloud computing reduces costs for your IT initially, when your data needs are not as substantial as they might be a few years down the line. Regularly evaluate your use of cloud computing to ensure it remains the most cost-effective solution.

Too often, businesses continue to use cloud computing environments long after it no longer makes financial sense for them to do so.

If you choose to use cloud computing, you want to be certain that the data you store in the cloud remains yours—you own it, not the host company. Ensure that, when you terminate the agreement, you get all of the data that you stored in the cloud. There should also be a provision for purging your data from the cloud once the agreement is terminated and all your data is back in your possession. The agreement should also provide for a service level agreement (SLA), which basically states that there is a quick turnaround for support and that you will have access to your data within a certain amount of time if the system should crash. Additionally, look for guarantees for access to data and speed of access.

You'll also want to make sure you back up and export your data on a regular basis. You want to keep your data outside the cloud in addition to in the cloud.

Securing Your Data

Of key consideration in determining your technology needs is keeping your data safe. You'll want to protect your customer data, information about your employees, and your business finances.

A firewall—hardware and software that blocks outsiders from accessing your data—provides a secure environment for your data while permitting those with authorization, such as your employees, access to information they need to do their jobs. If you decide to use a cloud computing environment, or host servers via a third-party collocation site, be sure that you get details on how data is kept secure. If you are uncomfortable with any aspect of the arrangement, don't take a chance. Losing sensitive customer data because of improper precautions or carelessness can drag you into lawsuits that can be detrimental to your business reputation and very costly.

Depending on the requirements of uptime for your system and the data, you may want to have a failover environment in place. This basically duplicates your systems, so if one system fails, the other picks up and takes over, allowing for uninterrupted operations.

BEST PRACTICE

Always keep a backup copy of your most critical data off-site in the event of a disaster at the business location. This may be at your own home, a trusted employee's home, or a bank safe deposit box. Renew the backup at least every 90 days.

Certainly you'll want to consider backup systems and software to provide you a regular backup of the data on your system. With a backup system in place, should something happen—such as a user deleting information by mistake or a system crash causing a loss of data—information can be retrieved from a backup. Consider Symantec Backup Exec for Windows or Macintosh environments (www.symantec.com). Smaller businesses might opt for Goodsync (www.goodsync.com).

Keeping Your Information Safe

If you retain customer information such as credit card numbers or other sensitive data, it is imperative that you keep that information safe.

BEST PRACTICE

There are several online payment services available for use by small businesses. Consider paypal.com or authorize.net. Other options include Google Checkout and Amazon, both of which allow you to create e-stores.

If you store any credit card information, go through a *PCI-compliance audit* to ensure you are following all protocols for storing the credit cards. Ensuring PCI compliance can be costly and might require you to hire a consultant, but it is worth the money, time, and effort to ensure that you have protected the data you store on your systems. See www.pcisecuritystandards.org to find out the latest version of standards and to get more information about PCI compliance.

DEFINITION

A **PCI-compliance audit** (or a Payment Card Industry Data Security Standard [PCI DSS] audit) ensures that you are following the PCI DSS to protect credit card information. Regardless of the size of your business, if you accept credit cards, you want to be PCI compliant! This audit is not a legal requirement, but it is a smart thing to do and is highly recommended!

Developing a Disaster Recovery Plan

Just as you need a plan for getting your business back up and running after a major incident, you need a disaster recovery plan for your IT. After all, any significant period of downtime can be very costly to the business. You'll need to have a plan in place should any of the following occur:

- Loss of all company financial data
- Loss of company customer data
- A security breach, such as someone hacking into your systems and stealing data or disabling your business systems
- Disasters such as floods, fire, or extended power outages

When developing a disaster recovery plan for your IT infrastructure, perform an analysis of your exposure to risk. What would an event such as a fire, flood, or hurricane do to your data? What would happen to your business if you suddenly lost all your data as the result of such an event? What systems are in place to keep that from happening? Include in the risk analysis how secure your systems are—your firewalls, authentication requirements, backup systems, and so on. The less secure the systems, the more likely you are to lose essential data.

BEST PRACTICE

Many consulting companies specialize in disaster recovery planning, and there are numerous books on the subject. Do a bit of research to learn about the benefits of disaster recovery planning for your business. You don't want to go overboard from a cash standpoint, but you shouldn't ignore the problem, either. Depending on the nature of your business, you may find hiring outside help in this area to be a good investment.

Here's another question to consider: how much time can you afford to have your systems down and unavailable? If you must be up and running around the clock with no exceptions, you might want to consider having a collocation site with a complete duplication of all of your systems running. If your business is located in Massachusetts and you cannot risk being down, you'll want to consider having backup systems in Maine or Connecticut pick up the slack should your systems in Massachusetts crash. This is, of course, a costly endeavor and is only recommended for companies (such as financial planning businesses) that have very sensitive information that cannot be lost or down for extended periods of time.

Once you develop your plan and have your backups in place, test it. You don't want to wait to find out if the system works when you really need it. As a best practice, run an audit of your disaster recovery plan on an annual basis to determine if it still meets your needs.

Updating Security

The IT industry issues security updates on a regular basis to protect its software from hackers, viruses, and *malware*. You'll want to have a system in place to regularly install these security upgrades.

> **DEFINITION**
>
> **Malware** is malicious software that is installed on a user's computer system without their consent. It may slow down the computer, steal passwords, or download important data.

Getting the Right Guidance

Unless you are an expert in this area, you should strongly consider getting some kind of (affordable) expert advice in making the best IT choices for your business. You'll want to select a consultant who …

- Has helped businesses in your industry and of your size.

- Is not partnered with any one technology provider but rather is an independent consultant (for example, you don't necessarily want a Microsoft partner for your consultant who is only able to recommend Microsoft solutions).

- Has worked with businesses to develop IT strategies.

- Has an understanding of the various options and the pros and cons of each.

- Has positive references for past work.

- Can work within your budget.

Spend time with the consultant before you hire him to ensure you are comfortable with that individual's working style. You should feel comfortable asking questions and being honest about your needs and your budgetary restrictions.

Several websites provide consultant directories segmented by industry. For example, Consultants Registrar (www.consultantsregistrar.com) provides a listing of consultants by industry and by state. Another option is Consultancy Register (www.consultancyregister.com) which enables you to search for consultants in a variety of specialties. But perhaps the best way to find an IT consultant is through references of others in your industry who hired a consultant and had a positive experience.

Planning for Business Growth

You don't want to invest significant monies now in an infrastructure plan and find out next year that your technology choices no longer support your business effectively. You must plan for growth.

If you are unsure of your needs, consider starting out with *software-as-a-service* (*SaaS*) applications. This reduces your out-of-pocket expense for costly technology solutions. As your business grows and you have a clearer idea of your needs, you can begin to make the investment in your own technology solutions.

DEFINITION

Software as a service (SaaS) are applications that are licensed to customers for use as a service on demand. For example, if you are unsure of the value of a CRM system for your business, you may choose to use a SaaS CRM system initially. You pay for the use of the CRM on a monthly basis, and if you decide that you do not need the CRM system, you can cancel the service. These services enable you to try out costly systems without having to purchase them.

Setting Up a Great IT Plan

Develop an IT plan based on your technology budget and your current and future technology needs. Update the plan on an annual basis to reflect changes in your business.

Take these steps in developing your IT plan:

1. Identify what technologies you currently use in your business and their purpose.

2. Think about future needs for your business as you grow based on the objectives of your strategic business plan.

3. Discuss technology needs with the various parts of the business. For example, what are the marketing group's plans over the next year? If they decide they want to start a blog, what technology is needed to support that blog? If sales staff will be traveling more frequently, what technology do they need so they can be productive on the road? If you know employees will be working from home within the next year, what technology needs to be put in place to ensure they can work from home as effectively and efficiently as they do in the office?

4. Develop a budget for your technology needs and develop a project plan to achieve your objectives.

Include the following additional information as part of your IT plan:

- Policies and procedures around technology use for your business (including a network security policy)

- Responsibilities of employees for protecting data, such as password protections

- A diagram of your network architecture—how computers are connected within the business and their locations

- A detailed inventory of all equipment, including model numbers, who that equipment is assigned to, and its location

- A complete list of all software in use by your business, including license numbers and agreements for the software

- All vendor agreements and contracts and all maintenance agreements

As a best practice, maintain a binder with all of this information; doing so makes it much easier to evaluate your IT needs on a regular basis.

Taking Advantage of New Technology

Technology changes constantly. There is always a new tool on the market with more bells and whistles. You can't possibly invest in every piece of new technology, nor should you attempt to do so, but some may provide great benefit to your business.

Let's assume that you are ready to upgrade your IT systems. Before committing to a certain plan, take a day or so to review all of your options. What new technology exists that would add value to your business? What technologies will be available in a year or two? Is the technology maturing quickly enough for you to take advantage of it given your limited resources?

Keep in mind that because technology changes so rapidly, you will always have appealing new options to choose from. Make the best choices you can right now. Don't let the blizzard of available options paralyze you. Make a decision. Create the best plan you possibly can, double-check it, then implement it. Then review your IT plan annually.

The Least You Need to Know

- Plan for your technology needs two to three years out.
- Seek out the services of a consultant who is an expert in technology and is familiar with your industry.
- Develop an IT plan for your business and review it regularly to ensure that it still meets your growing business's needs.
- Have a plan in place to ensure all data is kept safe and secure.

Best Practices for Bringing in Revenue

How do you create products and services that will drive your business's growth and connect you with the customers you want most? What do you need to do to hire, and hold on to, the perfect sales team for your business? How do you create a marketing campaign that is truly customer-centered?

If you don't have customers, you don't have revenue. And if you don't have revenue, you don't have a business. In this part of the book, you learn about best practices that are all about getting money in the bank by winning, and retaining, the right customers.

Product and Service Development

In This Chapter

- Using market research data to make decisions
- Determining what matters to your customers
- Using customer councils
- Pricing your products and services

If you're going to invest time, money, and energy developing products and services to offer your customers, shouldn't you offer what your customer wants? This is the goal, of course, but the challenge is to determine exactly what the customer wants. Certainly you may have some idea, but given the costs of development, you want a greater level of assurance than your own gut instinct that what you are going to develop will actually be successful in the marketplace.

One of the best ways to determine what your customers want is to ask them—get them involved in the decision-making process. This chapter shows you how you can reach out to your customers to get their insights and obtain the data you need to make good decisions on new or updated products and services.

The Benefits of Market Research

Market research enables you to gather additional information about a particular subject to make better decisions. Let's look at an example. You run a small shop that does screen printing on flags. You would like to expand your business to include screen-printed banners. You might begin to research the market for screen-printed banners by considering what companies would be your competitors in this area, the types of banners they produce, the costs of those banners, and what kind of customers they sell their products to.

This kind of research can be done fairly easily using the World Wide Web.

You might then ask your current customers if they have any interest in purchasing screen-printed banners. You can do this through voice-to-voice interviews with members of your customer council (our first choice; see Chapter 10) or by surveying current and past customers. The responses you get from your customers will inform your decision.

Getting and Using Data

There are a variety of resources for gathering market research data. Certainly you can get top-quality research reports on a variety of subjects from Gartner Group, Forrester Research, NPD Group, and other such organizations. But these can be costly, and in many cases you may need to be a member organization to purchase research studies.

PRACTICE MAKES PERFECT

The first step you should take in conducting market research is to delineate the purpose for the research. Make sure you know exactly what it is you want to find out, and what your end goal is once you have that information. Then, think about how you will collect the data you need and what sources you will use. Finally, consider how you will evaluate and analyze the data you gather.

Don't discount the variety of market research resources available to you at low or no cost, including the following:

- Public libraries

- Industry and trade associations

- U.S. Department of Commerce

- Marketresearch.com

- Your local Chamber of Commerce

- Company websites and annual reports of public companies

Idea Sources: Customers, Vendors, Others

Let's consider how you can use your company's customers and vendors to generate good product and service development ideas. Assume you sell project management training programs, and you deliver these programs both in person and as online tutorials. You want to do some research to determine the best options for expanding your services to offer consulting services in addition to the training programs. You decide on the following approach: you'll survey customers to determine their interest in hiring a project management consultant. (One best practice here is to use a powerful survey interface like the one offered at www.surveymonkey.com.) You will survey the following groups:

- Current customers who have purchased your training programs within the last two years

- Customers who purchased programs from you in the past (more than two years ago) but haven't purchased since that time

- Businesses who have never purchased from you but who utilize project management

For the last group of businesses you want to survey, you decide to purchase a list of names and e-mail addresses from a variety of project management associations. You are confident that these individuals will give you good information, since they already belong to a project management association. Because you purchased an "opt-in" list of individuals who have agreed to receive such queries, you can set up a survey for this group as well.

Additionally, you research competitors and the types of project management consulting they provide to their customers. This gives you an idea of the options available to support customer needs.

Vendors and suppliers are another way to collect data to make decisions around product and service development. Maintaining close ties with your vendors and suppliers is always a best practice and certainly one that pays off when you want to do a bit of information gathering. Vendors and suppliers work with other businesses besides yours and likely have some great information they can share with you. Although you can't expect them to share confidential information about other businesses or your competitors, they do see what is happening in a variety of businesses and may have a broader perspective of the marketplace based on the work they do. Any information they provide can help you decide where to invest money in new product development.

Continuing with our example, the company may choose to reach out to its own freelance instructors to learn about what they are seeing as project management consulting needs in the marketplace.

Don't forget about your employees when considering ideas for new products and services or for changes and updates to current products and services. Some of them are on the front line with your customers every day, and they often know what customers have on their minds.

Defining Customer Value

You probably know how much a specific customer purchase is worth to your organization, but have you ever wondered about the dollar value of your long-term relationship with a given customer? If your business model incorporates any form of repeat purchase—and most do—then you will want to understand the likely lifetime value of your customer. Understanding this value is an essential best practice that helps you make good decisions about your investments in customer acquisition.

Let's look at an example that will demonstrate how to determine the value of a customer for your business. Your business provides computer networking consulting services. Your typical customer spends $800 per engagement. You service your customers, on average, four times a year, bringing the business $3,200 per year in revenue per customer. Your net profit from that average revenue per customer is $2,000 per year. The lifetime of a customer is, on average, four years, making each customer worth $8,000 in net profit. This information ultimately helps you determine how much you should be willing to pay to gain a new customer. Let's say that currently you pay $300 in marketing and sales to acquire a new customer. Given that you have determined your customer's lifetime value is $8,000, $300 is quite reasonable as a cost of acquisition.

Of course, if yours is a new business, it is going to be harder to calculate the value of a customer. You should make an effort to start to gather the data, however. For now, make intelligent estimates. Keep records on your customers so you can, over time, track the value of a customer to your business with increasing accuracy.

What's Important for the Customer?

Now let's look at the other side: What is your value to the customer? Before spending a lot of time and money developing any new product or service, you will want to make sure it delivers *customer value*.

DEFINITION

Customer value is the benefit and the satisfaction the customer receives from purchasing or investing in your product or service.

In other words, why do people purchase from you? Specifically, when people make repeat purchases from your organization, why do they do that? Determining the answer to this question is another essential best practice for your small business. Suppose you learn, through surveys and conversations with your customers, that they keep coming back to you year after year for the following reasons:

- You charge a reasonable cost for consulting services.

- You are available when they need you—you are very responsive.

- You are trustworthy and helpful.

This information should affect not only your product and service development, but also your promotional, hiring, and planning processes.

You may think you know what is important for the customer—why they do business with you and purchase your products and services. The truth is, though, that you need to ask the question of the customer, and you need to ask regularly. Through in-depth person-to-person interviews, informal discussions, and annual customer feedback surveys, you must constantly ask variations on the question: Why do people purchase from your business? What does it take for them to recommend that someone else make a purchase?

PRACTICE MAKES PERFECT

Survey your customers on at least an annual basis to determine the following information: (1) Their level of satisfaction with their relationship with your business and its products and services; (2) What needs your business is currently not meeting for them but could be; (3) One thing they would change about their relationship with your business; and (4) Whether they would recommend your company to someone else—and if not, why.

Your customers probably include varying types of individuals or businesses. Each customer group may have different perspectives on what matters most. By segmenting your customer base—for example, by individual customers and business customers—you will be able to better track spending and repurchase behavior.

When you understand what is important to your customers as it relates to your products and services, you are in a better position to design your new products and services to suit their needs—to provide value. If you find in your research that your customers are purchasing from you simply because they have been doing so for a while and there are no other alternatives currently available, don't waste time and money developing new products and services until you figure out what's wrong with your current offerings—because you definitely have a problem. It's only a matter of time before another vendor enters the marketplace.

The authors know of a situation with a small business whose owner truly believed he provided a great service to his customers and thought they were thrilled with him and his business. After many years of offering the service but never really having an in-depth conversation with his customers, he started to talk to them and learned that they weren't completely happy with his service—particularly his business's customer service. Their perception was that service was poor or nonexistent. They bought from him because there was no cost-effective alternative.

This was a wake-up call for the business owner! Here he thought all was going well, only to learn that his customers felt cornered into contracting with him because of a lack of alternatives. He knew that if a competitor entered the market (and, frankly, it was just a matter of time), he'd soon find himself out of business. He spent a significant amount of time with his current customers to learn what they wanted from his business and made changes in his processes and procedures to satisfy their needs.

Using a Crystal Ball

The best way to understand the buying behavior of your customers—and therefore types of new products and services that would interest them—is to understand exactly who your customers are. That means learning more about your customers than you already know and being ready to do some digging to find the answers to these questions:

- Are your customers' purchases driven by individual or business concerns?

- For your business customers, is the person who makes the purchasing decision in Human Resources? Finance? Operations? Another business unit?

- Why do they purchase from you? Price? Customer service? Uniqueness of product or service?

The more you know about your current customers, the better you can predict what additional products and services they will purchase and where to target your marketing efforts to attract new customers.

BUSINESS BUSTER

Too often businesses develop new products and services without considering if a customer would be interested in them. If you have no buyers, the time and money spent on developing new products and services is wasted.

Partnering with Customers: Development

We know of one business that offers various business analysis training programs on topics such as requirements gathering and working with stakeholders. They took a copycat approach to developing new products: if their competitors came out with a new training program, they did the same. They didn't bother to ask their customers if they were interested in that new program. Instead, they simply followed their competitors.

The problem is that they invested significant money in the development of training programs for a specific discipline only to have their customers tell them, "Gee, that's great, but we already purchase that program from XYZ Company, have done so for many years, and are happy with the relationship." Had the company bothered to survey its customers, it would have learned that its customers would have preferred to see improvements made in the company's current training programs and even see those particular programs expanded. Customers were not interested in purchasing new training programs beyond the areas already offered by the company.

The lesson of this example is that it pays to partner with your customers. Invest money in development in those areas—products or services—that your current customers are interested in. Nothing does more to secure a relationship with your customers than listening to their needs and responding to them—whether by enhancing your current products and services or by developing cutting-edge offerings that address their challenges.

Creating Customer Councils

Customer councils are an excellent way to keep in touch with your customer and get feedback on developing new products and services.

For example, let's say you own a small deli and are considering expanding your offerings to add french fries, onion rings, and fried seafood to the menu. Before you make the purchase of a fryer and other relevant equipment, you want to be sure the investment will be worth it. You invite some of your regular customers to a free lunch to get their thoughts. You learn from these customers that they are actually trying to eat healthier and would prefer lower-fat, lower-calorie offerings rather than fried food. You decide to go a step further and survey individuals in town who might choose to purchase from your deli. A simple survey sent to them reveals that they, too, would prefer a wider range of healthier choices. After processing all of this information, you decide to offer a variety of salads, fresh veggies, and fruit for your customers.

BEST PRACTICE

Meet with your customer council on at least a semiannual basis to understand the challenges they face. Your goal should be to offer products and services that help them to solve their problems.

There are numerous best practices to draw on when setting up your customer council:

- Include a variety of your customers from different industries and different size businesses.

- Make it worth their while to participate on the council.

- Have regular meetings with an agenda.

- Rotate members of the council on a regular basis.

- Set ground rules regarding confidentiality at the first meeting.

Suppose your business sells employee assessments that gauge whether candidates for a position will be a fit for the business culture. You want to expand your services to include assessments for succession planning and employee development efforts. You meet with your customer council to determine their level of need for such assessments and whether they would purchase those assessments from you should you choose to offer them. Here's what you give back to your customers for the information they provide you:

- During the customer council meeting you provide them with a half-day training session on best practices for onboarding new hires, including tips and templates they can use.

- You provide them a free research report on how to provide professional development opportunities for employees at all levels.

Once you've developed a new product or service, ask members of your council to serve as beta testers at highly discounted rates or for free during a trial period. In exchange, they will provide you feedback and get a sense of ownership in the product or service, which breeds loyalty.

Using Wikis to Get Customer Input

Depending on your business, consider using a *wiki* as a collaborative environment between you and your customers.

DEFINITION

A **wiki** is a website that allows individuals to collaborate by creating and editing information on web pages. Use wikis to collaborate and share information with customers.

A collaboration site provides a place where customers can share information with each other and with you. Let's look at an example of how you might use such a site for new product development.

Suppose you own a business that designs and sells storage bags for camera equipment. Your customers are photographers—usually independent—but some are businesses, including newspapers and television stations that have photographers on staff. You are looking to redesign your line of bags to update them with more features. You decide to use a wiki so that your customers can go online, discuss the bags, and suggest changes they would like to see to help them in their jobs. You now have the information you need to design new camera equipment bags that fit your customers' needs.

Developing a Pricing Strategy

Developing a pricing strategy for your products and services is not an easy task. There is quite a bit to consider, such as how your competitors price similar products and services, what customers will pay for the product or service, and how much profit you need. Certainly, the quality of your product affects your pricing strategy. You may have competitors, but if their product or service is not as high quality as yours, you can charge a higher price than they do.

BUSINESS BUSTER

If you are in a market that is price sensitive, even if you sell a higher-quality product than your competition, you may not be able to price it much higher. Keep this in mind when determining the quality of the product or service you want to develop.

When developing your pricing strategy, have the following information at your fingertips:

- A list of your competitors, their comparable products and services (benefits and features), and prices associated with those products and services

- Your value proposition (see Chapter 5)

- Your cost structure for those products and services

PRACTICE MAKES PERFECT

Involve a variety of employees in your pricing strategy sessions, including your marketing group, salespeople, manufacturing, distributors, and resellers. They will all have valuable input on how to price products.

As a best practice, evaluate your pricing of products and services on a regular basis—at least annually. Things change in the marketplace—new competitors enter the market, customers' needs change, economic conditions change—all of which will affect your pricing. In addition, consider how your pricing affects your distributors or resellers. For instance, if you have minimum or maximum pricing requirements or discounting restrictions, you should review those on a regular basis as well.

You might price to get more profits from your current offerings, to increase the amount of sales per unit, or to gain a larger share of the market. Depending on your goal, your pricing strategy will vary. For example, if you want to gain a larger share of the market from your competitors, you may price your product a bit lower than your competitor to gain market share. Of course, as with any pricing strategy, there are pros and cons to such a decision. Think carefully about what you want to achieve and how it will serve your business in the long run. If you price too low now, how will you justify higher prices later? If you do offer introductory pricing, communicate clearly that it is for a limited period of time so as not to irritate customers when you increase the price later.

The Competitive Issue

You'll need to know the following to price effectively against your competition:

- How their products and services compare with yours
- How they price their products and services
- Who they target for marketing and sales

Much of this information can be found on websites, press releases, and public records (for public companies).

BUSINESS BUSTER

Don't make the common mistake of blindly charging exactly—or slightly less than—what the competition charges. You don't know what factors went into their pricing decision. Instead, develop a pricing strategy based on your own research, costs, and goals.

The Margin Issue

The price you set for your product (per unit) or service (per hour, per diem, or project cost), less the cost of goods sold determines the *gross margin* of that product or service. Refer back to Chapter 12 for information on determining profitability of products or services sold to customers.

DEFINITION

Gross margin is the amount of money you make (your profit) for each product you sell or service you provide your customers. For example, if your product sells for $50 per unit and the cost of goods sold is $10, your profit is $40, or 80 percent margin.

If the products you offer are of higher quality than your competitors', you may be able to command a higher price. Benchmarking information you gather can be of great value in determining how to price your products and services against your competition, and it can be very easy to gather. For example, if you operate a deli, you can certainly test your competition's quality of product by going to their deli and buying yourself lunch!

Setting the Right Price

You don't want to charge too little or too much for your services and products. Your goal is to find that happy medium. In addition to looking at what your competitors charge for similar products and services, consider the following when determining your price:

- Discounts offered to customers
- Profitability needs for your business
- Introductory pricing for new customers or for release of new products or services
- Your product's stage in its life cycle
- The pricing competition you face
- Your value proposition (a luxury product, for instance, is expected to carry a higher price tag)

All of these issues will have an effect on your pricing. For example, you don't want to set your "standard" price too low if you know you frequently offer customers discounts of 10 to 15 percent. Similarly, for products that are in a later life cycle and are moving toward becoming a commodity, you will not be able to set as high a price as a product or product line that is newer to the market.

BEST PRACTICE

Ask the experts at SCORE (www.score.org) to evaluate your pricing strategy. They will evaluate the price of products and services at no cost to you!

Let's assume that you sell Microsoft certified training programs, specifically Microsoft Office, Windows Server, and similar programs. However, many of these programs are commodities and are sold by so many training companies that you are forced to keep your prices low just to remain in the marketplace. This factor is affecting your business's ability to turn a profit. Therefore, you decide that to keep your business successful and increase your profits, you need to expand your offerings to products that are not as popular but still make sense for your business, in that your marketing and sales processes do not have to change significantly.

Based on your research, you realize that some Microsoft products such as Sharepoint, Project Server, and similar enterprise-level products are increasing in demand; however, very few people are qualified to train and consult in these products. By offering these products, you are able to command a higher price, differentiate yourself from the competition, move yourself out of the commodity market, and begin to offer advanced services that your competitors do not yet have. You are staying a step ahead of the competition!

Running a Focus Group

Consider holding a focus group session to determine how to price new products and services. Hire an expert to facilitate the session. Rather than focusing exclusively on your product, have the focus be on the type of product or service you offer. The focus group facilitator provides attendees with a detailed description of the product or service and asks the group a variety of questions to tease out what price range they would be willing to pay for that product or service under a variety of conditions.

The Least You Need to Know

- Use market research to make better decisions about your products and services.
- Gather data from customers, vendors, suppliers, and resellers to help determine what kind of new products or services you should develop.
- Consider what is important to your customers. If the products and services you offer aren't of value to them, they won't purchase from you no matter how low your price.
- Develop a pricing strategy for your products and services and evaluate your prices on an annual basis.

The Perfect Sales Team

In This Chapter

- Hiring the right salesperson
- Developing and investing in your sales process
- Sales compensation considerations
- Managing sales meetings

A strong sales channel is critical to any small business's success. Developing and sustaining this channel over time remains one of the most difficult challenges for any small business.

In this chapter, we move beyond the best practices necessary to launch a start-up's sales operation and delve into the best practices that will support your organization's sales efforts over time.

The Right Sales Hire

Choosing the right person for a sales job takes time and patience. One essential step to take before interviewing anyone is to develop a written job description for the positions you want to hire. The job description should include the specific behaviors and skills that you want a salesperson working for your business to have.

It is true that these needs will change over time and that you will need to refine and update job descriptions occasionally as your organization grows, but that is no excuse not to create the document in the first place!

Prior to developing a written job description, consider the most important questions—for instance, at this stage of your organization's development, do you need *hunters*, *farmers*, or a combination of the two? Do you have time to invest in training and guiding less-experienced salespeople, or do you need individuals who can produce significant revenue right from the start? Do you only want salespeople who have sold in your industry before, or will individuals who have worked in other industries who have strong sales backgrounds work?

DEFINITION

A **hunter** is someone who goes out looking for new business. Hunters frequently bring in brand new accounts for a business. A **farmer,** on the other hand, is someone who excels at maintaining existing accounts. Farmers are great at nurturing current business and do not focus on new account development.

Make sure your job descriptions specifically reference the responsibilities required to succeed in a particular sales role. Pay particularly close attention to the hunter/farmer issue. Is the salesperson going to be responsible for seeking out and developing new customers (hunter model) or nurturing income from within an existing account (farmer model)? Don't expect one salesperson to fulfill both roles at a level of excellence!

Other key responsibilities of salespeople include …

- Preparing weekly sales reports.
- Developing sales proposals and contracts.
- Generating customer referrals.
- Generating and qualifying leads for future business.
- Responding to phone or web inquiries from customers.

In addition, your job description should specify that salespeople should help to set up events for current and new customers. We're talking about the kinds of meetings that will help management grow the business: breakfast meetings, lunch-and-learn opportunities, product demonstrations for large groups, and so on. To make sure these events are successful for all concerned, salespeople must also be willing to share the information they have about customers with others in your organization (typically people in marketing and operations).

Your job description should encompass these responsibilities as well as others that are specific to your industry and your business. Complete the job description prior to interviewing candidates so you know exactly what to look for during the interview and the applicant knows exactly what is expected. This is an important hire for your company. You definitely want to get it right.

BUSINESS BUSTER

Unless you create up-to-date written job descriptions for your sales team, you will have a hard time recruiting and retaining the best salespeople for your business. This mistake will cost you time, aggravation, and lost revenue opportunities.

Traits of Great Sales Reps

Some job applicants are very, very good at selling. Specifically, they are good at selling *themselves*, which means they are good at interviewing. Selling well during the interview, however, does not necessarily mean selling well over time for your company. Your job is to use the interview process to identify a candidate who will shine not only during the interview but also over the long haul as a member of the team.

Start by identifying the basic skills and behaviors you want to see in a salesperson (including telemarketers) during an interview, whether that interview is held in person or virtually. The seven traits you will be looking for during the interview are summarized as follows:

The ideal candidate is a great listener. You need someone who is capable of carefully listening to the customer and understanding his or her needs. The last thing you want in a salesperson is someone who immediately assumes they know what is best for the customer and doesn't really listen.

The ideal candidate is a self-starter. You should not have to prod the salesperson constantly to perform key activities and make the daily numbers. You need someone who knows what the goals are and how to reach them—without you having to check in regularly to make sure everything's on track.

The ideal candidate is someone with a great attitude. The salesperson representing your business should have a superior attitude. He or she should be confident, optimistic, and purposeful. This individual does not let the word "no" get them down; they don't take adversity personally. He or she will be a social butterfly—someone who is outgoing, friendly, and a generally likable person who wants to be around others and whom others want to be around.

The ideal candidate has personal integrity. You want to hire an honest person with high values and personal ethics. The salesperson is, after all, the public face of your business.

The ideal candidate is a strong negotiator. Your salesperson must negotiate with prospects and customers regularly—on pricing, customization of products and services, timelines, and even when and whether the first discussion will take place.

The ideal candidate is someone with strong time-management skills. Especially when hiring salespeople who will be visiting clients in person, you must hire individuals who can manage themselves and their time in a way that does not inconvenience or disrespect prospective buyers. *Note:* The applicant's ability to show up on time for your interview(s) is a key indicator here!

The ideal candidate has strong follow-through. Here again, you can use the interview process itself as a skill barometer. Immediately after the face-to-face meeting, does the applicant attempt to clarify what is happening next and when it is happening? Does he or she follow up by phone to determine what is necessary to close the deal and get the job? These are skills that will definitely come into play during the sales cycle. You should see evidence of them during the interview.

BEST PRACTICE

Develop a list of the skills, traits, and behaviors your salespeople must have to be successful in your company, and hire individuals who demonstrate they have those skills, traits, and behaviors.

If your applicant is missing one or more of the seven critical selling traits—great listener, self-starter, attitude, integrity, negotiating skills, time management, and follow-through—it really doesn't matter how well the person handles your questions during the interview. The applicant in question is not likely to be happy or successful as a salesperson.

Traits of Great Telemarketers

If you are hiring salespeople who will be answering phone calls from clients and responding to web inquiries only, you will want to look for some additional skills. These are summarized as follows:

The ideal candidate should have a great personality you can hear in his or her voice. In many cases, these salespeople will never see a customer face to face; they will need to make a great impression immediately over the telephone.

The ideal candidate should have a strong team player attitude. People with these jobs will need to be able to work closely and harmoniously with your other salespeople and with people in other areas like operations and customer service. Additionally, these salespeople should be comfortable reaching out to people in product development, marketing, and senior management to share what they are hearing from customers.

PRACTICE MAKES PERFECT

Do not make an open-ended hire of any salesperson. Make the offer of employment contingent upon the salesperson hitting some modest but numerically measurable goal related to revenue generation over the course of a 90-day probationary period. Fire salespeople who don't meet the terms of their probationary period.

Behavioral Interviewing

Best practices for interviewing sales applicants include the use of behavioral interviewing techniques. These will help you to understand how the people you will hire will be likely to interact with your customers and other employees within the company. Chapter 14 gave you some general information on behavioral interviewing techniques; this chapter goes into a little more depth. Consider asking the following behavioral questions during your interviews:

- Describe a situation in which you were able to win business away from a competitor. (Here, you're looking for strategies that demonstrate the ability to add value where competitors don't.)

- Tell me about a time when a customer felt that you did not meet his needs and was angry about the situation. (Here, you're testing both the salesperson's poise and her ability to identify and solve problems.)

- Tell me about a time when you were not going to make your quota. What did you do to remedy the situation? (With this question, you're testing the salesperson's ability to do what it takes to make up lost ground by identifying new selling opportunities.)

- Describe a situation where you had to work really hard on selling a customer on a particular product or service. What were the issues and how did you overcome them? (Here, you're measuring the salesperson's tenacity, poise, and persistence.)

Another classic behavioral query is the "sell me this" question. Hand the candidate whatever is nearby on your desk—book, calendar, tape dispenser, pens, stapler, whatever—and then simply ask him to sell it to you. The best salespeople will ask you questions before they talk about the product they are selling, then they will tell you about the product and how it could meet your needs. You don't want to hire someone who starts out by telling you how great the product is! The salesperson's goal should be to understand you, your business, and the problems you need to solve. In this miniature role-play, the salesperson should work with you on how best to solve the problems you face.

With each of these questions, you will want to follow up with additional queries that will help you understand what the candidate did in the situation, how they reacted to it and managed it, and the behaviors they displayed.

Sales Compensation Basics

Finding the right compensation program for your sales team can be a tricky task. You need to find a balance between base pay and commissions and bonuses. Your ability to identify and maintain that balance can make all the difference in securing and retaining the best salespeople.

The Options

There are a variety of combinations to choose from:

- 100 percent salary, no commission, but with bonuses

- 100 percent commission and bonuses, but no salary

- Any combination of salary and commission

There are benefits and disadvantages to each option. For example, if you pay a salesperson only commission with no base salary, you will definitely be getting hunters; these tend to be very proactive salespeople who are eager to take the initiative.

They are likely to close the sale and move on to the next prospect. If you offer a larger portion of compensation as base salary, you may find individuals who are not as aggressive in sales (because they have a high salary to begin with) and are not as motivated to earn commission. These salespeople may, however, be better at maintaining ongoing day-to-day relationships with customers than the hunters.

As a best practice—and to save yourself a lot of headaches later—you will want to develop your compensation system before you hire any salespeople. This way the salespeople you hire know what the salary and commission mix is before they take the job.

The Draw

For new salespeople who need to get up to speed in the product or service being sold, many companies provide *draws*. If you decide to provide draws to new salespeople, you'll need to determine the draw amount, decide on what period of time it will be paid out, and decide whether it is a recoverable or nonrecoverable draw.

DEFINITION

Draws are money provided to salespeople against future commissions. They provide new salespeople a way to earn money while they are getting started in a new selling role. Draws may be recoverable (which means they are paid back) or nonrecoverable (which means the salesperson keeps the money no matter what).

Let's look at an example. You have hired a new salesperson who will likely take six months to get up to speed on your product given her past experience. You have provided her a draw of $5,000 to be paid over a period of six months. The draw will be considered nonrecoverable, meaning that even if the salesperson ends up resigning or being fired after earning only $1,000 in commissions, your company does not get $4,000 back.

Incentives

You may choose to incorporate some form of incentives as part of your compensation package, either regularly or on an occasional basis. These incentives could include prizes such as gift certificates, cash bonuses, or other perks.

One common approach is to use incentives as part of a team contest to drive the sale of a specific product or service. For the salesperson who wins the contest, you provide an extra reward (such as a luxury cruise).

Incentives can be tricky to get right. For example, you wouldn't want to use incentives simply to get a salesperson to generate activity (get leads); instead, you want them to do something with those leads—either move to the next step in the sales process (possibly get in for a meeting with key decision makers) or to close the deal. You don't want to make incentives too easy to achieve, such as getting more business from a current customer that regularly provides new business for your company without effort. Rather, you might provide an incentive to a salesperson who goes out and finds new accounts for the business.

As a best practice, do a bit of research into common incentives for salespeople in your industry and also for salespeople outside of your industry. By looking at what has and hasn't worked for other businesses, you can find creative ways to encourage your salespeople to make their numbers and bring in revenue.

Getting It Right

The right combination of salary, commission, and incentives will be determined by many factors, including what the salesperson is selling, who the customers are, whether the person is expected to contribute as a hunter or a farmer, the size of the average deal, the number of deals the average salesperson closes or is expected to close over the course of a year, and how long it takes to close a deal with customers.

Yes, that's a lot to take into account. As a best practice, consider following this core principle: the more demonstrated experience a salesperson has in successfully selling a given product or service, the higher the percentage of his or her income should come from commissions. Some senior salespeople may even be comfortable with a commission-only approach, but others with less experience may be intimidated by this idea.

Another best practice—and perhaps the most important of them all in this complex area of sales team compensation—is to be ready to change your approach if you notice that it isn't working. The whole idea behind your compensation plan is to give people an incentive to sell. If two months go by and the compensation plan you have selected is serving as a distraction and a magnet for complaints, it's in everyone's best interest for management to take a step back and reassess.

BEST PRACTICE

Review your sales compensation plan on an annual basis to ensure it is still working well and serving its purpose of driving revenue and profitability for the business.

Let's look at an example. You have noticed that your current sales team compensation, which is 40 percent salary and 60 percent commission and incentives to drive the sale of new products, seems to be affecting customer service. Part of what you want your salespeople to do is to ensure that they provide high-quality support to customers by checking in with them regularly and following up on their use of products sold. However, since the majority of their income comes from commissions, the salespeople are more focused on closing a deal and moving on to the next customer and the next deal. Your solution is to revise the compensation structure to include more salary and less commission (you change it to 50/50) and offer incentive plans focused on servicing the customer *after* the deal has been closed.

Invest in Your Sales Process

Your business's sales process is simply the workflow you follow when it comes to generating and closing sales. You may think you don't have a sales process yet, but if you've closed even one customer, you do. Some process must exist that salespeople use to get leads, follow up on them, and close the deal. You just may not have documented that process!

The following figure shows an example of a documented sales process for selling training classes.

The process begins with the marketing department generating leads through various marketing activities such as e-mail blasts, purchasing lists of potential customers, and website inquiries. Those leads are passed to the sales reps, who qualify the lead, determine the opportunity, do discovery, and submit a proposal for the work. If the proposal is accepted—the customer will select your business to deliver the training class for his employees—the delivery team steps in to do the training.

There are many benefits to having a defined sales process. You can see where sales are being held up in the process and can make adjustments, like additional training on products and services for salespeople or improved marketing messaging to potential customers. Additionally, you can see the value of the leads being generated from a variety of marketing campaigns and make adjustments for effectiveness. By having a sales process in place, you will know how long it should take for a lead to be worked by your salespeople until the deal closes; you can therefore more accurately predict how many leads are needed and how much lead time is required in order to generate revenue for the business. This information has important cash flow implications.

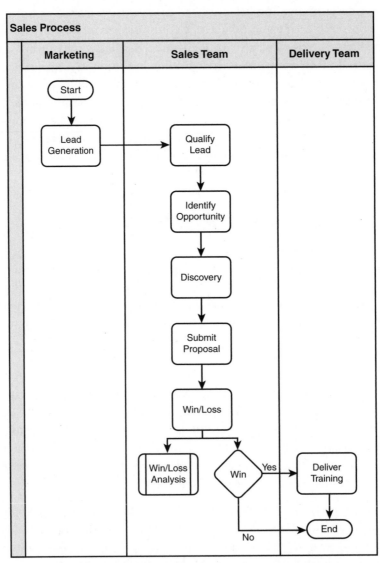

A sales process for a company that sells seats in public training classes.

Your sales process may vary from product to product and for each of the services you provide. Therefore, be ready to define multiple processes.

As your business grows and your customer base increases, some things will change; some of those changes may affect how you get leads into the process and how your customer buys from you. All of these changes affect your sales process. As a best practice, be sure to review your sales process on an annual basis to make any small adjustments necessary to ensure that your salespeople can do their job and meet their goals.

BUSINESS BUSTER

Failure to document and update your sales process will reduce your organization's ability to generate sales effectively and efficiently and reduce your company's revenue potential.

Training your salespeople in the relevant sales processes is an essential foundation of their success—and, ultimately, your organization's success.

Managing a One-Man Band

Assuming that you've made the transition from the entrepreneur-as-lead-salesperson model that we discussed in Chapter 8, you will find this the simplest of the sales management scenarios. No intradepartment competition exists in the one-person-band setting, and you can be solely focused as a manager on supporting that one individual.

Of course, it is important to train your salesperson in your products and services—the features, benefits, and value to the customer of purchasing from your business. Additionally, you will need to provide the salesperson with collateral—marketing brochures, flyers, etc.—about your products and services that they can, in turn, share with potential customers.

Let's say that your goal is to bring in $500,000 in total sales revenue in a year. Let's assume, too, that, your salesperson buys into this goal. You will need to break that figure down for the salesperson. Specifically, you'll need to determine how much of that revenue you expect the salesperson to bring in over the course of the year, and also what the corresponding weekly, monthly, or quarterly targets are. (The decision on how much revenue needs to be brought in each week, month, or quarter will depend on your sales cycle and the degree to which your organization's sales are likely to be seasonal.)

For example, let's assume you own a bicycle shop that sells high-quality parts to other bicycle shops, and that you are based in the Northeast. It is highly likely that the majority of your sales to the other shops are in the warmer summer months. Therefore, you will have lower sales in the winter months. After talking about goals with your salesperson, the two of you may decide to distribute your salesperson's quota as follows, assuming a calendar-based fiscal year:

Salesperson's Quota for the Year

Quarter	Quota
January–March	$50,000
April–June	$200,000
July–September	$200,000
October–December	$50,000

As can be seen in the preceding table, the salesperson's quota is higher during those months when more people are using their bicycles most, and shops are buying the most parts to meet their customers' needs.

BEST PRACTICE

To ensure your salesperson's success, provide regular coaching on her interactions with customers. Remember that every salesperson, no matter how experienced, needs your support to be effective.

Managing the Smaller Sales Team

As you move from one salesperson to two or more, the competition naturally heats up! As we discussed earlier, the best salespeople are go-getters. Their natural inclination should be to take the initiative and start working their territories, not to sit in your office and get coaching advice from you.

A brief (30- to 60-minute) weekly meeting with each salesperson is a good face-time target (or voice-to-voice target if your salesperson spends most of his or her time on the road); so is periodic professional development in the form of training or seminars. We particularly recommend the Sandler Selling System for sales teams of all sizes. You can learn more about the Sandler company's training and reinforcement regimen by visiting www.sandler.com or by checking out David Mattson's books *The Sandler Rules* and *Five Minutes with VITO* (co-authored with Anthony Parinello).

For businesses that employ salespeople from various areas who are unlikely to ever be in the office, consider weekly conference calls along with virtual training sessions to provide professional development opportunities.

Weekly one-on-one meetings with salespeople should be focused on the following issues:

- The salesperson's pipeline

- Progress toward meeting quota

- Problems sales personnel are encountering closing business

- What's working … and what tactics, tools, and resources will help the salesperson to do a better job

This is the time to really get to know your salespeople and understand what motivates them personally to get the job done.

Assigning Accounts

You will, of course, eventually need to work out a system for assigning customer accounts to your sales team. There are a variety of ways to do this:

- Vertical (finance, manufacturing, retail, etc.)

- Geographic (northeast, south, etc.)

- Named accounts (targeted, named companies)

You need to figure out what works best for your business and your specific customer base. Obviously, if you only sell your widget to manufacturing companies, it doesn't make sense to assign accounts vertically; you might instead choose geographic territories or assign named accounts for your salespeople.

Each salesperson on your sales team should have personal quotas; each quota should be the result of a private coaching discussion in which the salesperson helps to set the goal. More junior people (who just started with your company or are still learning the ropes about a given product or service) should have a less aggressive target than someone who has been selling the same line with great success for a number of years.

Some businesses find team quotas, along with individual quotas, to be effective in driving business. If you adopt this system, your salespeople should earn rewards for hitting the team quota, for hitting the individual quota, and perhaps a special bonus of some kind for hitting both.

Part of managing your sales team involves going out on sales calls with them. As a best practice, take a little time each week to spend a few hours out of the office with your salespeople visiting customers. This gives you the opportunity to see your salesperson in action. This also provides your salesperson with a learning opportunity. After the customer meeting, spend time debriefing on the following issues:

- What went well in the meeting?
- What improvements could be made?
- What should the follow-up be?

Continuous learning is important for any role and certainly is no exception for a sales role. There will always be difficult customers who need to be managed, new products and services to sell, and changes in competition that require a change in how you do business. For the members of a sales team to be effective you must continuously invest in their development … and focus relentlessly on opportunity.

Managing the Larger Sales Team

The larger the sales team you manage, the more work you have ahead of you. For larger sales teams, you will probably find it worthwhile to hire a sales manager to oversee the team and direct their actions on a day-to-day basis.

BUSINESS BUSTER

Being the top salesperson doesn't necessarily qualify someone as an effective sales manager. You are better off finding someone with a demonstrated record of success in sales management—a field that requires empathy, analytic ability, and administrative skills—than you are promoting your top salesperson to a supervisory position.

A common problem with larger sales teams is that training sometimes falls through the cracks. Even with larger sales teams, ongoing training and professional development must remain a priority. In addition to checking out the excellent Sandler Selling

System program, we recommend the following best practices for ensuring successful training of your sales team:

- Schedule regular internal training sessions (perhaps once a month) with the entire sales team, and include special sessions such as on time management, negotiating, and effective listening skills.

- Include other groups—such as product development (if new products are being released) or marketing (regarding a new marketing plan)—in your sales meeting to foster information sharing and relationship building.

- Practice role-playing scenarios so salespeople can try out new techniques or practice selling new products and services to their colleagues.

- Ask individual salespeople to share their own best practices for dealing with difficult customers, closing business with a new customer, or winning business from a competitor.

The Least You Need to Know

- Only hire salespeople who have the skills and behaviors necessary to succeed on the job.
- Create a compensation plan that makes sense for your organization and evaluate it on a regular basis.
- Document your sales processes and make adjustments as necessary as your business changes.
- Invest in ongoing training and professional development for your sales team.
- Use incentives wisely to drive revenue and profitability for the business.

Customer-Driven Marketing

In This Chapter

- Embracing Marketing 2.0 and the voice of the customer revolution
- Developing strong relationships with your customers
- Marketing best practices in a socially wired world
- Finding the right tools to get the word out about your products and services

For most of the twentieth century, the discipline of marketing was essentially a one-way push conduit that generated appeals to targeted groups of prospective buyers and then called on people to take action, usually by making a purchase that didn't involve a salesperson. Typically, there was no meaningful pre-sale communication between an individual buyer and the selling organization. Companies created products, services, and offerings, and then simply pushed various one-way media appeals—print advertisements, broadcast advertisements, direct mail appeals—that were designed to persuade people to buy.

In recent years, however, the game has changed. Advances in communications technology have allowed some marketers to augment these traditional appeals in a powerful way or even replace them altogether. How? By creating and supporting an ever-expanding ocean of conversations with prospective and existing customers.

These two-way discussions—whose speed, scope, and market influence are well beyond what could have been conceived in, say, the 1950s—represent nothing less than a marketing revolution. Some people have come up with a catchy name for this revolution, Marketing 2.0, but it is really a natural extension of what marketing guru Ernan Roman years ago dubbed the "voice-of-the-customer" movement. Roman, whose central teaching principle is "listen to your customer," is the founder of Ernan

Roman Direct Marketing (www.erdm.com) as well as the author of many influential books and articles, most recently *Voice-of-the-Customer Marketing*.

Whatever we choose to call the powerful two-way dynamic that has now emerged as the dominant expectation between sellers and consumers, we are ourselves part of it … as consumers. Our familiarity may come from our own experiences with sellers like Zappos and Amazon, who have an uncanny way of predicting what we will be interested in next, or from our typed responses to a chic local restaurant that posts Facebook photos of its mouth-watering menu selections. We simply expect more from businesses than consumers of yesteryear did: more choices, more specialization, and more interaction from our favored sellers. Someone trying to sell us shoes, books, Chicken Marsala, or anything else had better be prepared to engage with us.

Forget about technology for a moment. The phenomenon known as Marketing 2.0 is really all about becoming a favored, first-tier, top-of-mind provider for consumers within our target market rather than a member of the second-tier, "everyone else" group of sellers. The sellers in that second group are not yet in dialogue with us. They have not yet engaged us.

The same principle applies to the person we hope to turn into a repeat customer. Joining that person's elite group of favored providers means creating opportunities for two-way conversations, listening carefully to what we hear, and adjusting course frequently. It means fusing marketing, public relations, and customer service into a single coordinated effort. This is something large companies often have a hard time with; fortunately, it is something that smaller companies are perfectly positioned to pull off.

In this chapter, we show you how to join the winning side of the ever-expanding marketing revolution and how to harness the force of that revolution to become one of the winners in your target market.

The Voice-of-the-Customer Movement

Having a voice-of-the-customer program simply means having a process in place for understanding who your customer is, what your customer's most important challenges are, and what your customer expects from a relationship with you. Today, companies of all sizes have adopted voice-of-the-customer principles into their marketing and customer service initiatives, and many of those companies—such as Apple and Zappos—have emerged as market leaders.

BEST PRACTICE

Some consumer data may be captured via surveys or focus groups, but the most meaningful insights arise from extended in-depth interviews with individual consumers. For more information and resources on setting up voice-of-the-customer programs, visit Ernan Roman's website: www.erdm.com.

An effective voice-of-the-customer program uses in-depth, voice-to-voice interviews to discover what kind of personalized communication is most relevant to customers, including what channel(s) they prefer and the volume and the frequency of communication that meets their needs.

Harnessing the Voice of the Customer

Businesses use voice-of-the-customer information for a variety of purposes, including …

- Learning why people buy from us (and why they don't).
- Fine-tuning the value proposition.
- Ensuring the products and services developed are the ones that meet the customers' needs and address their problems and concerns.
- Determining how to improve current products and services.
- Keeping in touch with the customer by providing the right communications at the right time via the right channels.
- Creating new products and services, or adapting existing products and services, to fit the customer's requirements.

One important component of voice-of-the-customer marketing programs extends well beyond the initial interview. Not only must you gather feedback from the customer, but you must also be willing to consider changing your organization's practices, and perhaps even its structure, based on that feedback. This may not always be easy, but it is usually in the customer's, and your company's, best interest.

Let's assume you sell hand-painted furnishings. Thanks to extended in-person interviews conducted with some of your best customers and prospects, you have recently received feedback from a number of customers that, while they love the look and construction of the furniture they purchase, the colors fade rather quickly and the wood stains easily when glasses are placed directly on the table. You also learn that your customers would prefer to have some kind of personal input about the designs of the furniture they buy from you. Based on this feedback, you will not only want to change the materials and processes that you use to paint your furniture, you will also want to find some way to incorporate your customers' custom needs into the design process.

Tracking What Customers Are Saying Online

Interviews with customers are not the only way to uncover the voice of the customer. There are lots of free online tracking tools that can help you learn what is being said about your business, your products, and your services. Use any of the following to learn what prospects, customers, and others are saying about you:

- Google Alerts (www.google.com/alerts) enables you to track where your business name, your own name, or a product name appears online.

- Collecta (www.collecta.com) and Social Mention (www.socialmention.com) enable you to search for relevant terms related to your company, product, or service to see where they are being talked about online.

- Twitter Search (http://search.twitter.com) enables you to enter a search term, such as a product or company name, and see all conversations associated with that term.

Addressing Customer Comments

In our connected world, heeding the voice of the customer means responding quickly and effectively to suggestions, to compliments, and, yes, to the occasional complaint. Addressing a complaint is a marketing opportunity—make sure you make the most of it.

Let's say you receive a complaint via e-mail. Send an e-mail in reply immediately, even if it's only to report that you're aware of the problem and are looking into it.

An essential best practice here would be to follow these steps to address customer comments that come your way either because of a message to your organization or because of something you overhear online:

1. As soon as you receive feedback from a customer from any source, acknowledge the issue and provide a date when you will respond after you have looked into the matter. If possible, use the same communication medium the

customer used to reach out to you. (Of course, if the customer asks you to connect via a different medium, such as a personal phone number, you should respect that request.)

2. Provide the customer, by or before the date you promised, with your analysis of the situation based on your research and what you are doing to address the situation.

3. Make good on your promise. Once you have handled the situation, follow up with the customer and thank him for his feedback.

Make Customer Relationships a Strategic Advantage

Building your marketing initiatives, and indeed your entire organization, around the voice of the customer, requires that you look constantly for opportunities to interact with your customers. These interactions are not only short-term marketing opportunities, they can also help you generate good ideas about new marketing initiatives.

Best practices that will help you turn your relationships with customers into a strategic advantage include the following:

Have a customer council. This is very likely the best marketing consulting advice your company will ever receive … and it's absolutely free (see Chapter 17)!

Conduct regular customer satisfaction and other surveys via telephone, mail, or e-mail. These surveys, which you can conduct through sites like www.surveymonkey. com, are great because they give you something to measure. That's certainly important, but keep in mind that surveys are no replacement for a one-on-one conversation with your customer.

Hold as many informal, unscheduled discussions with customers as you can. This kind of unstructured interaction with customers is essential. If you have a storefront operation, you will want to chat with customers as they come into the store.

Express gratitude. With each purchase a customer makes, send a thank-you message along with the order that shows how much you appreciate the decision to make a purchase from your company.

These seemingly common sense best practices actually reflect an uncommon, or at least rarely implemented, piece of business wisdom: the better your relationships with your customers, the sounder your business's strategic position will be.

Building and Rewarding Customer Loyalty

There is no shortage of ways to reward customers for their loyalty to your business, but some of them do a better job of heeding the voice of the customer than others. Before you try to establish any rewards program, ask your customers what they think of it.

Panera Bread, for example, offers a card that earns points toward free food and drinks. CVS has a card that provides coupons and discounts for purchases at CVS. Both of these popular programs were tested in various ways, and both resonated positively with existing customers. By providing these incentives to customers, both businesses are now encouraging their customers to spend more money and more time in their business to earn discounts.

PRACTICE MAKES PERFECT

When talking to your customers, ask them if they would be interested in an awards program and, if they are, what that awards program should look like. Are your customers interested in discounts, points toward free products, cash back, or some other incentive that you haven't even considered? What kind of value will motivate them to buy more of your products and services?

Identifying Your Ideal Customer

To market effectively, you must have some idea of who your current ideal customer is so you can target more customers that fit that profile. In-depth discussions with your own prospects and customers will go a long way toward giving you the insights you need to figure out not only who your best customer is, but why that customer buys from you in the first place.

Identifying your best customer means being clear about the external identifiers. Is this someone who purchases a certain amount from your business each year? Or someone who refers you to others? Is this a business of a certain size and revenue? Let's look at an example. Let's assume that you sell meals to go. Your ideal customer may be a dual-income family with limited time to cook healthy meals and who have the disposable income to purchase ready-made meals from your business. (In-depth discussions with multiple customers may help you get even more clarity on what kinds of families you should be targeting.)

Identifying your best customer means understanding the motivations that drive both initial and repeat purchases. Talk to a customer who fits the external criteria you've identified thus far; ask questions that spotlight buying motivators. What inspired this person's first purchase from you? How was the decision to purchase finalized? What factors made it possible for this person to decide to do business with you a second time? An important note: the willingness to do business with your company more than once is almost certainly a trait of your best customer. Unless your business model explicitly precludes repeat purchases—and hardly any do—you should make sure this is the kind of customer you're interviewing. Find out what kinds of experiences support the decision to do business with your company more than once.

Developing Your Brand

Developing a brand for your business sets you apart from the competition. For example, United Parcel Service (UPS) uses the slogan, "What can brown do for you?" You hear that phrase, you immediately think of UPS. In fact, the acronym *UPS* is part of their brand, as are the brown uniforms the drivers wear and the brown trucks they drive. Of course, you should get voice-of-the-customer feedback about your brand and the messages it conveys to present and future customers.

Given the increasing competition in a global marketplace, you need a brand to distinguish your business from your competitors. But brands are not established overnight. You need to work on building your brand—it takes time, consistency, and careful planning.

Defining Your Brand

Defining and building the right brand is an art, not a science, but it is an art you can perfect with the help of your customers. By identifying what is most important to your very best customers through voice-of-the-customer interviews, you can evaluate (or perhaps re-evaluate) a strategically vital question: whether your brand is bringing you closer to, or taking you further away from, those kinds of customers.

Follow these best practices in developing a brand for your business:

- Keeps things visually and textually simple. Think of McDonald's golden arches, Coca-Cola's "dynamic ribbon" logo, and Capital One's "What's in your wallet?"

- Use your value proposition and mission statement to help in developing your brand.

- Test, test, test your ideas for branding in extended voice-of-the-customer interviews.

- Highlight the features and benefits of your products and services that voice-of-the-customer feedback identifies as the most important.

Using Your Brand

Once you have established a brand for your business, use it! Include it on your letterhead, in all of your marketing pieces, in presentations, in surveys you send, in press releases, on packaging for your product, on your website—everywhere. You want customers to see the brand and start to associate your business with the brand. Your goal is to ensure consistency in the use of your brand. If you have resellers, provide them with parameters for using the brand.

Inbound and Outbound Marketing

For your business to reach its full potential, you will probably need to do both *inbound marketing* and *outbound marketing*.

DEFINITION

Inbound marketing is when potential customers find you rather than you going out to find them. An example of inbound marketing is when people search on Google and find relevant information on your website through a natural search rather than a paid ad. **Outbound marketing** is the process of actively pushing out information about your products and services to potential customers. An example of outbound marketing is an e-mail blast to a list of potential customers.

In the not-too-distant past, businesses marketed mainly by sending messages through outbound channels—mailing catalogs to customers, sending e-mails about products and services, setting up booths at trade shows, and taking out advertisements in newspapers and magazines. While this type of marketing is still important, inbound marketing is now playing an increasingly essential role for marketers.

Effective inbound marketing channels include social media outlets such as LinkedIn, Facebook, Twitter, YouTube, and blogging. By participating in these social media outlets, you effectively accumulate a fan base, or a followership, that essentially becomes a captive audience that is interested in your discussions and therefore in interacting with you and your business. The following sections take a look at some of the media that, as of this writing, are helping small businesses support effective inbound marketing initiatives and create quality, long-term engagement with customers.

Search Engine Optimization

Search engine optimization (SEO) is the process and strategy of setting up your business website so that it ranks higher than other similar websites on *natural searches* on search engines.

An SEO methodology comprises:

- Defining keywords that are relevant to the products and services your business provides

- Incorporating those keywords within text appearing throughout the website

- Increasing *back links* to help your website rank higher in the search engine's results

DEFINITION

Natural searches occur when a person searches a specific term (such as "creating a business plan") on a search engine and the results that appear are due to the relevancy to the term being searched rather than a paid ad. **Back links** are hyperlinks that exist on websites other than your own that link back to your site or product pages.

We know one consultant who implemented a successful SEO methodology when she established her website. Thanks to the SEO methodology, the site became very popular quite quickly. After 18 months, the site was getting more than 3,500 hits monthly from organic search alone, which currently accounts for 50 percent of traffic to the site.

Pay-Per-Click Keywords

In addition to seeing organic search results when you search a term on Google, you can also see *sponsored links*.

DEFINITION

Sponsored links are advertising, also called pay-per-click keywords. Businesses pay search engines to advertise based on the keyword searched. The business has control over frequency, time of day, geographic location, and amount to be spent in a period of time for those ads.

With sponsored links, businesses pay for visitors to click through to their website based on a specific keyword or search term. The more popular the search term, the more costly it is for the business when an individual searching clicks through to the website.

As a best practice, choose your pay-per-click keywords carefully. We recommend you concentrate more on developing your SEO to rank higher in organic search rather than spending a lot on sponsored links.

Expanding Your Reach

Think of social media as long-term relationship building—not just with customers, but with anyone, anywhere in the world, who could possibly have an impact, either positive or negative, on your business. You should not expect immediate revenue to come from your social media efforts; rather, social media should be a part of your overall public relations plan.

Whether you like it or not, the quality of your marketing efforts is now all about the quality of discussions managed largely via social media channels.

Using Facebook, Twitter, and LinkedIn

Facebook (www.facebook.com), Twitter (www.twitter.com), and LinkedIn (www. linkedin.com) are the three most popular social media channels for businesses of all sizes. Regardless of whether you are a sole proprietor or have hundreds of employees, social media tools such as these enable you to reach out and connect easily with individuals across the street or around the globe. Through social media, prospects, customers, vendors, members of the media, and others can develop a personal relationship with your company.

Let's look at an example. In 2008, no one outside of a core group of companies had ever heard of Arment Dietrich (www.armentdietrich.com), a digital communication firm in Chicago. Today their CEO, Gini Dietrich, is listed among the top 10 communication experts—all because of Twitter. Spin Sucks, the company's blog, was launched in 2006 with no real purpose other than understanding blogging so they could recommend it as a tool to their clients. But in 2008, needing to try something new to drive business, they began to use Spin Sucks as a marketing tool, with Dietrich as the main author.

Dietrich began using Twitter to extend the blog's reach. She followed other PR and marketing professionals. She engaged in conversation with marketing and advertising professionals. She began to build an 80/20 content strategy that allowed her to showcase her thinking by tweeting what others had written 80 percent of the time and to drive traffic back to Spin Sucks 20 percent of the time. Dietrich used Twitter to help build traffic, awareness, and credibility. Spin Sucks now rivals (or exceeds) the traffic of its largest competitors and is in the top five engaged communities in the PR and marketing industries. By October of 2010, Spin Sucks had more than 22,000 visitors per month, with its primary traffic source coming from Twitter.

Other Social Media Resources

There are a variety of other social networking resources available. Don't try to get involved in everything that exists out there—you simply don't have the time and will not find value in it.

PRACTICE MAKES PERFECT

Two of the other popular social media resources include Ning (www.ning.com) and Squidoo (www.squidoo.com). Ning is an online platform that enables individuals to create their own social network. Think of it as a community page for people who share a common interest. Unlike LinkedIn, which is based on profiles of individuals, Squidoo is based on an individual's expertise in various subjects. Squidoo enables users to create lenses online around a particular subject of expertise. Lenses, by the way, are just another word, in Squidoo-speak, for a web page.

Social media channels provide a variety of benefits to help companies increase awareness around their brand and, eventually, lead to an increase in the number of customers buying their products and services. Your interaction in all of these arenas provides word-of-mouth marketing for your business and its products and services.

Setting Up Social Media Campaigns

Four best practices can support an effective social media campaign through websites like Facebook, Twitter, YouTube, and LinkedIn. They are as follows:

Engage person to person. Avoid over-relying on corporate accounts. By engaging with people at the individual level and communicating responsibly as a representative of your company, you allow others to learn about you as an individual and about your organization. Remember, people purchase from other people. By showing your personal side, customers begin to develop trust in you, and that trust will lead to interest in your company and its products and services.

Promote yourself and your business as a thought leader. By publishing original articles and other timely, relevant content of interest to your readers, you become known as a thought leader in your industry. People will begin to come to you as the source for information on the latest technologies and industry best practices.

Share interesting information. By sharing information relative to what your company does, such as tips for managing projects from a project management consulting company or tips for hiring and retaining the best employees from a recruiting firm, you provide your customers with useful information that helps them do their job better. This information may or may not connect directly to your products or services. Through these efforts you'll find that customers come to you because they have come to know you.

Interact with current and potential customers on a regular basis. Once a month won't cut it. Interact with others daily via social media. This kind of interaction doesn't have to involve a huge time investment. It could be as simple as a general conversation about a business book you are reading or a link to an interesting blog post. For example, a company that provides project management training may use social media to share information about increases in the number of individuals getting certified as project managers or the number and variety of organizations looking to hire project managers.

Direct Mail and Print Advertising

Direct mail and print advertising are used less frequently than in the past due to the high cost of such marketing and the prevalence of electronic marketing (such as direct e-mail, e-newsletters, pay-per-click campaigns, and SEO). It is still an important marketing tool, however, and one that many small businesses continue to use successfully.

> **BUSINESS BUSTER**
>
> Undifferentiated, untargeted marketing messages such as repetitive e-mail blasts or postcards may serve to disengage customers from your business. Today, we receive so much irrelevant e-mail and "junk mail" from a variety of advertisers that eventually we just ignore the messages.

The most important best practice to bear in mind here has to do with targeting. Any direct mail marketing you do must be targeted to those who want to hear your message—those individuals who opt in by asking to receive information from your business. The quality of the opt-in information you receive from people who join your list is directly proportional to the perceived value of the information, resources, and assistance you are offering them.

Advertising in newspapers, magazines, and industry journals can be an expensive and risky endeavor. However, with the right target audience and the right location in print media, the impact can be powerful—just choose your timing and location wisely.

Public Relations

In the past, the only way to get press for your business was to provide a press release to a reporter (and hope that the reporter found it interesting enough to print and share with others) or hire a public relations firm to help you get access to reporters and news agencies. This is no longer the case. Today, there are many resources on the web for posting and sharing your company news without having to rely solely on a news agency or a public relations firm.

To be sure you reach the widest audience and draw attention to your business, post only newsworthy information in your press release. This might include information about forming a new partnership, securing a well-known customer, releasing an innovative product or new service, hiring staff in key positions, expanding the business, or introducing a customer case study on your website. A customer case study introduced in a press release tells other potential customers that you have had success with another customer in a powerful, memorable, and credible way. It can be used to drive visitors to your website to learn more about your business.

Public relations, however, is more than just press releases. It includes social media networking (think Facebook and Twitter), sharing ideas and knowledge on LinkedIn groups, blogging, speaking engagements, company videos, and the like. As a business owner, you need to regularly engage with others in order to ensure that when they are ready to buy you are foremost in their mind.

Can You Do PR Yourself?

Yes, you most certainly can! There are a variety of online resources you can use to post your news and engage both traditional and user-driven media; some are available at no charge, and some charge a minimal fee. Some of our favorite resources for press releases include www.prweb.com, www.prlog.org, and www.free-press-release.com.

Using an Outside PR Firm

Choosing a PR firm can be a real challenge for small businesses. The cost of using a PR firm can be prohibitive and requires extensive monitoring. It's important to keep in mind that you know your business better than the PR firm does; do not rely on them to know all about your business and who your customers are. And don't expect them to be experts about your products and services. Instead, rely on the PR firm to help you develop creative ideas to promote your business and build your brand. The value you get from a PR firm is all based on how much you put into the relationship with the firm.

> **PRACTICE MAKES PERFECT**
>
> Once you have selected a PR firm, the work doesn't end. You must track the results. How successful are they in winning your company more visibility? What do they do that makes your company stand out from your competitors? Schedule regular meetings with your point of contact at the PR firm to discuss progress on current projects. Ask for regular status reports on what has been done to promote your company. Be sure to update the PR firm regularly with any new products or services you release to your clients.

When selecting a PR firm to work with your company, keep in mind these important considerations:

- Choose a firm that understands and will work with you on your existing social media campaigns.

- Choose a firm that will help you get articles and white papers into publications for your industry.

- Ask for references from customers in industries similar to yours.

- Make sure you meet the people who you would work with on your campaigns.

Your Website Is Key

Quite frequently these days, you don't hear directly from a potential customer. Rather, they perform a search on a search engine and, when they come across your website, they gather information there. If they don't find what they need, they are gone. In most cases, they don't call you looking for that information if they can't find it on your website. In other words, you rarely get a second chance to capture that potential customer.

Given this, your website must meet the following criteria:

- Maintain and promote your brand image
- Attract and keep people on your site
- Help them find what they need quickly
- Be search-engine-friendly

Your website is likely your main lead generator for customers. If customers submit inquiries via a contact form, you must be very responsive. If your site is an e-commerce site, you must ensure that purchasing a product is integrated seamlessly into the site to enable the user to quickly make the purchase as well as to continue shopping if they so desire.

Making the Website Customer-Friendly

Ideally, your website should be designed in such a way that your prospective customer is so intrigued by the (constantly updated) content that he or she keeps returning to the site. Eventually, the visitor engages by making a comment, sending you an inquiry, or making a purchase.

Does every small business have to follow this model for creating a content-driven website? No. But more and more of them are doing so, and this is certainly the direction in which the Internet is taking not only our economy, but also the global economy!

Your website doesn't have to be perfect right out of the gate, but it does need to be effective, user-friendly, appealing, and search-engine-friendly.

Good websites include additional content above and beyond information on your products and services. For instance, your consulting firm's website may include case studies, templates, newsworthy articles, and white papers that potential customers can peruse on the site or download for their reference. This provides you credibility and helps develop your reputation as a thought leader.

PRACTICE MAKES PERFECT

Ensure that you update content on your website regularly. In addition, include a site map (a list of all the pages on your site) and update it each time you add new information; doing so makes it easier for search engines to index your site. Fresh content keeps your customers coming back and encourages search engines to "crawl" your site more frequently.

If you are running an e-commerce site, you might choose to add a review section for customers so they can post reviews and get other customer's thoughts on the products. The feedback you get from these reviews gives you yet another opportunity to elicit voice-of-the-customer feedback and to demonstrate your company's ability to address and resolve complaints quickly and professionally.

You may also consider having additional information, such as videos on how to use the product or customer testimonials. For example, Amazon.com very effectively uses customer reviews to promote products.

Tracking Your Website's Progress

There are a variety of tools you can use to track use of your website. One of the most popular is Google Analytics (www.google.com/analytics), which is available at no cost. Google Analytics enables you to track …

- Visitors to your website and the source of the referral.

- The behavior of the visitor, including what pages they visited and which path they took to get there.

- The length of stay on your site and their geo-location (country, state, city).

- What computer platform (e.g., Microsoft), browser type (e.g., Internet Explorer), and browser versions (e.g., Internet Explorer Version 8.0) they are using. This enables you to ensure that your site looks best for the visitors to it. If you find there is an increase in visitors using Mozilla Firefox to view your site, and you have never tested your site on that browser, you'll want to make sure it looks good to them.

BEST PRACTICE

Consider hiring a consultant who specializes in search engine optimization and search engine marketing. You want to be sure you are capturing the information necessary to track the progress of your website. Without this information, you really have no idea how effective your website is for your customers. Once analytical software is set up for your website, you should be able to manage it yourself or turn it over to an employee to manage. One potential resource to find consultants is SEO Consultants Directory (www.seoconsultants.com), which enables you to search for search engine optimization specialists.

By tracking who visits your website, you can determine what marketing campaigns are effective (for example, do people click through to your website when they receive an e-mail from your business?) and which pages on your site attract the most visitors. This enables you to continue to enhance your website based on the user's desires.

New Options for Marketing

Today you hear quite a bit about content marketing. Search engines are interested in the quality of content on your website. When you put out high-quality, relevant content, you rank higher in the search engines, which drives more customers to your site. Content marketing includes providing your website visitors with information they can use—case studies, research, white papers—in return for their contact information.

By offering content that people want to view, you entice them to provide you with personal contact information in exchange for viewing that content. There is nothing wrong with asking the visitor to input their personal information—such as name, company name, e-mail address, mailing address—in order to access that content. This helps you build your lead database and gain a better understanding of who is interested in your business and what in particular they are interested in. For example, you may choose to provide visitors with an executive summary of a white paper; if they are interested in downloading the entire white paper, you ask for their contact information. Remember, the greater the perceived value of the information you are offering, the more detailed information about the consumer you can expect to receive.

A particularly important best practice to follow here is to ask only for information that is obviously relevant to the offer you are extending to the consumer. If people do not see the possibility of receiving real value, they will not share their personal information with your business!

Blogging Purposefully

Bogging is an example of content marketing. Research by Hubspot (www.hubspot.com) published in 2010 has shown that websites that have an active blog attached to them draw 6.9 times more organic search traffic than a site with no blog. Additionally, small businesses that blog generate 55 percent more traffic to their websites than those that do not. What does this tell you? You want to be blogging!

Blogs should be used to push out relevant information to your readers such as case studies, articles, your thoughts on current topics, and other topics of relevance to your business and industry. When you write about the current state of your industry, as a by-product you are at the forefront of innovation. This makes you a thought leader. When people want to learn more or are looking for new ideas, they will be drawn to your blog and your business, providing you a high level of credibility in the industry, and thereby bringing in more revenue over time.

Using Videos and Podcasts

Using videos and podcasts (audio clips) on your website or blog enables you to provide another outlet for distribution of content to your customers. Gina, one of the authors of the book, has effectively used podcasts on her blog (www.ginaabudi.com) as a tool to interview business leaders about their perceptions of current affairs in their particular industry. These audio clips have drawn visitors to her site interested in learning more.

One of the most popular video outlets is YouTube. YouTube enables users to share original videos with a large online community. Many businesses use YouTube to share videos about products, customer testimonials, presentations, and company events.

PRACTICE MAKES PERFECT

To see how you might incorporate YouTube into your business, consider this example. Let's say your business sells birdfeeders. You might post a video on ways to keep squirrels off the birdfeeders, or you might post a video of a squirrel creatively finding a way to get on to a birdfeeder to get at the bird seed. If your company sells lumber for building projects, you might have how-to videos for customers, such as how to build a bookcase or create unique picture frames from leftover pieces of wood. For example, Williams-Sonoma (www.williams-sonoma.com), a gourmet food and kitchen supply store, uses video clips on their site to demonstrate the use of some of their products.

Conferences and Public Events

Conferences and trade shows enable you to showcase your products and services to customers who are part of your target audience. For example, the Project Management Institute holds an annual North American Global Congress where individuals who are project managers, project team members, or executives in project management attend sessions to enhance their skills and learn more from others in the industry. Many vendors showcase their products and services at these events, thereby enabling them to reach out to people who are potential customers. There are many such events for nearly every industry.

When researching events in which you might participate, keep in mind these best practices:

- Look at the type of audience who attends and the expected number of attendees. Are they in your geographic area and part of your target demographic?

- Look at the longevity of the conference or tradeshow.

- Determine other vendors who are showcasing at the event.

- Determine if the cost of attending and showcasing your products and services is within your budget.

If you are unsure about the benefit of having a booth at an event, you may want to attend the event as a participant first to see the types of people who attend and the types of companies who have booths at the event.

The Least You Need to Know

- Have a process for capturing voice-of-the-customer insights (such as meeting regularly with a customer council) and a flexible plan that enables you to use the information you uncover.

- Identify your best customer's traits and preferences; find out what experiences are likely to lead to a repeat purchase from that customer.

- Consider a variety of social media channels to get the word out about your business; create and support good conversations with customers and prospects.

- Develop a brand image for your business and use that brand consistently.

- A website is essential to your business's success, even if you are not doing e-commerce.

Best Practices for Growing Your Business

How do you make innovation part of your organization's daily working culture? What can customers, vendors, and employees do to help keep your organization growing and thriving? How can you stay ahead of the competition in the areas that matter most to you? How do you create a realistic, and strategically sound, expansion plan for your company?

In this part of the book, you learn about best practices that lay the foundation for sustainable growth and keep your organization ahead of the game.

Innovate for Success

In This Chapter

- Innovating for long-term success
- Finding ways to be innovative
- Using innovation to stay ahead of the competition
- Developing a creative working culture

Innovation can mean a number of things to small business owners. To some, it means inventing new products or services. To others, it means making changes in the way you do things in your business. Even seemingly small changes can have a tremendous impact on the success of your business.

For small businesses, the best definition for innovation is this: a commitment to constant, never-ending improvement. It's the "how can we do it better" mindset that helps you to improve your own internal processes and the end-result experience you offer to your customers—or, preferably, both.

Today, more individuals than ever before are using smartphones—mobile devices that enable users to access their e-mail and websites and make and receive telephone calls. If you have an e-commerce site that's based on business models that date from the period before large numbers of people had smartphones, innovation means figuring out a way people can use these phones to access your website and make purchases. It also means finding ways to use your own smartphone to more efficiently manage your website, your marketing, your customer service, and your business as a whole. There are great ideas out there. Why wait for your competition to come up with them, refine them, and implement them?

This chapter gives you ideas for building, sustaining, and benefiting from a culture of innovation in your organization.

The Ultimate Best Practice

In this book, we've shared scores of best practices for your business. Some of them may fit your company perfectly. Others may not seem to apply to you. However, the most critical best practice—regardless of your business size, and the one that is definitely relevant to your business no matter what its focus—is to look constantly for new opportunities to innovate.

Innovation allows you to accomplish the following for your business, all of which lead to increased profits:

- Increase efficiencies
- Increase productivity
- Improve the quality of your products
- Increase your market share
- Open up your products and services to new audiences

Creating a culture of innovation can lead to significant breakthroughs for your businesses and for you personally as the owner of that business. Your challenge is to find a way to make innovation in your business something other than a one-time event or an occasional priority.

Here's an interesting experiment to conduct. Look once again at your strategic plan (see Chapter 7), your value proposition, and your mission statement (see Chapter 5). After you have read through those documents, ask yourself: "Where do I envision this business being 5, 10, or even 15 years from now?" The pictures and events this question summons up should excite you. (If they don't, you're probably not cut out to be an entrepreneur.) Now ask yourself: "What will have to change to get there?" The right answer to this question for virtually all business owners is: create, reward, and support people who innovate on behalf of your company.

Your Creative Working Culture

You want every one of your employees to be innovative. That not only means making innovation part of their working day but also providing them with the support and resources they need to be innovative in the first place.

Your people may need space—both literal and figurative—in order to be able to be creative. Ask your employees these questions to get them to start thinking a bit more creatively:

- How can we do our jobs better?

- How can we better serve our customers?

- What would make us stand apart from the competition?

- What small changes might we make in the business and how we work that will have a big impact?

Whenever your employees come up with good answers to these questions (or even try to), you must find some way to reward them publicly for their effort, whether that effort seems large or small to you. The rewards don't have to be expensive, but they do have to involve some form of authentic public praise that correlates to the effort and results generated. Any of the following make great rewards for your employees:

- Prime parking space

- Extra days off

- A plaque or trophy

- Gift certificates

No doubt you can think of many others!

PRACTICE MAKES PERFECT

Create innovation teams comprised of employees from all areas of your business. Ask the members of the team to work toward improving processes, enhancing a product or service, or finding creative new ways to reach out to potential customers. Provide these innovation teams with the time and resources they need to be creative. You might choose to pull them from their other daily work for a couple of days each month for six months to generate new ideas for the business. If you follow this approach, be prepared to keep following it for an extended period (say, three to six months). Whenever the team makes an improvement, even a minor one, be sure to reward each member publicly for his or her work.

Of course, you should never, ever punish or belittle an employee for suggesting a new way of doing things!

You may have heard the term *appreciative inquiry,* which supports many innovation-related best practices discussed in this chapter. The appreciative inquiry concept helps you to be innovative by challenging you and your employees to make a conscious effort to look at all the good things your business does, and to focus on ways you can work together to enhance those areas.

DEFINITION

Appreciative inquiry is a process within an organization that engages employees in looking at improving performance within the organization by modeling and expanding what is already working. The theory behind appreciative inquiry is that when employees begin to appreciate what is best about the business and focus on the things they do well, they are able to find new ways to enhance their efforts and improve the business.

Constantly encourage employees to think of new ways to do the job better or to provide ideas that will improve products and services. We know of one small business that employs about a hundred people that exemplifies this best practice. At the start of a new year, the business challenges their employees with the following: think of a way to enhance one of the business's products to open up new markets. The employees could work either alone or in teams. The winning employee or team would be granted two extra weeks of vacation the following year!

Be as clear as you possibly can about the specific areas where you are willing to reward innovation. It's easier for businesses to be innovative when clear goals and objectives are set and progress is measured.

Finding Innovation Partners

Plenty of consulting firms specialize in working with businesses and helping them to become more innovative. Before you shell out cash for such advice, however, consider instead looking to your employees, vendors, resellers, and customers for ideas.

You'll also find that, through industry groups and at conferences, you'll make connections with others who may be great partners in innovation. For example, perhaps you have a product for assessing candidates for certain job openings. You want to make your product available online; currently, the assessments are paper-based. You might seek out an application developer who can help you put your product online—this would be an innovation partner. You might choose to pay the developer for their development, or you might offer a mutually agreeable scale of royalties on every sale of the online product.

Great Ideas from All Over

In Chapter 1, we discussed how best practices may come from both inside and outside your industry. The same goes for ideas that promote innovation. You should look at a variety of sources for ideas that help you to innovate, and you should be ready to adapt those ideas from settings that don't connect directly to your business.

BEST PRACTICE

Does your business work on a variety of projects? If so, consider creating a secure online collaboration site where your employees, vendors, and stakeholders can share information, ideas, and knowledge. If someone has found a better way of developing a more accurate project schedule or getting information from customers for the project, you can use this site as a way to share that information. Such collaboration sites can be a great way to foster innovation on any number of fronts. You might consider starting with Zoho Wiki (www.zoho.com/wiki) to build an online portal for group collaboration.

Simply by reading blogs, newspapers, and magazines, you can come up with a seemingly endless series of ideas that can enhance your organization's capacity to innovate.

Don't hesitate to look globally for ways to innovate. For instance, as a small business with limited financial resources, you may choose to outsource some components of your processes to reduce costs and improve efficiencies. This is something large companies around the world are doing in countless industries. You might choose to outsource manufacturing of certain components to a vendor to lower your costs. This enables your business to focus on other areas. Or you might choose to partner with a similar business to be more competitive with global customers and bid together on larger projects that neither of you could do alone.

Great Ideas: Customers and Vendors

We've talked about reaching out regularly to your customers and creating a series of ongoing conversations with them. That's a great way to build strong relationships with them and build loyalty. It's also a great way to find ideas that help your company to become more innovative.

Through surveys and outreach efforts to your customers, you'll begin to garner ideas on how to better support your customers and meet their needs.

BEST PRACTICE

Consider asking your customer council (see Chapter 17) for their ideas about how your business might improve efficiencies and effectiveness in working with customers.

Vendors, resellers, and other partners may also have some suggestions on how to be more innovative. In addition to ideas for developing new products or services or enhancing existing ones, they might also have ideas for innovative ways to work with vendors and partners or even package and present your products and services.

Ask your vendors and other partners how they work with other customers. Based on their experience with other businesses, do they have ideas in how you might change or fine-tune your processes? For example, one of your vendors may tell you that one of his other customers has an automated system for tracking inventory that sends data directly to his office so he can be sure the products they need show up right before they run out. You might choose to implement that technology in order to improve the workflow between your business and the vendor and lower your inventory costs.

Great Ideas: Outside Your Industry

If you've been at this more than a year or so, you have likely developed a network of other business owners whom you know. Reach out to these people and talk to them about how they are working to improve how they run their business. What ideas might they be willing to share to improve processes, market and sell products or services, or open up new markets?

There are a number of groups to help business owners share ideas with others, address issues, and brainstorm ways to be more innovative. Consider Vistage (www.vistage.com), The Alternative Board (www.thealternativeboard.com), and Entrepreneurs' Organization (www.eonetwork.org) as some options.

Remember that innovation does not have to be some huge step toward something completely new and different. Small changes in how you take orders from customers, how you package your products, new ways to bundle your services, or even how you get things done in the office are all examples of innovation, and these kinds of inno-vations can have a massive cumulative effect. Look outside your industry for little things other entrepreneurs have done to grow their companies, enhance their products and service offerings, work more effectively with their customers, and increase their own efficiencies.

PRACTICE MAKES PERFECT

The search engine giant Google sets aside one day a week for its engineers to work on projects of their choosing. They can use the time to develop something new for Google or to improve something already in use. This enables their employees to be creative and innovative on Google's time! What a great way to support innovative efforts by your employees.

Staying Ahead of the Competition

Market forces are perhaps the strongest motivator of all when it comes to innovation. You must assume that your competition is changing and adapting to the marketplace all the time. You need to be doing the same thing if you expect to remain in business!

For instance: You are a provider of custom-imprinted business gifts, and you just read a survey conducted by a local Chamber of Commerce that showed that many small businesses don't like the low quality of custom-imprinted business gifts. The survey suggests that small business owners nationwide are beginning to look at alternatives to custom-imprinted gifts. What might you do with this information?

You could just assume that you don't need to do anything, since your own customers haven't complained. Perhaps your own recent customer survey showed that customers were generally satisfied with your company and its products. Does that mean you should ignore this data?

That would definitely be the wrong decision. You must use this information to enhance the way you do business now. You have an opportunity to gain market share if you can come up with some ways to promote truly high-quality products and compare and contrast it with the competition. This is an opportunity to learn more about the gaps and opportunities in your marketplace and get a clearer sense of the ways you can serve current and potential customers better!

For smaller businesses, it sometimes seems difficult to be innovative while accomplishing everything else necessary to stay in business. The smaller the business, the more hats it seems that you, the business owner, must wear. You may be tempted to complain that the job of identifying new opportunities for innovation is one hat too many. The more important reality, however, is that your competition is ready to innovate in any and every situation where you are not. And, as if that sobering fact isn't enough, you should consider that, in today's global economy, your competition is more than just the business a few doors down or in the next town. Your competition could well be another business halfway around the world. Through even small changes in how you do business, you might find new efficiencies in how you manufacture products, improvements in processes for marketing and selling to customers, new ways to serve your customers, and ways to increase your profits and reduce costs.

The Competitive Edge in a Tough Economy

Tough economic times and intense competition mean you should focus even more on innovation than usual. When your business faces a major obstacle—and it will—gather the team and draw on your organization's ultimate competitive advantage: the ability of its people to innovate.

Ask your employees to question everything. Why are things done the way they are? Why can't they be done differently? What if you changed the way you work with customers? What if you changed how you develop products and services? When new employees join your business, task them with looking at how you work with a critical eye. They may have some good ideas from an outsider's point of view.

Consider new technologies that may help your business, and read articles on the latest trends in your industry. You'll find plenty of new ideas that connect to innovation.

PRACTICE MAKES PERFECT

Think about Skype, audio books, e-books, Twitter, Facebook, and YouTube—these are all innovations. They provided a competitive edge to those who implemented the idea. (By the time you read these words, someone will have added a new item to the list!)

Innovation provides you a competitive edge by enabling you to do any or all of the following:

- Produce cutting-edge products and services for your customers

- Open up new markets or take market share from your competition

- Expand the reach of your business

- Become a thought leader in your industry

By working on innovative ways to do business during tough economic times, you are ahead of the competition when the economy improves and begins to grow again. For instance, imagine your business offers businesses health-care services by partnering them with the right provider to offer medical insurance for their employees. Costs are increasing and your customers want to find ways to reduce their health-care costs. You are getting pressure to help lower their costs. You develop a new line of business, a service focusing on in-house wellness programs. Specifically, you offer seminars and other services to help your customers' employees lead healthier lives, which leads to lower health-care costs for the businesses you serve.

Don't Follow, Lead!

In the final analysis, innovation means taking the initiative to improve your business. Let's assume you manufacture paper products. Everyone in your industry has been talking about going green in their manufacturing processes but haven't really taken significant steps in this direction. Why not lead the charge? Pull together representatives from the industry to develop green manufacturing processes that will benefit the industry as a whole.

When hiring employees for your business, look for candidates who are thought leaders in their field. Check on employees to see how active they are in utilizing social media channels such as Facebook, LinkedIn, or Twitter and whether they blog or not. Individuals who are innovative have an entrepreneurial edge—they are never happy with the status quo and are always looking for new ways to do things.

We know of one individual who had a blog focused on *lean process management*. An employer was looking for someone to lead innovation efforts in his business. Through a search on the web, the business owner came across this individual's blog, loved what he read, and made him a job offer! Why not consider snatching up the most innovative people for your own business? That's one of the best ways to stay ahead of the competition!

DEFINITION

Lean process management focuses on looking at the processes and procedures within a company with a critical eye to improve them to increase efficiency and effectiveness through eliminating tasks that add no value. In this way, not only are efficiencies realized, but costs are also reduced.

The Least You Need to Know

- Keep in mind that innovation doesn't just mean new products and services. Small changes in processes can make a big difference in your business.
- Involve suppliers, vendors, resellers, customers, and employees in your innovation efforts.
- Look for innovative ideas from both inside and outside your industry.
- Innovation should be a part of your overall business strategy.

Expanding Your Business

In This Chapter

- Planning for your business expansion
- Weighing your options for expansion
- Partnering with the right folks
- Expanding regionally, nationally, and globally

There comes a point in the life of any business owner when he or she faces a choice: should I expand?

For some, the answer is almost automatic—"Yes." For these entrepreneurs, growing the business is as much of a calling as launching the business.

There are as many reasons to embark on an expansion of your business as there are to start a business in the first place. For a sole proprietor who has spent a year or so playing "chief cook and bottle washer," there often comes a moment of truth that brings the answer to the question of expansion into clarity: you want your business to grow, and you realize that there is only so much you can do on your own.

To bring your business to the next level, you may decide that your situation justifies bringing on additional employees or even adding a partner. For other situations, expansion may take such forms as opening new facilities or storefront operations, licensing your intellectual property (IP), or franchising.

Just as you did when you were starting your business in the first place, you need to have a strategy and develop a business plan for expansion. There is always an element of risk when it comes to expanding your business, and you must have a plan in place to address those risks.

This chapter helps you decide whether it's time to expand your business and how to proceed if you conclude that doing so is the right course of action.

The Basics

At some point, you'll at least consider the question of expanding your business. It may be because you are looking to increase your market share, move into new geographic regions, or increase your revenue and profits. The expansion plan you eventually develop may be as simple as hiring employees so that you alone are not doing the work or as complex as opening up offices internationally. Certainly the more complex the plan, the more risks you are likely to face—and the more carefully you will need to plan for your expansion efforts.

BEST PRACTICE

Before embarking on any expansion plan, develop a business plan intended specifically for the expansion of your business. This plan should help you think through the available options, identify and evaluate the risks, and determine whether you will need to seek external funding. If you do require money from outside, this new business plan will be an essential tool for attracting loans or investments.

Address the following questions when creating a plan for expanding your business:

- What type of expansion makes sense for you: national, international, franchise, licensing your IP, hiring more employees, or merging with or acquiring another business?

- What will your business get from expanding? New customers? Increased profitability? New markets for your products and services?

- How will you fund the expansion? Do you have monies set aside or will you need loans? How about taking on a partner?

When Should You Expand?

There is no proven, hard-and-fast rule about when you should (or shouldn't) expand your business. One fairly reliable rule of thumb, however, is that if you notice that your competitors are expanding, you should at least consider the possibility of expansion yourself. Of course, the mere fact that your competition is doing something doesn't necessarily mean that imitating them makes good strategic sense for your business. Many terrible expansion initiatives have begun as misguided, emotionally driven efforts to keep up with the competition.

The only principle that definitely makes sense for all entrepreneurs who must evaluate the question "Should I expand?" is this one: stick to the facts! In keeping with this principle, you should do a fair amount of research first—and before you commit to any expansion plan, bounce it off your advisory board.

The authors know of a training company that decided to expand into a number of different areas simply because their competitors were expanding. Had they done their homework, they would have learned that the market for their programs was actually on the decline. Expanding at that time by opening new facilities and investing in new employees simply wasn't a good use of their time or money.

The owners ended up paying significant money for extensive leases they couldn't get out of. A better move would have been for them to look at expanding their product line in a smaller number of content areas—areas that were more promising for their company, given its history and past successes. If the owners were committed to embarking on a whole range of totally new training programs, they could have minimized the risks of doing so by creating small-scale pilot programs and then evaluating what had worked well (and what hadn't) before making all the investments associated with a full-scale program (such as office space, marketing materials, and employees).

Consider carefully whether you can afford the expansion you have in mind and what other projects you could be undertaking with the resources the expansion will consume. Do you have the financial means to carry out your plan? Do you have the time to invest in expansion? What about the political capital necessary to get managers, key employees, and customers to go along with the inevitable changes that accompany expansion? Last but certainly not least, consider that expanding your business is going to take a significant amount of your own time. You'll need to be able to invest in the process from all of these perspectives—not just the financial perspective—in order for your expansion campaign to be a successful one.

Meeting Your Investment Needs

You may be able to finance your expansion by using current cash flow or your own savings. Many entrepreneurs prefer this route for the same basic reason they prefer using their own money during the start-up phase: autonomy.

If you need to take out a loan in order to expand your business, consider loans through your local bank or the Small Business Administration. We discussed options for securing loans and financing for your business in Chapter 4.

> **PRACTICE MAKES PERFECT**
>
> Look at a variety of funding options to find what is best for you given your plans for expansion. Ask your advisory board and your own business network for their thoughts on funding sources. They may be able to point you to sources you never even considered.

You might also choose to take on a business partner who can help finance the expansion of your business. We'll talk more about the specific issue of finding the right partner for overseas ventures a little later on in this chapter.

Regional and National Expansion

Depending on your goals, you may choose to expand in your own region or nationally. For example, if you have a bakery business in Boston, you may choose to open up new locations in New Hampshire, Connecticut, and New York; if you do management consulting on the East Coast, maybe you have decided to take on a partner on the West Coast to cover that area of the country.

Franchising

Franchising is an option for expanding your business. Franchising enables others to operate an extension of your business using your logo, trademarks, and way of doing business. For example, Subway sandwich shops are franchised, and franchisees are taught how to operate Subway shops and are provided support by the home office of Subway.

Franchising doesn't work for every business. If you run a very complex business, franchising may not be possible. The simpler your business model, the more successful you may be with a franchise.

Keep in mind that you don't want your expanded business to compete with your original location. For instance, if you decide to franchise your retail clothing establishment, you would likely want to have franchises nationally (to help you expand your brand) but not in your immediate area (no sense competing with yourself!).

If you decide to go the franchise route, it is important to have a plan in place for how you will do the following:

- Select franchisees

- Create standards but still allow flexibility for innovations

- License your logo and brand

- Provide your franchisees support (such as marketing and training) in your business

- Evaluate and monitor franchisees

BUSINESS BUSTER

There are many challenges related to franchising your business. Too often businesses really don't understand what is involved. Each state has its own rules and regulations for franchises. You must talk to an attorney who is an expert in this area before you decide to move down the path of franchising your business.

One company we know of attempted to leverage the excellent IP it had developed over a period of about a decade by launching a full-scale consulting franchise operation that targeted every major city in the United States. The goal, according to the CEO, was to "show his competition a thing or two." (One of this company's major competitors had a national network of franchises.) Little planning or consultation with senior business advisors preceded this effort. Unfortunately, this particular CEO was completely out of his depth when it came to navigating the maze of regulatory obstacles presented in each state, and he was equally unfamiliar with the challenging task of managing a network of franchisees. No one on staff had experience in either of these areas, either. The effort sputtered, morale plunged, and the parent company's relationship with its franchisees quickly soured. The CEO eventually sold his interest in the company. He had lost more than a year of hard work, a substantial amount of money, and the good will of senior employees—many of whom had worked for him for over a decade.

Licensing

The CEO might have saved himself, his employees, and his network of franchisees a great deal of trauma and stress if he had opted instead to create, and troubleshoot, a plan based on licensing his company's IP. This would have been a far less complex, and far less risky, way to expand his business. It would have allowed him to create relationships with more new partners, avoid the legal and organizational pitfalls of establishing a franchisee network, and disengage more quickly (and gracefully) when expectations on either side were going unmet.

One great example of licensing as an expansion strategy can be found in the Ken Blanchard Companies, which license their Situational Leadership IP to other training companies and individuals, allowing them to train using the materials under Blanchard International. This has enabled the Ken Blanchard Companies to increase their revenue and profits through a network of partners (not franchisees) who pay for the privilege of using their materials but don't pay an up-front franchisee fee. If you have developed IP, such as training or software programs, you might consider licensing that IP to increase your profits and expand your business. Of course, you must have a plan in place that includes a contractual agreement with licensing terms and protection of your IP. For both franchising and licensing of your IP, see an attorney for assistance in creating the appropriate contracts and legal agreements to ensure you are protected.

PRACTICE MAKES PERFECT

To get more information on the best ways to license and protect your company's IP, visit www.cetus.org, the Intellectual Property Legal Center, which features an extensive selection of books, articles, and e-books on the subject. One standout, available as an e-book via www.cetus.org and www.amazon.com, is Poltorak and Lerner's *Essentials of Licensing Intellectual Property* (John Wiley, 2003).

Your decision to expand either regionally or nationally will be based on a number of factors, such as:

Competition: Where is the competition located? Are there areas that are not served and where opportunities exist? Or are there needs that are not being met by competitors?

Target audience: Where does your target audience exist that would benefit from you expanding your operations? Will expanding open up new markets for you so that you can increase your profits? For example, if you focus on consulting for pharmaceutical companies and are not based in Massachusetts, you may choose to expand operations in the Massachusetts area since many pharmaceutical companies are located there.

Capacity to expand: Do you have the resources and time necessary to expand effectively and successfully—especially if you choose to expand outside of your region? Will you be able to invest time in traveling to the other locations?

Choosing Locations

You want to spend significant time researching possible locations and really weighing your options.

> **BEST PRACTICE**
>
> The website ZoomProspector (www.zoomprospector.com) enables users to search for prospective expansion locations by entering a variety of business data. Also check with the local SCORE office for information on opening locations in those areas.

We can't emphasize enough the importance of doing your homework prior to committing to a new business location. Follow these best practices when choosing a location for your business:

- **Determine what you need.** Do you need a commercial location for a retail store or other storefront business, an industrial location for manufacturing or a warehouse, or office space in an office building?

- **Research the competitors in the area.** If you are moving to a new area, you'll need time to build brand recognition; that may be more difficult with many similar businesses in the same area.

- **Research the location for members of your target audience.** Does your business model require that you give your customers easy physical access to your facilities? Can they easily get to your location via car, via public transportation, or on foot? Is the area an attractive, safe area? Is it an area they would frequent?

- **Evaluate ease of parking and getting to and from the location.** This is important for both customers and employees.

- **Look at the surrounding businesses.** Do they complement your business? Is it a busy location? Ask those business owners their thoughts on the location—are they satisfied?

- **Consider the building you'll lease or purchase.** Is it updated? Is it aesthetically pleasing? (This is especially important if customers will be coming to the location.) How long a lease can you commit to? What kind of lease is the landlord willing to provide?

Legal and Tax Implications

There are usually major tax implications to consider when evaluating any plan to expand your business. For example, if you open up new storefront locations in different states, you'll need to pay taxes in those states, including sales tax. If you have a storefront in a particular state, you'll need to see what zoning and licensing requirements there are for your particular type of business.

If you license your brand or IP, and something happens that is attributable to your product, you could be held liable even if you are simply licensing.

Bottom line: Don't expand operations without first getting advice from your attorney and your accountant.

Going Global

If you are thinking of expanding your business internationally, you'll need to consider a variety of issues besides what we discussed earlier in this chapter. First off, hire an attorney who specializes in international business development and expansion. There is really no excuse for not getting good legal representation right from the start in this situation.

You'll also need an experienced partner and/or consultant in the country you are considering operating in, so you will need a plan for securing a relationship with someone you can trust. In many situations, a local partner with an equity stake in the business is required by law. Check with countries as to ownership requirements of businesses. For example, in Kuwait, the majority of a business must be owned by a Kuwaiti citizen.

PRACTICE MAKES PERFECT

If you are considering expanding your business internationally, check out the various U.S. government sites for resources that will be of value: Office of International Trade (www.cbp.gov/xp/cgov/trade), International Trade Administration (http://trade.gov), and the U.S. Department of Commerce (www. commerce.gov), to name a few.

Get information for any country where you are considering expanding operations. What regulations exist? What are the tax laws for doing business in that country? Can you get money out of the country easily? For example, does the country have a free zone—an area specifically designated to encourage business development—where you may be able to own 100 percent of the business and/or be taxed at significantly reduced rates? Can you easily export product to that country?

BUSINESS BUSTER

Every culture has customs and nuances in how business is done. What might be an acceptable business practice in the United States might be considered offensive somewhere else. The book *Kiss, Bow or Shake Hands* by Terri Morrison and Wayne Conaway is a good guide to doing business in more than 60 countries.

Draw on the variety of resources available to you, including consultants from SCORE, government websites, and certainly an attorney and accountant well-versed in international law in the country you are considering for expansion. Check out the U.S. Department of Commerce site's grants, contracting, and trade opportunities (www.commerce.gov/about-commerce/grants-contracting-trade-opportunities) page for a variety of resources for doing business overseas.

Don't jump into expanding internationally without a strong business and strategic plan in place.

Finding the Right Partners

Finding the right partner will be the most difficult part, especially for global operations. Unless you know someone personally or have a personal recommendation, you really need to do your due diligence in securing the right partner for your business.

BEST PRACTICE

Be sure to check references, investigate financial background, and learn all you can about the partner's reputation for doing business. You'll have less control of overseas operations and you must have someone you can trust representing your interests overseas.

You might ask vendors, resellers, suppliers, and your attorney or accountant for recommendations for partners. Your best bet is going to be to find a partner through someone you know and trust.

Consider also the possibility of partnering with another small business overseas. For example, if you are a technical services firm, you might find another small business that complements your services or extends your services overseas.

In order to reduce your risk, you might choose to work with a potential partner on a few projects prior to formalizing an agreement. For instance, you may initially enter into an agreement to refer business to each other prior to entering into formal partnership agreements.

PRACTICE MAKES PERFECT

For some good advice on selecting the right business partner, or improving a current partner relationship, see David Gage's fine book *The Partnership Charter: How to Start Out Right with Your New Business Partnership (or Fix the One You're In)*, available from Basic Books.

Is Your Business Model International?

Are your products or services culture-centric? For example, if your business sells memorabilia and historical products from the American Civil and Revolutionary Wars, there's not going to be a lot of international demand for them. On the other hand, if your business sells specialized hiking and adventure trips, you may find that your business expands well in areas, such as Europe, where there are well-established hiking trails.

You will more than likely need to make changes to your product or service offerings to accommodate overseas expectations and norms. Especially with products, think clearly about why you believe your product will sell in a global marketplace. Is there no similar product available in that country—or is your product superior?

You'll also need to consider pricing. Your pricing will need to be adjusted for overseas markets; some countries will require a much lower pricing model. If you have many costs associated with either development or delivery of your product, you may not be able to price competitively enough in certain overseas markets.

Think carefully about what changes you'll need to make in your business model when planning for global expansion, and get advice from a business ally with direct overseas experience before committing yourself. Do not make the mistake of assuming you can simply transplant your existing business model without making any changes. The question is whether the changes are minor enough for you to expand overseas … or major enough for you to conclude that it simply doesn't make sense for you to expand globally.

Last but not least, don't forget that growing as a person is at least as important as growing your business!

The Least You Need to Know

- Develop a business and strategic plan for your expansion.
- Monitor what expansion plans your competition is putting into action.
- Don't expand for purely emotional reasons.
- Seek advice from your attorney and accountant before finalizing any agreements or contracts related to expansion.
- Take significant time to research before committing to expanding your business internationally.

Glossary

accrual basis accounting   An accounting method in which income is reported in the fiscal period during which it was earned regardless of when it is received and expenses are recorded in the fiscal period during which they occur, whether they are paid at that time or not.

advisory board   An informal group of individuals who provide guidance to a business by acting as a sounding board and bringing their own expertise to bear to assist in making strategic decisions.

appreciative inquiry   A process within an organization in which employees look at ways to change and improve performance. The theory behind appreciative inquiry is that when employees begin to appreciate what is best about the business and focus on the things they do well, they are able to find new ways to do even better and improve the business.

balance sheet   A snapshot of the business's assets and liabilities for a particular time period.

behavioral interviewing   A way of interviewing that takes into account a candidate's past experiences to determine his ability to perform a role. Past experiences are often good predictors of how the candidate will perform in the future. These kinds of probing questions enable you to gain a deeper understanding of how a candidate handled a particular situation.

benchmarking   Measuring a business's processes, procedures, and practices against the processes, procedures, and practices of companies considered the best at what they do in the particular areas being measured.

benefit   As it pertains to products and services, what problem a product or service solves or what need it fulfills for customers.

best practice   A specific method that improves the performance of a team or an organization and can be replicated or adapted elsewhere. Best practices often take the form of guidelines, principles, or ideas that are endorsed by a person or governing body that attests to the viability of the best practice.

brand   The identity associated with your business and its products and services. It can be depicted by a logo, slogan, specific colors, and a name.

break-even analysis   A technique used to analyze how much must be generated in sales in order to achieve enough revenue to pay expenses and generate a profit.

budget   A list, broken down by product, service line, or category, of all planned revenues and expenses associated with a business.

business economics   *See* managerial economics.

business owner's policy (BOP)   A package insurance policy that combines property, liability, and business interruption insurance for small- to medium-size businesses.

business plan   A formal plan that describes a business's strategic goals, marketing and sales strategy, operations and management, products and services to be offered, and financial information.

cash basis accounting   An accounting method in which income is recorded when it is received and expenses are recorded when they are paid out.

cash flow statement   A document which shows how the cash of your business moved (in and out of the business) over a specified time period.

change management   A structured managerial strategy for getting employees to transition to a new way of performing their jobs. It involves introducing people to change gradually and gaining their acceptance as it takes place.

cloud computing   Using programs and data stored on servers connected to computers via the Internet rather than storing software and data on individual computers.

COBRA coverage   COBRA refers to the Consolidated Omnibus Budget Reconciliation Act of 1985 that provides terminated employees with the ability to temporarily continue health coverage at group rates.

competency-based interviewing   *See* behavioral interviewing.

cost of goods sold (COGS)   The direct costs associated with producing and offering your products and services.

critical success factors (CSFs) Activities that your business undertakes with the aim of meeting strategic long-term goals. CSFs are measured with performance indicators.

customer relationship management (CRM) system A software program that enables businesses to track and manage their interactions with current and prospective customers. CRMs are used to ensure a coordinated interaction with customers.

customer value The benefits and satisfaction the customer receives from purchasing or investing in your product or service.

dashboard A visual representation of how a business is performing at a particular point in time. For example, a dashboard may include sales metrics, revenue numbers, or marketing metrics.

disability insurance Insurance on the earned income of the policy's beneficiary against the risk that personal disability will make it impossible for that individual to work and earn money.

draw In sales, money a business provides to its salespeople against future commissions. Draws may be recoverable (which means they must be paid back) or nonrecoverable (which means they do not need to be paid back).

emotional intelligence A gauge of an individual's ability to control his or her emotions and evaluate and manage the emotions of others. Individuals with high levels of emotional intelligence do an outstanding job at leading teams, managing others, and working with customers.

employment-at-will This U.S. legal doctrine allows the employer or employee to terminate an employment relationship at any time with no liability. There are certain exceptions to this doctrine.

enterprise resource planning (ERP) system An integrated software application that serves as a business management tool, helping to track resources, tangible assets, materials, finances, suppliers, vendors, customers, and employees.

entrepreneurial edge A person's spirit and drive to identify and create business opportunities.

farmer In sales, a salesperson who excels at maintaining existing customer accounts.

features The specific attributes of a product or service.

firewall   Hardware and software that blocks outsiders from accessing your data and creates a secure environment for your data while permitting those with authorization, such as employees, to access information as needed.

fixed costs   A business's overhead or sunk costs. Examples of fixed costs include lease payments and salaries of employees.

franchise   An extension of a business in which others pay a fee to use its logo, trademarks, and methodology for doing business.

general liability insurance   Insurance that protects a business's assets in the event that it is sued for something it did (or failed to do) that caused damage to property, injury, or a combination of the two.

go-to-market plan   A plan for introducing a product or service into the marketplace and for selling and delivering that product or service to customers.

gross margin   The amount of money a business makes (profit) for each product or service it sells.

hunter   In sales, a salesperson who is responsible for getting new customers or clients.

inbound marketing   A situation in which potential customers find a business on their own rather than through any marketing initiative on the part of the business.

income statement   A statement showing the revenue and expenses for a business for a specific period of time.

innovation   A commitment to constant, never-ending improvement.

intellectual property (IP)   Copyrighted materials, trademarks, patents, and trade secret protections.

key employee insurance   Insurance to ensure continuation of the business operations if a key person(s) passes away, becomes seriously ill, or otherwise cannot participate in the business.

key performance indicator (KPI)   *See* performance indicators.

lean process management   A focus on improving the processes and procedures within a company by eliminating tasks that add no value.

lessons learned   Information from past projects, such as problems that occurred and risks that were encountered, that can inform future projects.

malware   Malicious software that is installed on a user's computer system without the user's consent. It may slow down the computer, steal passwords, or download important data.

managerial economics   How business decisions are made by managers to achieve a business's goals and objectives. It is also referred to as microeconomics or business economics.

mediation   An informal process led by a third party mediator to help two or more parties resolve their differences. The mediator helps the two parties come to an agreement on resolution, but it is not necessarily a binding process.

mentoring program   A program in which junior employees are partnered with more senior employees; the senior employees provide the junior employees with guidance in performing their roles and responsibilities.

microeconomics   *See* managerial economics.

mission statement   A written statement that describes the business's purpose and provides a sense of direction for the business. It helps management to develop complementary strategies.

natural search   When a person searches a specific term on a search engine and the results that appear are based on relevancy to the term being searched, not as a result of the business paying for an ad to appear based on the same term.

onboarding   A process for effectively assimilating new employees into a business in the shortest time frame possible. Onboarding includes helping people to understand the culture of the business, and providing training on products and services, as well as on relevant processes, procedures, and policies.

opt in   Permission granted by current or prospective customers to receive messages from a business about its products and services. It is understood that the recipient will continue to receive messages until such time as he chooses to opt out and be removed from the mailing list.

organic searches   *See* natural search.

outbound marketing   The process of actively pushing information about products and services to customers. An example of outbound marketing is an e-mail blast to a list of potential customers advertising your products or services.

pay-per-click   *See* sponsored links.

PCI-compliance audit   Also known as a Payment Card Industry Data Security Standard (PCI DSS) Audit; an audit to ensure that a business is following the security guidelines meant to keep credit card information secure.

performance indicators   Quantifiable metrics used to measure the success of activities undertaken to reach strategic goals.

positioning statement   Statement that includes information on what a business does (products and services offered), who the target customers are for those products and services, how the business brings value to its customers, and why it is different from its competitors. Positioning statements are used to develop sales and marketing strategies, but they must also be well understood by everyone with frontline customer service responsibility. In essence, these statements represent a company's promise to the customer.

professional development   Opportunities provided to employees to help them further develop their skills and knowledge and grow both personally and professionally.

profit sharing   A program that enables employees to share in the profits of a business by receiving a one-time bonus or percentage increase in salary based on how well the company has performed that year.

scenario-based interviewing   *See* behavioral interviewing.

search engine optimization (SEO)   The process and strategy of presenting a business on the web to improve the ability of potential customers finding it through natural searches on search engines such as Google, Yahoo!, and Bing.

SMART objectives   Business objectives developed to be specific, measurable, achievable, relevant, and timely.

software as a service (SaaS)   Applications that are licensed to customers for use as a service on demand.

sponsored links   Advertising, also called pay-per-click keywords. Businesses pay Google search engines to advertise based on the keyword searched. The business has control over frequency, time of day, geographic location, as well as amount to be spent in a period of time for those ads.

strategic direction   A course of action to move forward with a strategic plan that allows for flexibility to account for changing marketing conditions and customer demands.

strategic plan   A long-range plan that serves as a business's road map for the future. It includes the product lines and services, the number of employees, technology requirements, industry trends, competitor analysis, revenue and profitability goals, types of customers, and long-range marketing plans.

succession plan   A plan for identifying, developing, and retaining individuals who have the ability to take on key leadership roles within the business.

SWOT analysis   A planning method used to evaluate the strengths, weaknesses, opportunities, and threats involved in a particular strategic direction for your business.

talent management   The long-term process of recruiting employees, onboarding them into the business, providing them professional development opportunities, managing their activities and career path, and doing succession planning.

tax law   The Internal Revenue Code and other state and federal statutes, rules, and regulations that apply to taxation of businesses and individuals.

value proposition   A three- to five-sentence statement that conveys to customers the value and benefits that a business brings to them. The value proposition should convey why the customer should purchase that business's products and services over the competition's.

variable costs   Costs that vary depending on output. Materials required to manufacture products and temporary employees hired for certain busy times are examples of variable costs.

venture capital (VC) firms   Firms that provide financial funding to start-up firms with high potential for future success. In exchange, the partners of the VC firm (with interest) get equity in the business. Many VC firms also provide oversight of business operations to ensure the appropriate use of the investment monies.

vision statement   A statement describing the long-term view of a business—where it wants to be in the future. It is the reason for the business's existence.

voice of the customer   A program that includes a process for capturing—via interviews, surveys, or focus groups—information about the customers' perceptions, expectations, and needs. This information might be used to develop products and services.

Voice over Internet Protocol (VoIP) A set of technologies and protocols that allow for communication over the Internet. VoIP allows for telephone communications, multimedia communications, faxing, instant messaging, and video communications.

wiki A particular website that allows individuals to collaborate by creating and editing information in web pages.

workers' compensation An insurance policy that is provided by the employer to ensure for medical compensation for employees injured on the job.

Resources

The Alternative Board
www.thealternativeboard.com

A group that brings together business owners to get advice and brainstorm for innovation.

Amazon Services
www.amazonservices.com

An alternative online e-commerce solution without having to build your own e-store.

American Bar Association
www.abanet.org

A resource for finding an attorney in your area.

Authorize.net
www.authorize.net

Online payment services.

Business Plan Template for a Start-Up Business
www.score.org/pdf/Business%20Plan%20for%20Startup%20Business_08.pdf

A template for a start-up business provided by SCORE.

Career Builder
www.careerbuilder.com

An online resource for finding candidates for jobs and posting job openings.

Chamber of Commerce
www.uschamber.com

Use this main site to find a local Chamber of Commerce.

Collecta

www.collecta.com

An online service to search for relevant terms related to your company, product, or service to see where they are being talked about online.

Consultancy Register

http://consultancyregister.com

A registry to search for consultants in a variety of industries and with a variety of specialties.

Consultants Registrar

www.consultantsregistrar.com

A directory that provides listings of consultants by industry and by state.

Dice

www.dice.com

An online resource for finding information about technology-focused job candidates and for posting IT job openings.

Dun & Bradstreet

http://smallbusiness.dnb.com

Small business products, services, and resources.

Entrepreneur's Organization

www.eonetwork.org

A global group of business owners offering support, advice, and coaching to each other.

Equal Employment Opportunity Commission

www.EEOC.gov

Information on employment laws.

Experian

www.experian.com/small-business/services.jsp

Services and resources for small businesses, including doing credit checks, obtaining credit reports, and getting leads for customers.

Facebook

www.facebook.com

A social networking site founded in 2004.

FindLaw

http://lawyers.findlaw.com

A search engine to find an attorney.

Free Press Release

www.Free-Press-Release.com

A free resource for creating and sending out press releases.

Good Sync

www.goodsync.com

A nonenterprise backup solution for securing your individual computer data. Good Sync does have an enterprise solution, but they are better known for their nonenterprise (individual-machine) backup solution.

Google Alerts

www.google.com/alerts

Set up alerts to track where your business name, your own name, or a product name appears online.

Google Analytics

www.google.com/analytics

A resource to track use of your website.

Google Checkout

http://checkout.google.com/sell

An alternative online e-commerce solution without having to build your own e-store.

HubSpot

www.hubspot.com/marketing-resources

A great resource for free marketing information and how to set up and effectively use LinkedIn, Facebook, and Twitter for business. Also includes information on how to structure your website.

Internal Revenue Service
www.irs.gov

Information on U.S. tax laws.

International Trade Administration
http://trade.gov

Information for businesses looking to expand internationally.

Lawyers.com
www.lawyers.com

A legal resource site plus a resource for finding an attorney.

Lending Club
www.lendingclub.com

A peer lending service that partners individuals looking for investment monies with those interested in investing in them.

LinkedIn
www.linkedin.com

An online networking site and resource for finding employees and promoting your business.

Monster
www.monster.com

An online resource for finding candidates for jobs and posting job openings.

National Venture Capital Association
www.nvca.org

A directory of member venture capital firms.

Ning
www.ning.com

An online platform that enables individuals to create their own social network.

Office of International Trade
www.cbp.gov/xp/cgov/trade

Information for businesses looking to expand internationally.

PayPal

www.paypal.com

Online payment services.

PR Log

www.prlog.org

A resource for creating and sending out press releases.

Prosper

www.prosper.com

A website for finding funding options for your business. This site connects people who want to invest money with those who need to borrow money.

PRWeb

www.prweb.com

A resource for creating and sending out press releases.

SCORE

www.score.org/index.html

Resources, free advice, tools, and templates for small business owners.

SEO Consultants Directory

www.seoconsultants.com

A directory of search engine optimization consultants and specialists.

ShareFile

www.sharefile.com

A secure resource for transferring and sharing files over the Internet.

Simply Hired

www.simplyhired.com

An online resource for posting job openings.

Skype

www.skype.com

An Internet-based telephone communication alternative that enables video communications and conference calling.

Small Business Administration
www.sba.gov

Information on loan programs and many other resources and advice for small business. Many articles on how to start and manage a small business.

Small Business Administration Insurance Information
www.sba.gov/category/navigation-structure/starting-managing-business/
managing-business/running-business/insurance

A comprehensive online guide to insurance for small business owners.

Social Mention
www.socialmention.com

An online service to search for relevant terms related to your company, product, or service to see where they are being talked about online.

Society for Human Resource Management
www.shrm.org

A variety of resources for human resources professionals.

Squidoo
www.squidoo.com

An online platform that enables users to create web pages around a particular subject or expertise.

Symantec Backup Exec
www.symantec.com

An enterprise backup solution for securing your data.

Twitter
www.twitter.com

A social networking and microblogging site founded in 2006.

Twitter Search
http://search.twitter.com

Enter a search term, such as a product or company name, and see all tweets associated with that term.

U.S. Citizenship and Immigration Services
www.uscis.gov

Information on hiring employees and the I-9 and other forms for download.

U.S. Copyright Office
www.copyright.gov

Information on applying for copyright and searching for existing copyrights.

U.S. Department of Commerce
www.commerce.gov

Information for businesses looking to expand internationally.

U.S. Department of Commerce—Grants, Contracting, and Trade Opportunities
www.commerce.gov/about-commerce/grants-contracting-trade-opportunities

Information and a variety of resources for doing business overseas.

U.S. Department of Labor
www.dol.gov

Resource for employment law information that must be posted in the workplace and a wide range of information on labor rules and regulations.

U.S. Patent and Trademark Office
www.uspto.gov

Information on trademarking logos and names.

Vistage
www.vistage.com

A membership group for leaders and business owners to share information, get advice, and brainstorm and problem solve with others.

YouTube
www.youtube.com

A website that enables sharing of original videos.

Zoho Wiki
www.zoho.com/wiki

A website to create online portals for group collaboration and knowledge sharing.

ZoomProspector
www.zoomprospector.com

A website to help you find a location for your business based on a variety of characteristics and other information you enter into their database.

Index

C

D

F

G

H

M

Q-R

X-Y-Z